DEDICATION

To Kalee, thank you for the tough love. For your grace, for holding your lines, for being the example.

To Sophia and Rick, may your inspirational stories of courage be shared this fully some day.

Introduction

At 39, I have done nothing special, with the exception of walking away from "the money" in favor of pursuing my dreams of world travels in the face of long odds. The truth is, I know no other way to honor my calling than by sharing my life's journey and experiences, compiling and presenting them in this manner: the wins and losses—far more losses than wins—some things I have learned along the way that fall outside of what is deemed acceptable by mainstream society. While my travels were amazing and ultimately my time away from home provided me with that which I was seeking, they weren't that extraordinary. I'll be the first to admit it. I didn't even make it to the Far East; an uneventful layover in Turkey was as close as I could muster. Some fresh Baklava and a grainy Turkish coffee would have to do. No Egyptian pyramids, Thai monasteries, or Tibetan caves. What I did manage to find, however, I believe is far more valuable than anything else: freedom and purpose. And the peace of mind that came from this essential, but ever elusive and uncommon, feat. In times where so many are disengaged and "stuck," struggling to find their way, I now find myself content and firmly rooted in my truth, freely living a life of purpose and meaning in service to my fellow humans.

A life I have patiently designed from the ground up.

This book is a distillation and synthesis of my life to this point. Along the way, I'll share important teachings that I have found to be valuable, teachings that have served as inspiration for me on my path less-traveled.

In these pages, I'll openly and honestly share my story, my experiences, what I have seen and done firsthand, all remembered (some details many years later) and presented to the best of my ability.

My life radically changed at 35 years old when I felt love for the first time. This was a shocking realization, as I have always been surrounded with love and the most loving and caring people. How is this so, at this stage of my life—a grown man in my thirties—feeling love for the first time?

I had diligently toed the line of conformity and followed all of the rules set forth by the society that raised me. The first instance where I stepped outside the pale to discern for myself what was real, I came alive. I became aware of just how special the human experience can truly be when you follow your heart and live in your truth.

This love that I will speak of doesn't properly fit the definition that has been adopted by our modern world. This love: universal, expansive, free from conditions and limitations.

The love beyond words.

Before I left for my travel journey, I was "stuck," poorly defining love, unaware of the potential that lies within my own heart. I was duped by Bullshit, Inc.: disengaged with work, overwhelmed by familial expectations; defined by past hurts and limiting beliefs; consumed by crippling fear and incessant worry—all of it far too heavy to carry. Way too much a burden on my soul and mortal heart.

It was "jump" or die. Death without ever knowing for sure what lay beyond the pale seemed like cowardice. So I said "Fuck it!" and jumped. In doing so, I called the bluff of Bullshit, Inc.

It was time to figure out what this human experience was really about. No more hiding. No more pretending.

Many people are hurting: We are at a crossroads, a time of peril with grave challenges environmentally, socially, economically, and politically. It's truly a "shit or get off the pot" moment for the human race. These words are all I have. With a grateful heart, I humbly share them.

Thank you for reading and giving this book a shot.

PROLOGUE

We just went over the rules. Everything we needed to know, what to expect for this night and the hours to come had been laid out for us, a gathering of international seekers. The day's blazing heat finally subsiding, an ominous mountain breeze reminded me why we were encouraged to wear long sleeves and bring blankets to the temple. We sat in a large circle listening intently to this important instruction. The hand drums and many musical instruments were set up like a concert about to go down. A beautifully ornamented altar prepared with candles, pictures of wise sages, precious stones, and crystals was presented gracefully. The hosts, Nicole and Vismay, the medicine workers at this seemingly enchanted spiritual healing retreat in a remote forest in Costa Rica, put everyone at ease, a reflexive gesture to combat the tension we all felt. They were clear and deliberate about what was to transpire during this unconventional healing ritual; they delivered all the instructions in a calm and friendly spirit. Everything, that is, except their stern warning not to leave the safe space and container. There was to be no venturing into the jungle or going down to the river or returning up the hill to the cabanas and our belongings where we all slept the night prior. This notion irked me, leaving a moment of concern—have they lost others in the past? Has something gone wrong before—perhaps a psychedelic mishap that may have left an unprepared seeker lost in the jungle? It was crystal clear that under the influence of this medicine, we needed to be supervised by those facilitating this ceremony;

there needed to be accountability when we were in this vulnerable altered state, where everyone had to trust in this obscure and foreign process.

This was a crossroads. A most important impasse had been reached in my life back home, leaving me all in to the notion that there is something more to this human experience, something that would require some ardent pursuit on my end.

While their warning was perplexing, in all honesty, I didn't give it much thought at the time. I was consumed in my own dramas. My near-constant, dire pain. Unable to hold on much longer, as the pressure kept mounting each day, drifting at sea further and further from my truth and feeling something had to be done, I had made the bold decision to explore an extreme course of action, stepping outside of what was "socially acceptable" to investigate for myself. With my baseline reality in peril, I needed help. Something drastic had to be done.

There were 30 or so international travelers, mostly Americans and Canadians, who traveled long distances to engage this medicine with a group of strangers. All of us were here for a reason, seeking relief from something. A common thread was our unwillingness to settle for what others have said—we were doing something about our dismay, our angst. We refused to remain lame-duck sitting targets.

Traveling solo this trip, it was different from any other I'd taken. There were no golf clubs, expensive resorts, or fancy dinners. This was about the reclamation of that which had been lost many years prior. I was there to figure out my "what and why" for living, what is it that I am here to do with this precious life of mine. This trip was a desperate plea for guidance and purpose, for something bigger than my all-consuming selfish indulgent habits. This unorthodox healing method had to be explored. Everything I had tried to this point had failed me. My weary soul feeling like it couldn't hang on much longer with things the way they were. With this unorthodox treatment, though, I heard of people getting better, finding relief from depression, PTSD, and addiction. I had to try it.

Only a few friends of mine knew that I was making this trip, that I was willingly subjecting myself to potentially throwing up and shitting myself in the name of healing and getting better—in the name of my mental health. This time was different, I knew this had to be done. Bypassing sharing with anyone I suspected might object to this bold move, I refused to subject myself to the dogmatic psychobabble of others. There had to be more. I was missing something, completely unable to wrap my hands around my caving world. My existential dilemma was on the front burner with boiling water pouring over.

During this unconventional healing experience, everyone would have to trust in these two leaders and their team of guides. For me, this was all worth the shot. I had tried everything at home, twice. Nothing worked. Nothing could quiet my mind's chatter. There was nothing that provided sustainable relief to my human condition.

Since arriving at Florestral the night prior, I had been on high alert, keeping a close eye on the others, scanning for anything that might be a clue that danger was forthcoming. All my radar picked up was love and gratitude. All of it felt almost too good to be true. There had to be a catch. I knew I was either in for an ambush or something truly beautiful and awe-inspiring.

This idea was fucking crazy! Whenever pondering this notion, though, I thought of how unhappy I was back home. In the midst of abundance, I was fucking miserable. My last-second thoughts of backing out were squashed. No turning back. This was my time to man up, to trust what lies within. To take my medicine.

After the medicine workers recited an incantation, we said a few prayers of gratitude and thanksgiving, then lined up to drink this plant medicine. I nervously waited in line, trying to breathe and stay present. When it was my turn, I held up a shot glass nearly full of this dark, thick medicine. I looked Vismay in the eyes and said thank you with a gesture of cheers, having absolutely no clue what I was getting myself into. Down the hatch like a shot of whiskey. Here we go!

TABLE OF CONTENTS

1

TRUE TO MYSELF

"Everyone knows that a broken heart can't see."
— DAN AUERBACH, SINGER/GUITARIST/POET

MAY 2011

The greatest distance in life is the distance between knowing and doing. For years, I hid from this hard truth. Likely, an entire lifetime would have been spent in avoidance of facing this quandary if it weren't for my pursuit of love and a deeper connection. It was easy to hide. We all do it to varying degrees. We wear masks to protect ourselves so we can more safely navigate our respective realities. It can be a mean and challenging world to face without any cover.

It is often easy to ignore what we believe to be true in a society that doesn't always value honesty and integrity. We go along with the status quo and meander through life pretending we aren't gifted with this most incredible human experience. We pretend we aren't made of the same stuff as the stars in the sky. In our complex and distracting modern world, it can be a grave and dangerous challenge to live an authentic life aligned with our values, our highest commitments, and what we believe to be true.

When my life was in near shambles, as though part of a natural progression I sought out help in an effort to better understand the mess I had created, finally engaging the services of a paid listener. I felt backed into a corner and had no other option but to seek unbiased assistance. I wanted to better understand my behavior and my continuous, repeating struggles—vicious cycles of unending drama. I could no longer do this alone. Years of infidelity and deception with myself and others had finally caught up. I was a liar and a cheat. And this wasn't just my mess anymore; my lowly actions were causing grave disharmony for my loved ones as well. Only objectivity from the outside could save me now. I was finally man enough to admit I could not do this alone—I needed the help. My past was too much to deal with by myself.

Working with a therapist, together, month by month, we peeled back layers. In time, I could see more clearly how I was playing a role in the perpetuation of my own disharmony. For so long, I was in denial unwilling to accept responsibility for my actions and my role in my own disharmony.

Through many long conversations with my therapist, it became clear just how much I was suppressing my childhood trauma. My whole life to that point was full of pretending this unresolved trauma wasn't a big deal and wasn't ruining my life. I had subconsciously adhered to inhumane cultural rhetoric: "Be a man and don't feel"; "Be strong and repress anything that gets in the way of your pursuits of money and material wealth"; "Do what you are told, stay in line. Push down feelings that could be a sign of weakness." At last, this toxic and erroneous way of thinking was decoded, seen for what it really was.

I could finally breathe again.

Emotions are meant to flow and move. The word "emotion," in fact, comes from the Latin word *emovere* ("move out, remove, agitate.") No different than a powerful water source that is dammed, our emotions will eventually find a release point. Truth works in a similar manner as well. This is best summed up by the following simple but profound quote from Buddha: "Three things can't be hidden long, the sun, the moon, and the truth."

After many months of talk-therapy, I realized my unresolved childhood trauma was at the root of all my problems. Failing to address this pain from yesteryear kept me from connecting with intimate partners on a deeper level. Trauma in the early years of development distorts and warps the victim's truth, and does until it is addressed head on, healed, and finally let go. When we compromise integrity in one area, the whole system is affected—and infected. The ego says, "I can compartmentalize and discern which feelings and emotions are felt. I have this under control." For too long, my ego and faux self completely ran the show. But when you numb pain, you also numb joy. Selectively numbing? Nope, we aren't wired that way. I was ready to do it differently.

I was prepared to handle the truth. I was prepared to

deal with any of the myriad of possible outcomes stemming from this declaration. It was time to fully address my past and, in doing so, confront head-on the childhood sexual trauma that had long garbled up my nervous system. After giving much thought to the myriad of potential outcomes and scenarios, I decided there was no way besides an intervention of truth. For the first time in my life, I didn't really care what would happen. I was prepared to deal with whatever transpired. No matter how ugly it got, I would hold my ground and lead with the truth. Matters of the heart require trust and letting go of expectations of a desired outcome.

My heart was breaking. I could feel my heart slowly dying; continued silence would mean imminent death, my remaining days lived as a coward, never knowing what lay on the other side of my biggest fear. I had reached "the threshold" where the pain of more silence and inaction was far more dangerous than confronting my past and the subsequent unknown. This reckoning was a moment of grace. Rumbling with my past was the most courageous thing I'd ever done.

Intent on freeing myself of the heavy burden I had carried in silence since my youth, I felt an immeasurable weight of shame and guilt. Last-ditch thoughts of wavering from my truth or "chickening out" were met and swiftly dealt with in a gangster-like manner; there was no denying what needed to be said and done. This was my life's first hardline. I knew this burden was not mine to carry alone; this burden was my family's to share and bear. As a family, we would intervene in the toxic falsehood of how the past was to be remembered.

It was time to shake things up with no expectation of anything in return. My immediate family had to be made aware of the sexual abuse that I encountered by a close family member. I arranged a meeting with my parents, also informing my older brothers by phone of my intent: our family's deep, dark secret would soon see the light of day.

My family was probably not that different from the typical American family. It had its many flaws and problems, real-life middle-class struggles, but everyone did their best. Now, though, pretending we were some picturesque family and that my upbringing was picturesque too was no longer an option.

It was an unpleasant day for me. I was nervous and scared, but fully prepared to speak the truth. Something inside of me clearly communicated that this was the right thing to do. All of this was an integral part of my healing process and could not be bypassed. It was a defining moment that I couldn't cower away from.

The day before our meeting, fears about how everything would shake out ran rampant in my mind. My hands were shaking; my palms were sweating. But when the time came to share this painful hidden truth, I was surprisingly calm. I said what needed to be said in a clear and grounded manner. My parents listened, taken aback. My mother was curious and engaged, while my father was seemingly confused, in a sort of indifferent shock. I can't blame him. This came out of nowhere, and our truths can indeed be shocking.

Sharing this was unpleasant, but it was probably the most honest moment of my life. This is my truth, our truth. Ugly or not, this was and is our reality.

"Why didn't you tell us?" came the obvious first question from my mother. I responded calmly, "There was too much fear. I didn't feel safe sharing this in my youth. In time, the fear turned to shame." Repressed shame had garbled up my nervous system, making honest communication nearly impossible for most of my lifetime.

That day of reckoning was huge for my personal healing. It was like the weight of the world was lifted off my shoulders now that my family also shared this truth, though this was a challenging situation that would take many years to properly heal and let go. Still, I know this: when words come from the heart, it really doesn't matter if they are received, acknowledged, or accepted—it's just truth. That spring day when I informed my parents, I'd unknowingly set my soul in motion through "right action," by telling the truth and therefore declaring that I was worthy of living an honest life. That I was worthy of love.

In also confronting the perpetrator, I learned that the same abuse that happened to me had happened to him: a messy, unsavory situation indeed.

Child sex abuse is extremely common. It carries a heavy emotional weight of shame that doesn't jive well with our material world. "Let's just push that one under the rug and pretend we didn't see it!" is the sentiment mostly shared by our collective culture. Because it is ugly and nasty, childhood sexual abuse doesn't get talked about, and, in silence, victims of abuse can't heal. This atrocious epidemic is a symptom of our sick society, especially the Church, perpetuating this systematic child abuse by blocking the flow of the natural sex energy in its clergy/leadership, the same people commissioned to watch over our vulnerable youth. We all know this is a HUGE problem, yet the Church defends their biggest assets—the sick clergy/priests. You better believe they know there won't be any real repercussions for their deviant behavior thanks to the deeply lined pockets of the Vatican.

In silence, victims are continually tortured by their memories of traumatic events, memories that play on repeat; In effect, these people relive the trauma again and again, until it is addressed head-on.

When met with silence, pedophiles have carte blanche to deceive and inflict harm on trusting and unsuspecting families, families that are too disconnected or distracted to sense this wrong happening in their very home. Because of the victim's shame and, often, inability to communicate about these evil acts, especially considering that most often the perpetrator is abusing from a place of authoritarian power, childhood sexual abuse is rarely reported until later in life when the weight of carrying this heavy emotional burden becomes too much to bear. It's a sneaky and subversive sickness. Many child sexual abuse survivors will never have the courage to say, "It is not mine to carry alone; it was not my fault. I was a child!"

One in five Americans are sexually molested as a child. The actual number could be even higher. This statistic is deeply troubling to me and is the reason I have chosen to write this book and share my story with the world. In good conscience, if these words inspire one person to look within and challenge their truth, then this arduous task of writing the story of my healing journey will have been worth it.

2

THE FRUITFUL DARKNESS

"This is the most simple and basic component of life: our struggles determine our successes."

— MARK MANSON

DECEMBER 2009

"Cheers, brother! It's gonna be a great night, I am feeling it!" I said to my brother Ben with faux confidence, laced with fear. This fearful confidence, although fake, was as real as I'd ever known. "I am ready to talk to some ladies," Ben responded in forward manner, quieting his voice as our waitress arrived at our high-top table, dropping off our third round of drinks: tall vodka sodas with some citrus fruit, though I can't recall whether lemon or lime. Our drinks, our then-medicine, went down like water. We were two of maybe ten people in the bar, having arrived early to warm up our livers and get the most out of the drink package. Staggering tables lined the outer edges of the long and narrow tavern. Cheesy New Year's Eve décor indicated we would close out the year in this establishment. The empty bar meant more frequent access to refills. Our base-level anxiety slowly faded with each sip.

This night, New Year's Eve in Chicago, was a top-shelf night. We clanked our glasses, looking one another in the eye. "How are you feeling? ...Are you ready for this?" My pep talk: motivational words intended to fire us up. Like warriors going into battle, we prepared for this evening's fight, but what were we fighting? "Let's do this!" Ben responded after a deep breath.

We were at a bar in our neighborhood that would serve us drinks all night till the midnight ball dropped; a drink and food package, hopefully with many pretty single woman. Or married women. It didn't matter. We had little shame when under the influence! All of this combined to make a perfect night to overindulge in some state-sanctioned chaos.

Ben was unhappily married with two kids. As for myself, I was a single man, reeling from a recent break-up. Hurting. Struggling big-time. *Tonight will be different. I won't feel anything. Tomorrow does not exist. Just tonight.* This had been my life approach since first engaging alcohol in my late teenage years.

Our unconscious strategy: find the line and own it! You know that line of intoxication: where you can still function, but your conscience is offline, your inner voice dumbed down. I had gotten really good at owning this line, diligently practicing this art without a clue of any other worthwhile pursuit. When crossing the line: a rough encounter with the porcelain gods. When on the line: rowdy fun and, at times, unsuspecting strangers in my bed, cornbread pancakes served gleefully in the morning. When below the line: an excruciating boredom, a stagnant state of indifference, an emptiness.

Nothing was worse than living below the line. We drank heavily to avoid that excruciating indifference at all cost.

Like professional athletes, we had done our stretching and had faithfully gone through our pregame routine. Not really, but figuratively; our drinking had us warmed up, our inhibitions had almost completely fallen to the wayside. Ben had a distinguished and fearless charm to him: part pawn, park rook; his strategy was to dive right in, unafraid to look stupid, unafraid of rejection. Perhaps it was the six years of additional heartache he had on me as my elder. Or his unhealthy marriage had a role to play. I'm not sure.

"Have you met my kid brother, Matt?" Ben said with a smirky grin, introducing me to two beautiful blonde women.

"No ...I haven't," one of the nameless wide-eyed beauties responded in a shy tone. This was a clear invitation to stride closer. As the docile and demure prey, these women played their role in our drama to a tee: coy, passive, with a sort of scripted nonchalance, so as not to be over-excited. But obvious signaling gave away their interest—head twists and look-aways, as if practiced thousands of times. Both of the finely dressed women had matching wrist bands, and, likely, they also matched our deviant and dishonorable intentions: love in the big-city. All of us played the only game we knew how to play, with carefully crafted rules, conditioned and programmed from the moment we took our first breaths as newborn babies.

"I am Heather. This is my friend, Karen." By this time, it had been two, maybe three hours of drinking, *Have these girls been here the whole time? How could I have not seen them?* I quickly pondered. It didn't matter now.

"So wonderful to meet you ladies." I always played the nice guy, true to form, the "Eddie Haskell" type, pleasant and well-mannered. Diplomatic. The dating gods looked down upon us all in favor. It was going to be a great night! From the word go, I was stricken, but pulled back from being too overt, so as not to give away my excitement. "What are you boys up to later tonight?" Heather had asked. Now this opportunity was a clear upgrade, our most promising scenario yet.

For the next hour, Karen, Heather, Ben, and I sparred with qualifying surface conversations: weather, favorite sports teams, recent vacations, go-to libations, cocktails, and spirits; all this lifeless conversation a practical exercise to build trust, a formality, a protocol, to show these ladies that we weren't sex-crazed ax-murder maniacs. If these ladies were going to come home with us, we needed them to feel safe.

By this time in the night, Ben and I were approaching double-digit drinks. A hazy fuzziness surrounded us all. Our female counterparts consumed just as aggressively as we did, which made for easy-flowing conversation with both Heather and Karen. *This is all too good to be true,* I thought. Out of the corner of my eye, I thought I saw Ben outside. *Why does he have his fists in the air like a boxer, like the "fighting Irish" mascot?* "Ladies, please excuse me." I darted outside to investigate, to protect the honor of my brother. Ben, the middle child, at times had anger issues. Even in his 30s, when we got drunk together, he often got sentimental about my arrival as our family's youngest, the unplanned baby who came, even then disrupting the status quo. My mother, in her mid-thirties, encouraged by some to abort me, never gave it a thought. She named me Matthew: "The gift of god."

Welcome to my twenties. Actually, nights like this were quite typical and persisted into my early thirties. With this as our culture's breeding ground, it is no wonder why we collectively fail so miserably at love and monogamy.

While I could write more about what happened outside that night or what would transpire in the hours later, just know that Ben and I were out till 4am that night and I held the line. We were lost. We honored our powerful evolutionary urges to procreate, trying our best while mating in captivity, adhering to the cultural norms and societal programs set forth: Bullshit, Inc.

For my entire life, people, mostly my family, prodded me in the direction they thought best fit. They gave me projections of how to live life and what it meant to live a good life. What this human experience was all about. This resulted in much confusion, since most everything I had seen and experienced aligned poorly with the instructions and expectations of others. So I didn't listen. I went my own way, looking to fill this infinite emptiness with anything— my way.

I would do anything just to feel something.

The walls of truth were closing in on me. No longer could I deny this obvious lack of sustainability. My behavior was despicable, but I had a free pass. That hurt from yesteryear gave me a sense of entitlement, not having to follow the rules and common courtesies of polite society. I rarely gave this notion any thought; with near-constant numbing and avoidance, I got really good at pushing it under. It had been my way of life since my teenage years when the heaviness of life became too much to bear sober. My circle of influence mostly shared the same values, although outliers existed on both ends of the spectrum. Nearly every waking thought I spent on scheming: how to make money and how to get laid. There was not much room for anything else. My actions were applauded, my sexual obsessions not as deviant as others—this was the unsustainable manner in which I rationalized my plight.

Every opportunity that called for me to speak up with honest expression was passed on like a vegan at Thanksgiving dinner. My cowardice had honed into a reflex while climbing a soulless ladder of success in an American big city. I got so good at passing the buck to others; I was an expert in not having an opinion or an original thought. An expert at being agreeable with others, complying even when I knew in my heart of hearts that I was doing wrong. Because of the pain and trauma in my heart, I made many poorly constructed commitments, unsustainable agreements that aligned perfectly with Bullshit, Inc. All this made me the perfect aspirant in our over-competitive world that values success by dollars rather than character, right action, loving our neighbor, and being a productive member of society, working toward the collective good. The childhood trauma I held in my heart was my buffer; it made me resilient by protecting me from getting too close to others. But I was resilient in relation to the values of my culture, not in relation to what lay in my heart, or to that of my evolutionary impulses. What makes this resiliency unsustainable, however, is how it buffers us from everything human: emotions, feeling, love, and empathy. This can be good when your motives are based on insecurity and consumption, not on what intrinsically makes us happy. My trauma helped me ignore my heart at an early age, but my values suffered as a result. I was as much a victim of Bullshit, Inc. as I was my childhood trauma. I complied and conformed. It was easier that way.

A typical day for me: work from 8-6, come home, pour a drink, and jerk off (my way to relieve myself of the edginess and existential malaise)—all this before napping for two to three hours almost every workday. It was only on the weekends where I actually slept through the night. During the week, I walked into the fire each day with heavy anxiety, making my way as a "professional" in the big city of Chicago. I picked an occupation that required very little soul but paid nicely, at least three times more than that of a teacher or policeman. I worked in sales, selling legal copy and imaging and e-Discovery services for law firms and corporate legal departments—a job pretty close to the bottom of the rung in terms of careers offering meaning, purpose, and fulfillment.

At this time, I lived with my brother, Ben. Yep, fists-in-the-air Ben. I ought to note both Ben and me got kicked out of the bar that night in question because Ben was defending the honor of a woman who was being mistreated by her aggressive male partner in a domestic abuse scenario. We lived in our Old Town apartment in Chicago's near northside. Old Town was a major upgrade from my roach-infested studio apartment in Uptown that I had lived in prior. Norm, the shitty landlord, didn't do anything about those sneaky little critters. Reflecting back, however, maybe the nearly constant pile of dishes in my sink had more to do with the vermin. Often, I felt lethargic. On the weekends, I'd lie around with epic hangovers, which made me a procrastinator or stuck in abusive, negative thought loops: struggling with crippling anxiety, doubts, and bouts of depression.

Although Old Town was not the best neighborhood, at least I didn't hear gunshots nightly. Ben, whom I had grown close to after my years at university, took on a contract and assignment in Chicago, giving us a unique opportunity to be roommates as adults. Ben and I commiserated together with boozy nights; we shared the same values: sex, binge drinking alcohol, devilishly rich foods, illicit drugs (when available), beautiful women, and a deep insecurity of not having enough. True Americans. Our bond and connection: the troubled upbringing in the class divided suburban Northshore of Milwaukee, Wisconsin.

I hated my life. The best proof of this hate: my actions, especially how I treated myself. I was consumed by a deep self-loathing and self-abuse. In my late 20s, I was drinking heavily, probably near 50 drinks per week. I fit in perfectly with everyone else. Thursday through Saturday, I hit it hard, and then a little Sunday fun-day afternoon boozy fun to stave off the intense anxiety I'd feel for the approaching workdays. If I had an invitation for state-sanctioned chaos, an excuse to push the limits, I accepted it. Early days in the week, however, were off-limits, as my life's biggest fear was that of poverty and failure, not keeping on a career path. At all cost, I never wanted to disappoint my father. Ever since my freshman year of college, I drank heavily like this. Sometimes more, sometimes less. That is just what you did. By doing this with others, it made it a way of life that came with a badge of honor for balancing this excess with an acceptable career path, mostly with other people who suffered from the same sickness.

At that time, I had a girlfriend. Her name? Karen. Yes, the girl from the bar. She came home with me that night. Our relationship grew on a very shaky and questionable foundation.

She was from nearby Michigan but also lived in the Windy City. We met during that drunken New Year's Eve celebration, a debauchery-filled night filled with Olympic-style excess and indulgence. Nights like that are perfect predictors of like chaos to come. When you build a house that has giant cracks in its base-level infrastructure, why would anyone be surprised when this house falls through the widening fissures?

Karen, the unsuspecting and sometimes naïve participant in my drama, got caught in my web of deception. Although looking back, she was equally guilty. She had her shit. We all do. Both of us were adults; it takes two to tango.

Our troubled relationship looked perfect from the outside. Enough so that Ben once gave us 60,000 frequent flyer miles, flying us both to Hawaii. He thought I was going to propose to her on that trip. Actually, I broke up with her a few weeks later. Typically, three break-ups were my calling card and that was my first strike. Katy Perry had me figured out: I was a "love bipolar." On one day. Off the next. A vicious cycle of highs and lows made building the trust necessary for love and connection nearly impossible.

While immensely painful at the time, I don't regret any of it. All of this was a training ground for my spirit. Every experience was useful, a lesson to behold. "The road of excess leads to the palace of wisdom. The tigers of wrath are wiser than the horses of instruction." William Blake knew that it is only through living and experiencing firsthand that we grow, learn, and become wiser. There is no substitute for doing, for trying, for action—for failing.

Things were really fucked up with Karen. I was far more interested in online porn than making love to this long-legged, six-foot-tall beauty. She was gorgeous, tall, slender, and strong, with very fair skin. Having played volleyball in college, Karen had a lean, athletic build. Country strong would be a fitting description of this country girl. Karen had a big heart, and she was very well-intentioned. Although a challenging time in both of our lives, we did have a lot of poorly aimed fun; we laughed hysterically all the time. She had a warmth and lightness to her.

Again, on the outside we looked content and fulfilled. An All-American couple poised to make babies and live happily ever after. But what about the ick? That gross feeling I felt during intimate moments of closeness? Our closeness needed the constant shroud of alcohol, some kind of distraction to be bearable. Her grace was far too much to behold while sober.

From the first night I had met her, she—only after excessive drinking—would initiate deep conversations about life and love, trying to get a pulse of my heart's intentions: "Feelings" talks, things I strictly avoided.

I cheated Karen by living life this way. And I cheated on her. By doing so, I cheated myself. Connecting with her was scary. Being honest seemed to bring up all sorts of unprocessed emotions, so I lied. And, we drank—a lot! She smoked lots of cannabis, too. Nearly every day, she got high. This probably helped her cope with all that was "unsaid" in our dishonest communication—it was her way to check out, to alleviate the pain of our truth. We did our best.

Since my youth, I had been addicted to porn—multiple online trysts, almost daily. I knew it was shallow, but I needed hits of dopamine to regulate my brain chemistry, to walk the line set forth for me by my family and the society that raised me. I first found a porno magazine at six years old. Porn is a far bigger a societal problem than we give it credit for. It is a tool used to control the sick and unaware. It zaps one's essence; one's inner powers are stymied by an action that doesn't align with our hardwired evolutionary drivers to procreate.

This unsavory excessive habit distorted my definition of beauty, leaving me only available for surface connections, too fearful and uninterested in anything deeper and more substantial. Most of my friends were no better than I was. We shared in our common affliction and sickness, many deceiving themselves and their partners as to how detrimental this addiction was. We laughed and joked about our shared plight and inability to connect with the women we were attracted to. That was all we could do, just laugh.

A disproportionate amount of those who experience sexual abuse in their early years of childhood development find themselves addicted to porn. They have an insatiable craving for more and more. As humans, we love novelty. We are wired for novelty. But, unknowingly, many become fooled and addicted by the feel-good neurochemistry that porn yields, ruining lives and sabotaging efforts for authentic connection. This leaves afflicted men without the "chi"—the lifeforce—necessary to properly channel their sexual energy in the direction of intimacy and exercise one's creative powers aligned with one's life purpose.

I was lost and nearly always in pain when not under the influence of some external substance. In my twenties, those quiet, still moments were agonizingly uncomfortable, almost unbearable, while sober. So I'd go hunt for another drink, another lover, anything to quell the ache, however temporary the relief might be.

The Sound of Settling

"Matt, I don't have the money to buy that plane ticket," Karen exclaimed with a bit of shame while we conversed in my high-ceiling loft apartment, our morning coffee in hands. She struggled financially ever since meeting me. Unable to balance our relationship and her work life, it didn't take long before she was fired from her job after only a few short months of dating. "This trip will be expensive." I retorted in an almost defensive manner. "I already have to pay for a hotel room. And there will be lots of drinking, partying." I drew the line with this, unable to tell her how I really felt. I stalled, constantly delaying my honest expression, my true feelings. Of course I had the money, but I didn't want to take her to Puerto Rico. I resented her, judged her for her struggles, but lacked the courage to break it off. To be real with her. Although we had fun, I never envisioned her as a long-term partner. But since she fit the mold of what I was supposed to have in a partner, I went with it, stringing her along, telling her what I thought she wanted to hear rather than my honest, heartfelt emotions.

My friends and family adored her. My pain was supposed to go away when I found the right woman—it didn't! "You will be missed. I really wish you could be there." I said with a fake sincerity. "It is only five days ...it is not that big a deal." Karen also was in a habit of swallowing her words. She took a couple of deep breaths and complied, stuck. "Have a great time! Please call."

I traveled to Puerto Rico as the best man at my friend Matt's wedding. It was a torturous weekend, then, since I was deathly afraid of public speaking, but I had to prepare for a best-man speech. My torturous fears tormented me for most of my time away. During that wild weekend, I binge-drank with Matt and our friends. Celebrating Matt & Kristen's holy matrimony with a destination weekend getaway in Puerto Rico provided plenty of outside distraction to numb the truth. At that time, I was completely broken. Cool and calm on the surface, but in shambles, in dire pain. My weight near 240 pounds, I was as heavy as I'd ever been, feeling sick all the time, pressure coming from every angle, in every aspect of my life—I could not hide. As I approached my thirties, my maturity and life responsibility wasn't growing in proportion to my substance abuse. This was obviously not good, an unsustainable equation. And the tide could not be slowed down.

That weekend I lost control. All of it, far too much to bear. After a wild night that came with 20 drinks and a $500 tab at a strip club and one Blackberry phone lost in the dark-strip-club-underworld-abyss, I was reeling, without a grip on my reality. The wheels were starting to come off. No longer could I deny that it was time to seek out help; my excessive childlike indulgent behavior was out of control; my denial was killing me; my trauma was endangering my survival and human dignity.

I had been in therapy before, and it helped a little. It started to give me a voice. But, just like a defensive all-star, I protected my deep, dark secret, afraid to go near those thorny and shameful memories even with a paid professional whose job was to get to the truth. It hurt too much. When I broached my past, I felt this intense, suffocating feeling in my chest, a dire constriction. I probably would have held this in forever, had it not been for the excruciating pain. It is pain, and only pain, that demands immediate change in every living species. My cage, the one that I created with my lies and deception, shook, rattling louder than ever: I needed help!

Returning home to Chicago from the Caribbean, I was fucked. Completely cornered, no longer could I outrun my conscience. I had cheated on Karen, making out with a stripper while on this wedding getaway. I paid $200 for an hour of conversation and open-mouth kisses. The stripper had looked at me like I was insane when I told her she was the most beautiful woman in the world, and I wanted to kiss the same dirty mouth she used to do whatever a woman of the night does. I had no shame when under the influence, and the most intense shame when sober: Matt 1.0. She complied with my request. "Lauren the exotic stripper," a very expensive, lusty hour of passion, had taken my money and moral dignity. I crossed the chasm of truth, now, in the grave danger of living without a working code of conduct.

This truth was too heavy to bear. I had to tell Karen about my infidelity. But in doing so, I packaged up a lifelong secret as a bartering tool. You want to hear the good news or the bad news first. "I have something really important to tell you. And I don't know how to say it." Karen listened intently; she really cared for me. "Whatever it is. You can tell me." I listened, while in bed, seated upright. I didn't have the courage to look her in eyes. "You can trust me. I am here for you." My heart beat out of my chest. My breath came short. I sat in front of her scared, shaking; a visceral response to the unbearable task of bringing to the surface a lifelong hurt.

This intervention-like conversation was completely out-of-character for us, having never really fought or had much in the way of depth in our conversation while sober. She had no idea I was about to drop a bomb on her. It took about 15 minutes of stalling, but I knew I had to hold this line. But I was literally unable to get the words out, no matter how hard I tried. It was really awkward. Maybe the most uncomfortable experience of my life. Karen knew this was important, a crossroads moment in my life. Her eyes were wide open, her focus and attention crystal clear. She had great compassion and patience for this suffering human being sitting within arm's reach. Looking back, I am ever grateful for the caring saint of a woman.

I led with the abuse. And just said it. "I was sexually abused in my youth ...I was just a kid." For the longest time I thought I would die with those words. I really did. "I am fucked up. I have done a lot of fucked-up things." Karen listened, her jaw dropping as her lover just released a lifelong secret. It was intense, a powerful cathartic release. My hands shook. She immediately started crying the tears I couldn't for all these years. She felt my pain, my desperation. A lover's embrace had me release tears that had been held for over 20 years. I am forever grateful for her grace, her ability to sit with my shit.

I agreed to get help, to see a therapist with the sole intention of fully addressing the childhood trauma. Karen, while disgusted with my behavior, was still willing to stick in out. To help me get better. While I never cheated on her again, I wasn't fully honest about just how ugly things were. At that point, we had too much for us to bridge. We couldn't last.

3

STAY ALIVE

*"Love is the only sane and satisfactory answer
to the problem of human existence."*

— ERICH FROMM

SUMMER 2014

My soul was on the bartering table. I was troubled and shallow and misguided, with a surrounding army of people to reinforce every misstep. I blindly followed the herd, dangerously reliant on approval from others to feel whole—completely lacking the courage and confidence necessary to express myself authentically.

I had been doing cocaine off and on for a few months; I really liked the high. I wanted people to like me. I wanted so badly to fit in so I crossed that line I said I never would. With cocaine, for a short while, the excruciatingly painful emptiness was gone; the cocaine filled me with life, clarity, and a sort of faux inspiration accompanied with a feeling of belonging. I belonged, only to be left emptier once the high wore off. Cocaine creates a synthetic version of yourself that brings with it a multi-day self-loathing hangover; two steps forward, three steps back, a sort of fool's gold. For me at least. Besides, there is blood on the hands of everyone who engages this ego drug. While I am no moralist, I can't and won't ignore this obvious fact and thus perpetuate its evil: sex trafficking; vicious cycles of gang violence; families and communities destroyed; the underlying power of the "war on drugs," which has failed by wrongly victimizing minorities perpetuating an unfair class division.

At that stage in my reality, money and sex were still all that occupied my mind. And this was mostly the same for those I associated with. The Problem: I had much of both money and sex, and I was still miserable. I was stuck. I mean really stuck, unable to free myself from endless negative feedback loops from Hell, seemingly having to rehash in my mind every conversation I had. *Should I have said this? Hope she didn't take it that way. Was he offended? Did I say thank you? Did she get the text?* Constant and unrelenting feedback loops bombarded me. It was exhausting. Many interpersonal relationships were running my life. I sorely lacked the tools and awareness to deal with the complexities of life and my relationships in our "always on" world. As I climbed higher and higher on my career path, becoming more and more our societal definition of success, I was sinking further and further into a black hole of despair and nothingness. As a means to protect myself and the pain and trauma in my heart, I pushed it under the rug and mostly pretended this wasn't the case. I'd put on a mask like many of those around me. That is what I had always done, what most people do. This inability to honestly communicate what I really thought was crippling—this indecision and doubt was slowly poisoning myself, and with each hesitation I betrayed my truth. It was overwhelming and tiring, so much so that I resigned myself to submission: to others, to my unhealthy and destructive habits, to pretty much everything. All of this had created vicious patterns of addiction with seemingly no way out. Welcome to the mind of a troubled but functional addict: here are your front-row seats and backstage passes.

No matter how hard I tried, I could not stop drinking. While I was drinking far less than during my terrible twenties, I still didn't have the courage to intervene and set healthy boundaries. Alcohol undermined my willpower. I was a leaf in the wind, at the mercy of the next social event and my inability to say "NO."

Each social invitation pulled me further from the shore, until I found myself in more and more dangerous waters, away from my truth. It was much easier to follow others and rely on their code and creed—consigning my power of thought and my ability to discern to others, completely unaware that I was slowly making my way to the slaughterhouse.

There was much confusion as to the steps necessary to get back on track. Where would I even begin in my desperate attempt to regain a sense of hope that had been absent since my youth?

This memorable day in question was typical, a Sunday I planned to spend staring at the ceiling in a state of complete hungover indifference, feeling the infinite blah and hopelessness, an aftereffect on my transgressions the night prior: snorting lines of cocaine while washing down my fear with cold beer. Another unsavory night out; I was barreling down the wrong path and heading for real trouble.

Instead, I clearly recall the conversation with Joe, who called out of the blue that Sunday: "One can't experience the deepest depths of romantic love unless he loves his brothers [fellow humans], as himself." Joe posited in the least preachy way possible. This is the first time I'd ever pondered brotherly love and what that even meant to me. Immediately, I was thinking, *How on Earth does the notion of romantic love have anything to do with brotherly love?* Joe went on and on about his personal experiences, what he was up to and so on—stating emphatically that he can't fully love others as himself. "Nah, it is just too much ...it is taking this love thing too far." True to character, Joe's response was honest and forthright. *But I can do that!* I thought reflexively.

Joe was a dear friend from my youth, my best friend growing up until we parted ways after our days at university. Since then, we'd have a token phone call every year or so to rehash old memories and we'd meet up for dinner on a few occasions. It was comforting to reconnect with someone with whom I shared such a strong familial bond. Laughter filled every get-together we had. It was like going back in a time warp to our preteen days when you just say and do anything and everything was hysterical. How life was before the never-ending seriousness set in, before we had to grow up and fulfill our respective societal roles and positions.

As children, in his family home's basement, we would toss a half-deflated Mickey Mouse ball around for hours and hours. This dilapidated ball that was less than half filled with air would faithfully complete our triad. Something was really special about those times. No cares in the world. We'd talk about life and the girls we liked and what we aspired to do and be when we grew up. Sometimes I wonder: *What ever happened to that ball?* ...And *whatever happened to those days?*

As we grew older, both of us knew we had very little in common except our past: lots of great memories, an insane amount of laughter, much mischief.

Therefore, this phone call was exceptionally memorable for me on so many different levels, a lifeline of sorts. It was serendipitous timing to be given advice from a dear old friend when I was struggling immensely, completely void of purpose. I was lost, alone, feeling so little inside.

After the minimum of niceties and small talk, Joe cut to the chase, clearly sensing my dismay. "I am not sure if this would resonate with you because of your upbringing with religion [implying my close-mindedness in my youth], but *The Art of Loving*, by Erich Fromm has been a special book for me, it's helped me make better sense of our world and my place in it." I listened intently. Truth is, I had been done with dogmatic certitudes for many years. While I had lived freely in many ways, I was still very much a prisoner to fear and the dogmatic residue of a lifetime of shame and guilt. In the midst of many blessings, I knew little peace of mind, stymied by errant and erroneous beliefs festering deep within my subconscious.

At that time in my life, I was oblivious to the fact that all of my disharmony was caused from my own short-sided thinking about life, leaving me unaware of how much a fearful, closed mind limits opportunities for growth and true adventure, for the exciting things that make us feel alive—for love! In my day-to-day routine, anything challenging my comfort zone would be strictly avoided.

Like a hawk, from miles away I could sense social interaction that would require authentic expression—interaction that would expose me for who I really was and what I truly felt inside. I did the easy thing, followed others, and hid behind alcohol. I avoided scenarios that caused dissonance, as any dissonance meant a potential disruption in my financial earning power. I didn't have the bandwidth for distractions, so I tuned out my surroundings and held steadfast to an intolerant mind, mostly unwilling to acknowledge my place in this world in relation to my fellow man. This completely closed me off to the whole brotherly love notion.

Joe's compassionate angle was perfect—it was pure genius, going a little something like this: "This worked for me," "I found benefit from this," "You might want to read this," "This might help," and so on. Indirect, patient, and understanding, this tactic perfectly flew under my ego's highly effective and sensitive radar. Speaking from his personal experience was a breath of fresh air; his honest and authentic sharing and tender approach stood out in a world where we have collectively taken righteous indignation to epic heights: "I am right; you are wrong," "My way is better," "This is the only way," "My god is better than yours," you get the point.

What made this call even more meaningful was the fact that I had been dodging contact from this old friend. Joe had crossed lines and been rude and tasteless on calls years earlier. I didn't have the time or energy to engage this nonsense; my boundaries were set and I was okay with letting him go. I had made a conscious intention to cut people out of my life who didn't treat me with kindness and respect, no matter who they were or what they've meant to me before. Something was different this year with that call; in my sad and desperate state, I graciously welcomed it as a life raft from an old friend.

Through an indirect challenge of sorts, our conversation left me with an immense amount of excitement and hope for what lay ahead on my path. It left me with an invitation for more.

This unsuspecting carrot dangled in front of my face would be all I needed, just enough to invite me out of the cage of smallness that I had been living in for too long. Ten dollars and three days later, *The Art of Loving* arrived at my doorstep in a small cardboard box delivered by Amazon. This little love book was a godsend, my invitation to figure out where I was going so desperately wrong in my search for romantic endeavors and overall life satisfaction; an opportunity to figure out why I was stuck in unhealthy patterns—dating often and repeating the same painful mistakes over and over. Never appearing any closer to the societal definition of success: wife, suburban home and 2.5 children. Like many in my social circle, dating and trying to find that perfect mate or find happiness with the mate you had became sort of an obsession.

Something clicked with this classic love book. In a concise and eloquent manner, it puts into nonthreatening words a deep message that summarizes many Eastern philosophies I later came across. Fromm, a philosopher and psychoanalyst, is largely regarded as one of the greatest thinkers of the twentieth century. The pragmatic approach of this book completely drew me in; real, direct, and honest, I could immediately apply these resonant words to my then-shitty life. It was particularly impressive how this little 125-page book served as a sort of guide/handbook for the next couple years. I read it several times over, a chapter here, a chapter there, pondering quotes and notions. I found so much relief in having words on paper that could help me make sense of my path, words that would help me realize I wasn't as lost as I thought. All of this paved the way for a semblance of gratitude; through my own eyes, I was now able to see much progress that had been made over the past few years, and even developed a sense of appreciation for my struggles and slow progress. Seeing my shortcomings and also my strengths through another's words and vast experience came at a perfect time. I connected the dots. Most of all, this book helped me deal with the fear of judgment and criticism from others. I now saw more clearly how spirituality could be used as a tool to foster more out of my life in relation to our busy modern world; nothing was lost in translation for me with *The Art of Loving*.

At that time, I had a weak stance in my religious affiliation, like almost everyone I had known to that point in my life's journey. Talk is cheap. Few around me actually lived in alignment with their words. I had grown weary of all the judgment and hypocrisy; the phony bullshit, the broken paradigm of belief I pretended to adhere to. This disturbing notion was strangely liberating. It was the start of identifying the problems that plagued my existence.

We live in a time where many people have a great challenge sitting with themselves without distraction for longer than a minute or two. Why is this? What is so scary about those quiet moments alone? Looking at all the busyness in my life and the lives of my loved ones only compelled me to deepen my very early understanding of what spirituality really was.

The book Joe recommended was the first one I had read that truly spoke to me, having practical application that could immediately be applied to my life. The notion of love as an art to "practice" gave me great hope. I had been called "coachable" on many occasions during my upbringing, and I knew that I could work toward the attainment of important goals. I had been doing that my whole life through school, sports, my career, and various tasks/objectives that I had taken on. Concentration, patience, and discipline: the three required attributes necessary to cultivate an environment where love can be realized. Man oh man did that resonate deep inside of me. Trusting this simple and profound message, I started to ponder a daily practice, slowly seeing outside of this shadowy haze of fear that I had carried into adulthood. Much work would be needed, but I'd found a great place to start, working each day to cultivate life attributes and better understanding the virtues needed to create the conditions necessary for love to blossom from within. All the while, I built faith in myself and my experiences and place in the world. I understood more clearly that everything in my life's journey had been a lesson to that point. All of it—everything had been a lesson to teach me, to help me grow. From that point forth, my thoughts and actions were now part of the equation; I started to shed the victimhood I had clung to since my youth.

What impressed me most about Fromm and *The Art of Loving* was his observation that we live in a society where it is valued more to *talk* about God and religion than it is to live a godly life in accordance with the doctrine itself; blabbering about going to church is strangely more highly regarded than living aligned with the word itself by incorporating the teachings into our daily thoughts, words, and deeds—ACTING in accordance, not talking in accordance, with the divine.

How backward is this?

Looking back, I am not surprised that this important guide in the form of Erich Fromm was introduced by my closest friend from childhood in that synchronistic fashion, a friend who credits me for being there during his horrendous time of pain after a serious break-up with a high school girlfriend. We joked (not funny) that I would keep him from taking the toaster into the bathtub. It was that dire for Joe. For a month or so, I would check in on him in a regular manner to ensure his wellbeing and safety. During a college break-up, he was confronted with the harsh realities of the existential dilemma. He had an early spar with the human condition—an unavoidable war we all face at some point. Joe needed someone to hear him out so he could make sense of his own pain. He needed somebody he trusted and valued to be present for him. Unknowingly, many years later, he would return the favor when I was struggling, calling at the most perfect time when I found myself in crisis, stuck in the muck of life and getting deeper and deeper into it.

At the time of that surprise phone call I was insane—actualizing fully Einstein's definition of insanity: "Doing the same things over and over with an expectation of different results." I fell deeper and deeper into a dark abyss, without any clue as to how to get out. Joe offered much comfort and support, sensing that his old friend from yesteryear was down and out and needed some simple advice, needing to be heard. That timely conversation and that subtlest challenge to investigate brotherly love became my saving grace, a most worthy objective to channel my energy toward. Through that conversation, many seeds of truth were planted in my fertile mind. That moment reinvigorated my desire for reading. I felt inspired, devouring books in the self-improvement, spirituality, science, and inspiration/positive thought arenas. I had been hurting and waiting patiently for that spark, an insight into a way out of my anxiety-ridden prison of extreme highs and lows that I had accepted as my reality. Then the phone rang and everything would be different. Connection is that powerful—one conversation kept me from reaching an even deeper low in my then-freefall.

4

WHATEVER IT TAKES

"Don't let joy be an accident. Create it."

— TOM BILYEU

It was my 35th birthday, October 16, 2014, the day I sold my business. I worked my ass off for that business for many, many years. It was a momentous night, finally finding a larger national company to purchase our company, effectively setting me free to pursue my heart's desire and a greater purpose. Although a business owner, my shift out of corporate America to free-spirit traveler in search of truth, might have been the perfect choice as researchers have found that "purpose" is an indistinguishable quality that builds resilience. And Yuval Harari, a historian/futurist and the author of *Sapiens and Homo Deus*, sees emotional intelligence and the ability to recreate oneself as the most important skills to have in this rapidly changing world of exponential technologies and artificial intelligence where many of our jobs will become automated.

What follows is my approach to untangling myself from a loveless career and the mess I had created of my life. Coming to grips that everything was my fault was strangely, one of the most empowering narratives I've adopted: a scary, disturbing, difficult truth. This openness to the truth, my plight, to what was: unknowingly, a catalyst for positive transformation. Shifting from a state of denial to acceptance allowed me to feel what I was unwilling to feel for so long; properly acknowledging my anger and frustration and this endlessly expansive emptiness I felt for too long. All of this positive change seemed chaotic at first but would get better with time.

This special night marked the beginning of the end of my business partnership with Gary, although there would be much work ahead as I had verbally committed myself to many more years working with the new management. Gary, a perennial underachiever with our work dynamic the way it was, would thrive in the new work environment; he was a "thoroughbred salesman" who needed others to compete against in order to perform his best. His deepest motivator was competition, and the new dynamic brought forth when we merged our company with a more established national network surely would provide that.

My partnership with Gary had been a very productive one. I learned so much from this man, and he was likely the best teacher I ever had. The two of us worked hand in hand, side by side, for the better part of 13 years. I learned the "ins and the outs" of entrepreneurship. We went through a lot together. My uncertain life path out of college led me to Chicago in pursuit of money and status, and Gary had been there the whole time.

Although we made money and met our objectives, it

wasn't a great long-term fit with Gary. Our relationship was dishonest. We were co-dependent in many respects—I was unable to express myself authentically on a consistent basis and Gary was maybe over-expressive. A seasoned expert at confrontation after growing up in the rough Southside of Chicago, Gary could be a bully. His own personal trauma was too deeply rooted to fight against. I was no match in a physical fight or a verbal altercation. We all have shit and pasts, pain in our hearts. I love the man, but knowing this background will add needed context for the words to come.

While he was probably the most entertaining storyteller you'd ever meet, almost all of his stories would leave you saying: "What the fuck? Did that really happen?" His life provided a far contrast to the north-shore suburban life where I had come from: we were definitely the "odd couple."

As a youth, Gary microwaved gerbils while conducting a middle school science experiment. He still insists that his science and methodology were sound. The Catholic school authorities, priests and nuns, informed his parents that he was a bad seed—even going as far as calling him the antichrist.

In probably the strangest story Gary proudly tells, he once picked up a helmet that had a human head in it, while holding a chili dog in the other hand. A motorcyclist, the older brother of a friend, was riding his motorcycle and had an unfortunate, life-ending encounter with a hanging wire that severed his neck and spine. Pretty gruesome, and probably true.

Gary would also share about the abuse that he would endure from the hand of his father. He grew up in a time and place where it was more acceptable to beat the shit out of your children. His father, an Italian immigrant who had his own boxing career cut short because of a faulty heart (rheumatic fever), pushed his son relentlessly. Bursts of uncontrolled anger, under the guise of "discipline" and "tough love," would have had him locked up in the sensitive times in which we now live.

Of course, I heard repeatedly Gary's countless stories about his sexual escapades and conquests when he was a single man, reveling in the glory of yesteryear. Gary was in a band. He played guitar. I need say no more. I'd be the first to admit that Gary's autobiography would be a much more entertaining read than the book you are holding in your hand.

Many years in the Catholic Church left him, at times, disgruntled and estranged from his family. Even in his mid-forties, many of his friends have died, having been met with brutish ends. It seemed that almost monthly he was heading out to a funeral. Morbidity abounds in Chicago's south side, making me wonder just how rampant childhood sexual abuse was in the parishes that dominated the schools in that proximity. My guess is Gary's circle of influence, where most attended Catholic schooling, is far more affected than the national statistics that say 1 in 5 are subjected to childhood trauma, but I am not sure. No one really knows just how expansive the reach of Church sex abuse is.

Despite his colorful past and penchant for sharing it, our time together was full of positive takeaways and insights gleaned; Gary taught me a brand of tough love and pragmatism that prepared me to embark on my life's journey and subsequently do this work. For a stretch of 13 years, we ate more amazing food and had more laughs than one could ever imagine. It wasn't all that bad. It wasn't my calling, but we made it work. All the while, our time together inadvertently schooled me for what was next in my life, preparing me for more meaningful lessons that surely lay ahead.

Everything started to change with Gary (and all my other relationships) once I found meditation. It was as if good things just effortlessly happened in every aspect of my life, everything shifting in the subtlest of manners. It didn't take long to meditate myself out of our at times troubled relationship—the transformative power of peace!

Once incorporating this inner peace practice, I no longer blamed him for my plight, for my being stuck. Again, I assumed all blame for my problems. Taking accountability was a challenging step, but in doing so I found almost immediate benefit and clarity. Gary and I were stuck in negative loops; the same issues bounced between us on repeat. And either he was not open to honest communication or I lacked the courage to honestly confront. Either way, we were stuck. Gary had a wicked temper, but even he would admit he had a long wick. Meaning, it took a lot for him to blow up, but when he did blow his top, it was a sight to see. A trained fighter, Gary boxed until his was 19 years old. All Gary knew was pain. Everyone around him had died: father, mother, sister. Only he and his estranged sister were left.

Gary's problems were my problems for many years while we struggled to grow our business. There was a Cold

War that he was completely oblivious to. I felt it. Nothing was getting done and we had little prospects for anything more than a company that would yield two generous livelihoods and nothing more. But I wanted more. I wanted to know what freedom would be like, so I worked my ass off, knowing that at some point the work would pay off and I would be compensated fairly by way of selling my business. I effectively became an indentured servant to fear and my past. I had to work hard for a really long time without ever knowing if my work would pay off. This was an invaluable, golden lesson that helped me develop grit and resilience—I had to develop faith if I was ever going to know freedom.

One day it just made sense. Peace, it is that simple. I needed to cultivate the inner peace to be the change, so I could be the solution. No more looking outside, from that point on, I was intent on running experiments from the inside out. We would be in business meetings and I would not yield from a non-violent resistance stance rooted in peace. Whenever Gary would get angry and confrontational, I'd maintain my equilibrium as if my life depended on it. In those challenging times where Gary was triggered, and my own anger arose, often resulting in belligerent unconscious behavior, I would breathe and pause, holding steadfast to my stance of peace. I'd ask him, with a slight smirk on my face, "Gary, why are you getting angry? Aren't we supposed to be partners? Aren't we supposed to be working together?" This simple adjustment ended the overplayed cycles; our negative loops were no match for intentional peace. From that point, Gary could see clearly his own actions through me, as if I were a calm, still lake. He could see his reflection in my non-reactivity, my peaceful disposition serving as an unsuspecting mirror. This way, Gary wasn't told that he was being an asshole or an angry man. He was shown this through my peace and presence and was able to error-correct on his own. A man like Gary, who has been through hell and back, can't be told anything; their ego has become too defensive. The man had mental grooves as deep as the Grand Canyon, and these grooves needed to be avoided and worked around at all costs.

This strategy is an extremely powerful stance used by Gandhi to free India and Martin Luther King to lead the Civil Rights charge of the 1960s. To date, I believe it is the only methodology that has proven effective for enduring change. When you combat fear with fear, you get a multiplied and worse form of fear. That is the same insanity that has been used in the countless failed attempts: "The war on Drugs, Crime, Terrorism," you name it, this approach only makes the situation worse. Fear can only be productively dealt with by love and understanding. This principle is far easier said than done, but from firsthand knowledge I know it works and all parties are better for it at the end. Jesus encouraged everyone to turn the other cheek, and he was right. Peace is the strategy that works.

All of this is about peace. All of it. And it can only start from within. Peace is our easiest, most natural state of being, contrary to all that we have been programmed to believe about our brutish human history and past. In peace, there is effortless action and abundance of clarity. From peace, we can bring forth our creative inspiration and channel the divinity that lies within us all.

Once Was One

I had food, shelter, and sex for the foreseeable future; my most basic biological and physiological necessities were sufficiently satisfied. I was supposed to be happy, grinning from ear to ear. But I couldn't deny my misery, still stuck in my loveless work that occupied so much of my time and energy.

These realizations were indeed a mind-fuck: the more I attained from the outside, the more miserable I was. My life had become a strange inverse of what cultural wisdom told me was true.

This all posed some serious questions for me: How is this so? Am I being true to myself? Whose definitions of success am I adhering to? Am I living the life of my dreams—do I even have dreams? How willing am I to honor and trust my intuition, this "Feeling" that something more—something greater—awaits me? And, yes, am I batshit-crazy for pondering these notions?

Shortly after the sale of my business, I had a series of synchronistic events and chance happenings like never before. Things were about to get interesting...very interesting!

In my many years in Chicago I had gone on many hundreds of dates; seemingly one every week or two. It was always nice to meet new people. An active dating life yielded much adventure and novelty, but, still, I found no fulfillment, or even a satisfactory level of intimate connection—the closeness my heart and soul yearned for.

In a city where I cordially knew hundreds of people, my social network included people from many walks of life. People often set me up on blind dates. Everyone knew I was single, eligible, and looking, and probably sensed my desperation, too. It had been an often-tiring 15 years of dating with a few long-term relationships sprinkled in my constant pursuit of a deeper connection. It was getting more and more apparent that I replayed the same dramas over and over, never getting any closer to settling down or finding that special person to share my life with.

This wave of synchronistic encounters started while out on a date with Jess. We had been set up by our mutual friend Lina. Jess was lovely, kind, and sweet. We met at a bar in Chicago's Logan Square, sitting belly up at the bar. Like me, she was on the free-spirit side and loved to travel, so naturally Lina thought us a perfect fit. Jess had many adventures that took her around the world and back a couple of times. About halfway through our date, I was taken aback and awe-stricken. Not by her beauty or charm (although she was very pretty), but by the breadth of her experiences she shared so generously: "I just got back from an adventure in Peru. Machu Picchu was the most incredible of sights and natural wonders," Jess shared with an enthusiastic sparkle in her eye. To that point, our date had been a bit of a pissing contest as to who had more adventurous travels under their belt. She clearly had me beat; I was thoroughly impressed. My concession brought forth marvel at this worldly adventurer. Sensing there much to learn, I interjected with curiosity. "What a special opportunity. That sounds absolutely incredible! What was the highlight? What were your thoughts and impressions?" Like a curious kid, I attentively waited for her response. The travel experiences of others have always inspired me. We see and understand ourselves much better through the differences of others. This is how we grow. This is how we evolve. Jess responded in a hesitant and cautious manner, projecting her obvious discomfort while recalling this particular time and adventure. "The trip was incredible and, yes, of course I would love to go back. The people were lovely and the nature was incredible. The Andes were special like none other. I will definitely stay away from San Pedro next time, though. It was awful, ...I threw up. It was really awful."

"San Pedro?" I quickly responded, cutting her off before she could get another word in. "What do you mean by San Pedro?"

"It is a hallucinogenic cactus that is used in healing ceremonies by the Peruvian natives. We tried it and it was awful. I got really sick. I'll never do that again."

Interesting, very interesting! For the remainder of the night, my anxious, one-track-mind would only think: get home and research "San Pedro"!

"Check please!" I asked our server in an almost impatient manner, more focused on my pending Google search to investigate her claims than on our potential relationship.

After our date, I dove in and stole a goodbye kiss, letting her know my intention to call and see her again.

That would be the last time I would see Jess. My life was about to drastically change.

Heading home, I could barely conceal my excitement. What is all this San Pedro talk about? Motivated to make sense of this and quell my curiosity, my search didn't take long to come up with satisfactory answers. How was it that I never have heard about this cactus? I had heard about peyote in racist/judgmental snide remarks from others mocking indigenous cultures. Maybe this was the same? Is this San Pedro similar to the magic mushroom I've ingested at concerts with friends? I kept posing these questions as I aggressively filtered through a labyrinth of content. My curiosity was intense: searching countless websites and message boards for the hours to come, scouring for trustworthy information. In searching for San Pedro, I came across another intriguing plant medicine called ayahuasca, a medicine from the Amazon Rainforest having purported healing effects against depression, trauma, and addiction. Get out! How come I've never heard of this? This was irresistibly compelling for me, as I still struggled with addiction and depressive episodes. Although I binge drank much less than years prior, I was still an alcoholic who would drink to get drunk, to numb my fear and anxiety over life, to cope. I was still numbing myself and hiding from my truth, this could not be denied. *Was there really something out there that might help me?* I pondered before closing my laptop and going to bed. After much time researching, I let this all pass. It was too far-fetched to give any more attention. I had work in the morning to gear up for.

Only days later, I came across another online article that spoke to the incredible healing effects of ayahuasca, grabbing my attention once again. It was inviting to see this publication in a mainstream news source and outlet; apparently this plant medicine from the Amazon was offering tremendous relief to traumatized U.S. veterans and victims of sexual abuse and childhood trauma. These psychedelic medicines were helping people confront old traumatic memories by healing the root of the trauma. This notion was fascinating. Psychedelic which means "mind manifesting" were just starting to come on my radar. Although I had done much inner work by this point, I found myself captivated at these scientific claims that this psychedelic, taken as medicine, could heal what I had barely begun to confront. Many of these studies indicated that these medicines were highly effective in safe and controlled settings. These notions corroborated my limited personal experience with psychedelics—the temporary relief felt from ingesting psilocybin, the active healing ingredient found in magic mushrooms—these incredible experiences partying with friends. Still, all of this was a lot to take in— it caused a feeling of dissonance. *How is it even possible that illegal drugs could be used to heal depression and help people heal from trauma and abuse?* Again, skeptical, I'd let this all pass and resume my life as it was. I had work to do.

A week or so later, meeting up with my friend Courtenay, I would get slapped in the face by karma and another chance happening, while meeting for beers and pizza at a West Loop Chicago pizza parlor. It had been some time since we last hung out and I could feel our friendship slowly drifting apart. Courtenay was nicknamed "The Wildcard," but I'd call him CK. We spent much time in the years prior playing golf and getting drunk together, chasing girls while taking weekend getaways to warm weather to hit a white ball around with a stick. We always had fun together. CK was a straight shooter, while still managing to live up to his nickname. A solid and loyal friend, a good guy to have on your side during life or in a bar-fight. I once saw him knock out an obnoxious drunk idiot at bar closing time with an impressive right jab; he had a temper, but this guy had it coming to him. Afterward, he was in shock. I got him up to speed quickly. "Dude, you have to leave now—they will arrest your ass."

After catching CK up to the happenings in my life, the new developments with work and romantic escapades that I was surely bragging about, he eagerly shared some well-timed news.

As if he couldn't hold it back much longer, CK unleashed some heavy truth on me, excited about a documentary-like TV program he had watched weeks earlier. A CNN episode, This Is Life—Jungle Fix (www.cnn.com/videos/bestoftv/2014/10/23/lisa-ling-jungle-fix-2.cnn) took a news camera into a medicinal healing ceremony in Peru and reported their findings. Hosted by Lisa Ling, she investigated the claims that numerous Westerners, especially U.S. combat veterans seeking relief from war trauma, were claiming about the powerful transformational healing effects of this potent psychedelic medicine. Yes, you guessed it: ayahuasca. Again, this mysterious plant medicine returned to the forefront of my mind.

"Have you ever heard of ayahuasca?" CK asked me. "Apparently its this super strong psychedelic that people are using to heal from trauma and find inner peace."

It was shocking to be having this conversation after all the research I'd been doing. "Yes, I was reading about this in the last couple of weeks. What do you think about this? It seems pretty far out."

CK didn't have an opinion either way, but broached the subject because he sensed the changes in my life. Years later, CK would affectionately admit that at that time he sensed I was into that "peace shit," sharing candidly with a friendly grin on his face about my shifts toward yoga and meditation.

At that West Loop pizza parlor, I consciously asked for the first time, *Is the Universe trying to communicate with me?* It was getting eerie. After never hearing about ayahuasca in my life, this medicine presented itself three times in the course of a few weeks. (I've since heard from many others that this medicine typically shows up in one's life three times, usually in an abrupt manner.) Along with these chance happenings, I felt this overwhelming guidance and urge from within, the whole thing resonated as honest and right, coming from the deepest depths of my being.

It was abundantly clear that this medicine was calling to me. That night, I booked my retreat and flight to Costa Rica. (This destination seemed a little less intimidating than Peru's Amazon Rainforest, where apparently this medicine healing tradition began). Whatever I was seeking, I would find it in the foreign lands of Central America.

It was time to shake things up. No longer could I delude myself with encouraging words and affirmations I didn't fully believe in. My soul was growing weary. I had to act, to do *something*. Shake shit up by trying something new. Without a bold move on my part, how was anything ever going to change? How would I ever really truly know if there was something greater for me without stepping out of my comfort zone? These questions bombarded my psyche as I arranged the logistics for my ayahuasca healing retreat and adventure in Costa Rica, pleasantly surprised to find that Costa Rica, a country that I always dreamed of traveling to, had many psychedelic healing options.

There was a sense of immediacy, with having only a seven-day window of available vacation days, just after Christmas and before New Year's. This may have been the last time I had the freedom to travel for the foreseeable future before getting sucked into the new business and the increased responsibilities and expectations of my new employer: *now was the time.* It was time to jump into the deep end of life, to see just how well I could swim.

For the next couple weeks, I got serious about my intentions. I wasn't naive to the fact that I was going to embark on a journey to a faraway land to drink some jungle juice that makes you puke.

Ayahuasca is a medicine that indigenous peoples have been drinking for many hundreds, possibly even thousands, of years. Its active ingredient is DMT—dimethyltryptamine, a molecule that is present in every living organism, plants and animals alike. It is said to be the "spirit" molecule. Everyone has surges of this naturally occurring psychedelic molecule upon dying.

There was a solemn and intensely focused seriousness

that permeated my being as I prepared, making me dialed in like a laser for the weeks prior to this healing adventure, as if my number was called. For what? I didn't know. But who was I to question all this? Did I really have it all figured out? I would submit and trust this intuitiveness, with a strong knowing that I would never forgive myself for not going *big* one time in my life.

I made a long list of all the supplies that I diligently gathered before my pending flight. I found there was a pre-ceremony diet you were encouraged to follow: no alcohol, meat, dairy, or sex before the medicinal healing ceremony. Basically, no fun, as it is advised to eliminate most everything that stimulates the body. The consensus on the message boards was that it is best to abstain from your vices for as long as you can before engaging this powerful healing plant medicine, but the minimum abstaining should be for a few days to ensure your system is clean before engaging this potentially volatile medicine. This abstaining from creature comforts supposedly makes your energies more sensitive to the medicine's healing effects, deepening the overall experience. I intended on fully abstaining from these creature comforts for two weeks beforehand...but, it ended up only being only five days or so. I found myself unable to resist holiday drinks and the sexy time that would come after too much red wine.

Nearly every website I read stressed the importance of having clear intentions: What would you like to experience? Why you are engaging this healing medicine? All of this served as fair warning, reinforcing the potential of this medicine that falls outside what is accepted in our Western healing paradigm.

My intention, the reason I was embarking on this obscure journey, would slowly crystallize after days of contemplation.

I skipped my usual family Christmas that year in Milwaukee, Wisconsin. My mother would visit me in Chicago, thus making it easier to honor my diet, eating clean in the days leading up to this maiden voyage. I was vague about my pending travels, only letting loved ones know that I was going to explore Costa Rica's abundant nature. At that time, I had a good poker face, intent on keeping other people's opinions and fearful projections at more than arm's distance. I felt crystal clear about this decision, as assured in this bold move as anything I had ever done to that point in my life. It felt prudent not to have others worry, or potentially muddy my inner waters of clarity about this most important life juncture.

As a grown man, this was something I had to do.

With the importance of the intention emphasized so emphatically, I made much time for meditation and inquiry, time for tuning out the outside world to look within. Really, it was the first time I had done something like this. To my chagrin (and then delight), just days before heading to Costa Rica I had a profound meditative experience in my Chicago bathtub; this completely caught me off guard, when my slow and intentional breathing had my body buzzing, hands shaking in fearful surprise. It was probably the first time in my life I had calmed down my "always on" sympathetic nervous system by accessing my parasympathetic nervous system with my intentional conscious breathing. Though this experience is basic biology to me now, this was scary, even freaky, at the time. Was I losing my shit before my journey even began? Nope, this phenomenon was merely a product of my actually slowing down, turning off my phone, and getting serious about life, for the first time really looking within.

With my intention firmly in hand, I was ready to jump into the unknown. Prepared or not, here I come—Let's do this!

5

FROM
THE GROUND UP

"Most unhappiness is caused by people listening to themselves....instead of talking to themselves."

— WILLIAM JAMES, FATHER OF MODERN PSYCHOLOGY

DECEMBER 2014

Landing in Costa Rica, all I could think was, *this is happening.* Whatever "this" is. It was Christian, the gracious taxi cab driver, and I, and a three-hour ride from San Jose to Florestral, the remote healing farm where I'd spend the next five nights. Traveling logistics were a challenge. Costa Rica has limited options—an infrequent bus schedule, limited roads/routes, airports, etc., and then of course the language barrier—my Spanish is awful. It was easier for me to just take the $200 cab ride than deal with the headache. That was largely how I operated at that point in my life: just throw money at the problem.

We took the short way through the mountains, approaching San Isidro at 9pm or so; the city, a near ghost town, surprisingly dark too with its limited street lights;

we were definitely not in the U.S.A. After getting lost, Christian and I found some locals that gave us directions enough to Florestral. Being in a foreign land still struck me as eerie. Then we drove down a long, remote, unpaved road to a destination I had so many questions about. It was fortuitous that it wasn't raining, or Christian's taxi surely would have gotten stuck in the mud. It was suggested to only take a 4x4 vehicle if raining; we were chancing it in a taxi. It was a beautiful and clear tropical night. The road was insanely bumpy, the night sky pitch-black dark. Our cab only drove five miles per hour as we trudged forth on the barely usable path/road; the bottom of car hit the earth enough to make me squirm every minute or so. I kept thinking, *What am I doing right now?!*

Finally, after an unanticipated adventurous cab ride, we arrived at the retreat and the much-anticipated healing adventure could now begin. As much research as I had done, still, I was coming in blind; all I knew was there were two ayahuasca ceremonies with an option for a third, and plans for a traditional Native American sweat lodge. Sure, I read a lot about what was to come, but words do no justice in articulating what would transpire in the coming days. This was an experience that required a leap of faith into the unknown with a significant exposure to risk. To my relief, I found much comfort when seeing an international crowd of twenty to thirty other travelers upon my arrival in this seemingly hidden enchanted forest. People talked and engaged in what appeared to be positive-spirited conversation. *...I am not the only crazy one*, I thought to myself. The presence of more women than men made this unfamiliar place seem even more inviting.

A lovely woman name Nicole, slender and petite with sandy blonde hair and noticeable bright eyes, greeted me. She gave me a warm embrace before swiftly investigating to ensure that I had paid a fair price for my cab ride. I did indeed.

Nicole, I learned, was one of the medicine workers and the "matriarch" of the healing farm. I'd later find out she was from South Africa and had spent the better part of her life helping others heal holistically from PTSD, depression, and other emotional challenges with the sacred plant medicine ayahuasca. Nicole was the wife of Vismay, the shaman/medicine-man whom I had emailed while setting up all of the logistics for this healing retreat. Shortly after arriving, I met their three children who called Florestral home, too.

This was all far out, drinking jungle juice with a forest family in a sparsely populated part of the most beautiful country on Earth. Why the fuck not!?

Although feeling much trepidation and unease, I fully made my way through the group; leading with my typical big smile, introducing myself to many of the other participants, finding an almost overly warm greeting wherever I looked. Everyone seemed happy and content. I had never hugged more strangers in my life. The majority of those at this retreat were from the U.K. and the U.S.A./Canada. The others had traveled from all around the world. The obvious diversity had me enthusiastically relishing the opportunity to engage these free-spirited travelers. Immediately, the atmosphere had a similar exciting/nervous feel to the European travels I was accustomed to. It felt like a "fact-finding" mission, wondering:

"How do you do it? You know, break free." Sensing that many there were untethered from a 9-to-5 existence, I'd scour and survey, hoping to pick up tools and techniques that may lead me to more personal freedom.

With my flashlight in hand, I was led to the dorm I'd be sharing with five others—simple, no frills, a large concrete slab with three walls, a roof and mosquito netting/screens. The mattresses on the beds were thin and pillows a tad dingy. At that time, Florestral would have had a hard time applying for a two-star hotel rating. I didn't care. I was tired, and far more interested in solid rest and the adventure that lie ahead. This felt like camp—rugged outdoors, minimalist living aligned with the natural environment.

The next day, I awoke rested and recharged, intensely curious for what lay ahead. We had a full day of settling in and meeting more arriving travelers before an orientation covering the retreat plans/itinerary, laying out our adventure to come. Three times daily, we gathered as a group to eat. Their communal-style eating was different, but I enjoyed seeing everyone getting along, engaging each other in a friendly and spirited manner. Florestral is strictly vegetarian, and most of the meals served were vegan, so as not to interact with the plant medicine diet: which is a special diet with recommended prohibitions, discouraging foods that don't interact well with ayahuasca.

Around three quarters of the participants were completely new to this plant medicine healing ritual, alongside me, tasting this bitter brew for the first time. During the day I spent much time making my rounds, socializing more with the other travelers, again, trying my best to glean insight as to what the heck the others were thinking: *What were their intentions? Were they also looking to heal from childhood sexual trauma? Did they also struggle with alcohol, addictions ...authentic connection?* While pondering these notions, I kept a stranglehold on my original intentions, my "what and why" for retreating from my day-to-day to take this bold leap into the unknown.

My intentions were clear: find a *way out* of my struggle back home by addressing my mental health straight on.

Before our first ceremony, Nicole and Vismay, gave us the run-down of rules to follow, or, better stated, suggested guidelines to adhere to. Forestral really had only one rule: stay in the allotted and supervised space during the healing ceremony. There were many apparent and potential dangers that may arise if unsupervised in this altered state of awareness. This made total sense, having done and seen people do really stupid things while high.

In a calm and grounded manner, Nicole and Vismay, assured everyone of what was to come the best that they could. They noted the importance of singing along with the music, encouraging active participation and giving your best effort to stay present and engaged in order to make the most out of this unconventional healing experience. And, of course, they presented a common theme for the days to come: surrender to the medicine. Whatever that meant. Sure, I had heard the word surrender many times in cheesy love songs back home, but had no real idea what is was, nor had I ever thought of surrender in practical contexts.

As people started making their way into the makeshift temple, this became real to all of us. You could feel the apprehension, the tension in the air; everyone bringing in their emotional baggage from big-city living, stepping outside of their normal routine with hopes of finding relief. A break, a retreat from the busy world of incessant deadlines and expectation, everyone looking for comfort and healing in nature.

Most people were wearing all-white shirts and pants. It is thought that wearing white protects energies. I wore a supposedly mosquito-proof, white, long-sleeve shirt, and a pair of my trusted cargo pants; the all-white wasn't for me, it seemed a bit over-the-top, more unnecessary clothes to purchase.

The temple was comparable to a large tent that one might find in the parking lot of a large stadium in the Midwest, comfortably fitting up to 30 people or so. We all had our own mats and resting/work space to safely go within. Most people had sleeping bags; it got surprisingly chilly at night. This healing farm was in the mountains, elevated from the sea level's extreme heat. In addition to the medicine workers, and the participants, a few musicians played inside the temple and a team of helpers were on duty to supervise everyone who would be under the influence of this strong potion.

All good, ready or not, here I come—this is game time! I thought anxiously. I had no further questions; I was as ready as I would ever be, everything felt right to me—it was time.

That first sip of ayahuasca was brutal! My whole body quivered, a reflexive somatic response to its overpowering first taste impression: liquid Earth in a shot glass.

During the ceremony, men were on one side, women on the other. It was their tradition, in yin/yang fashion, to separate the sexes as a means to keep at bay any touching or over-communication between couples. I sensed this medicine work was intended to be done solo, although there were four or five couples jumping into the unknown together at this weekend's retreat.

My first night with the medicine was a great struggle for me. I had put too high of an expectation on this unknown experience by bringing in an attitude of entitlement instead of gratitude. This left me in borderline shambles at night's end. I expected a color show, a fun experience similar to other psychedelic experiences I had years prior in social settings. Ignorant wishful thinking. This was not at all the case. This, a deeply humbling experience, shredded me, ripping me apart without any reference points to lean upon. I'd experience the loudest, most intense and violent rounds of power-barfing—easily surmounting any previous vomiting while in my teens or twenties while over-indulging in cheap beer, boxed wine, or rail spirits. To that point in my life, I had done my fair share of throwing up—and yet this medicine crept up fast and hard, barely leaving me time to exit the temple.

All of this was on a completely different level from anything I'd experienced beforehand; it was no joke. It felt like I was purging from the deepest depths of my soul. After the powerful cathartic release, I expected safety from my inner turmoil and struggle—thinking: Bedtime? I was wrong. Very wrong. This unorthodox healing experience wouldn't let up over the next three to four hours, merciless, until the medicine determined I had enough abuse, then the nausea slowly faded, finally allowing for rest.

The ayahuasca took an hour or so to come on, but once it did, I was greeted with cold flashes and mild tremors that would accompany my mental anguish. It wasn't pretty. I was self-conscious at first but realized that many others were experiencing the same harsh effects, some worse. We were all being humbled and beaten down by this medicine they affectionately call: "*The Mother.*" In my mind's eye, I saw flashing computer code that would not relent, 1s and 0s, geometric shapes—it was horrifying, it wouldn't stop. It was as if the curtains of my subconscious mind were pulled back for me to objectively see the inner workings of my mind. It felt like my internal hard drive was going through a defrag, purging excess files and data no longer needed and making conscious the unconscious.

In an effort to seek relief from this terror, I bravely ventured outside of the temple to sit by the bonfire. I felt intense nausea like never before and tried my best to keep it together; my original intention now a million miles away, my focus was only to keep from completely coming undone. Whatever this was, whatever was happening—it scared the shit out of me. Literally.

During the fourth or fifth intense round of vomiting, I was standing over my feet outside of the makeshift temple asking myself, *what have you gotten yourself into this time?* While tripping balls, the grass looked like sharp crystals. In bare feet, it felt like I was standing on broken glass, with the ominous bright moon shining overhead, the stars brighter than I'd ever seen.

All of this was very strange; even more strange, though, was how natural and honest this beating was—I felt safe during this entire ordeal. Almost like I had been here before, and this was a necessary part of my evolution.

My first ceremony was in the books; my inaugural journey with momma aya was painful and unpleasant, but I survived. It could only get better.

I woke the next day shaken, unsettled and confused— but yes, ALIVE! *What the fuck just happened? What was that?* The intense jungle symphony and the rising Costa Rican heat made lying in my healing work-space an unsavory option. It was time to get up, mingle and try my darnedest to figure out what I was up against in this most unfamiliar of foreign lands.

It would not be long before my first integration circle. This, a previously unknown phenomenon to me, was a special opportunity where everyone could share their personal experiences to the group, in essence, an intentional time and place to talk "feelings." While I had spent the better part of my life avoiding the "feelings" talks at all cost, this time was different. I welcomed an opportunity to open up and talk about last night's onslaught. During the sharing, some of the others absolutely lit up while speaking about their journey from the night prior; many had the most incredible of nights—overflowing with revelatory insight and clarity, beaming with joy and bliss; you could really feel love emanating from their pores. Not me, though, and many others also listened in borderline disbelief of the accounts of others. I felt the urge to be jealous but quickly checked my ego, actively listening the best I could, looking for clues, wondering: *How does this all work?*

My turn came and I shared my plight and concerns, my struggles and insecurities; opening up about the intense challenges from the night prior, my doubts about what I was doing there...would I find what I was looking for? I shared the pain of feeling "stuck" when I should be happy and grateful, with all the abundance and blessings in my life. My background and experiences were quite in contrast to that of the other attendees. That said, it still felt like a safe space without judgment where we could all just let it fly. This "open" expression was really helpful, definitely an important part of this healing process—vulnerability builds trust.

Everyone shared openly and honestly, understanding that we would all be heard and our words honored and accepted: some said a few words, others gave full accounts of nearly every detail. All this made me realize how often we aren't truly listened to in our busy modern world—always running to and from this or that, largely distracted and not present with others or, most importantly, ourselves.

"There is no competition in spirit." Vismay uttered these subtle but powerful words in our first conversation days after my arrival, likely sensing my overly competitive energies. At Florestral, the shared ethos leaned more toward cooperation than competition. It was refreshing to see this firsthand. Everyone seemingly engaged this healing process in a spirit of harmony, working together as a group as fellow earthlings, all having our "shit" to deal with. Competition has run through my veins since I was a small child. If I was going to "get" this, it would likely take a different strategy than what I was accustomed to using back home. Vismay, the humble soft-spoken leader of Florestral, was from Israel. He found the medicine many years prior, having studied in India, and having worked under an ayahuascero in Brazil for many years. He was, along with Nicole, very slender; this lifestyle—living holistically on the land and eating vegetarian—made optimal conditions for impeccable health. He was passionate about this work, the night prior playing and singing his heart out for everyone. Nicole and Vismay made a formidable team, holding incredible healing space for their guests.

Although still rattled, I couldn't shake this feeling inside that something special awaited me. I was committed to giving my best effort and making this time count; having traveled nearly 5,000 miles, the idea of giving up never crossed my mind—I had literally come way too far. So I suspended any judgment until the weekend was over.

In between ceremonies we were encouraged to rest and spend time in nature. It was free time to do whatever we felt necessary to prepare for another night of intense healing.

It was time to dig in and get focused. I embarked on this journey for a reason, determined to leave with the healing I sought, an understanding into a way out of my personal prison back home. My first ceremony with ayahuasca was humbling and painful, so I was content to let it go and move my focus toward the next healing ceremony, now just hours away. There was no time to wallow in last night's horror. Many people were saying the second ceremony is usually better, whatever that meant. This gave me hope for what was forthcoming.

That day we ate light: fruit and porridge in the morning, yucca stew in the afternoon. Standard medicine retreat food had no salt and sugar on days of ceremony. Some of the others whined and complained about the bland food on those days. Apparently salt and sugar diminish the effects of the ayahuasca and aren't to be consumed for 24 to 48 hours before ingesting the medicine; our senses are more sensitive to ayahuasca when having abstained from the salty and sweet. Many people don't eat at all on days of ceremony, no doubt getting a stronger effect from this powerful plant medicine in that case.

After a long day of mostly solo soul searching, I was feeling much calmer and more prepared for doing this all over again. Sensing it important for me to be grounded and centered, free from distraction, I created some space between myself and the others. I didn't embark on this healing journey to make friends: this was about my own healing, doing whatever work it took to figure my shit out. For much of the day, I sat in meditative contemplation, looking within for guidance and clarity. All of this spirituality stuff was still new to me. Still, it seemed the more I would practice and breathe into the discomfort, the more relief that followed. It didn't make any sense. All of this was completely counterintuitive to how I had been programmed to think. But it felt honest and good, offering relief and comfort. Who was I to challenge that?

For most of the time in between ceremonies I could be found by the river resting on this massive rock—a huge boulder that had a perfect incline, making lying back and enjoying the Costa Rican abundant sunshine most ideal, while listening to the birds chirping and the strong bubbling current racing by. This is one of the most special places I have ever been, a dreamy secluded natural sanctuary of peace.

After withdrawing from the others for some time I meandered back to the group. Many could see clearly that I struggled greatly the night before. My emotional state was pretty obvious: I am not shy about expressing my enthusiasm and it was near absent after getting shell-shocked. At first, I was taken aback, as many sought me out to give me words of encouragement and assurance, almost reacting in a defensive manner: "I don't need your help"; "I got this under control"; "I know what I am doing" narratives ran through my mind.

This environment was so foreign—emotions and healing, all these feelings out in the open. I could feel myself slowly warming up to this compassion container that our group was creating.

Those inspiring conversations with some of the loving participants had me more at ease for round two. This phenomenon of openness and vulnerability was fascinating; while everyone clearly had work to do on whatever issues they brought, they had a surprisingly strong willingness to help those around them as well. This was so uncustomary in the busy world I was from, a world where we often run over anything and everything on the way to the top, in our endless pursuit of money and material possessions, status and power.

One conversation in particular stood out. I was consoled by a tall and lovely British woman named Bonnie. "How are you holding up, Matt?" she asked sincerely.

"It was a total shitstorm of the mind last night. It was really scary. I am not sure if I am doing this right. I don't really know what to expect tonight, but will give it a go and trust in this process." I admitted in a half-defeated state. "You seemed to have a good night, how was the experience for you?" I eagerly inquired.

"It was deeply healing. Lots of letting go. It was a good night," she had said in a humble spirit before offering some loving advice: "Remember to surrender. Remember to breathe. Trust this."

Remember to breathe? I am always breathing. What the heck does surrender mean? I thought. "What do you mean by surrender?" I asked like a small child. Sure, I had been meditating back home, but nothing can fully prepare you for this deep inner journey. This medicine humbled me to the ground, challenging everything indiscriminately.

"Just let go—trust whatever comes in. You are here for a reason...to heal. Focus on your breath and the singing, that works for me. Surrender to the medicine," she shared in her British accent. I love British accents. Bonnie's presence carried a level of authority. She had other experiences with ayahuasca and other plant medicines. She carried herself with a powerful, dignified confidence. Bonnie had an attractive lightness; her inner contentment made everyone around her feel at ease. I left that conversation thinking, *Matt. Just breathe and surrender...that is all you have to do!*

So there we were again gathering as brothers and sisters sharing in this humanity and unconventional retreat experience, trying our best to make sense of our respective realities and experiences with no official guidebook in hand. Nearly all of us embarked on another journey into the deepest depths of the subconscious mind. Some people left the retreat early—this experience clearly isn't for everyone—while others had arrived later. It was a Saturday and many locals would come and sit in for the night. So despite some people leaving, there was a much bigger crowd than the night before. Probably closer to 40 people, some even had their mat and healing space just outside of the makeshift temple. This strong familial and communal atmosphere was quite welcoming: "the more the merrier," similar to the holiday season sentiment back home when anyone and everyone is welcomed. After last night's experience and another day of everyone getting to know each other, an invisible bond was slowly growing stronger and stronger. It was inspiring to be around others who were also addressing "their shit" head on. Brave souls determined to find the answers they were seeking.

I arrived for the second ceremony many hours early, taking time to breathe and rest and meditate more. I took more time to center, time for focusing on my intentions. I felt a slight air of confidence from having been there the night prior. Tonight would be different. I was certain.

Just before the ceremony began, I approached the Brits who were sitting in a small circle: Bonnie, Esther, Rachel, and Craig, AKA "Team Brit." Though all of them were from the U.K., they had traveled solo and separately, banding together once they arrived to support each other and encourage each other's individual healing adventures. It was inspiring to see how quickly they bonded and how open they were to engaging all the other travelers. Whatever it was they had, I wanted some.

When I reached them, I offered some niceties to Bonnie. "Thank you again for today, Bonnie. Your words were very helpful. I am feeling more at ease and prepared for all this. Thank you. Thank you to all of you." I then shifted my focus from Bonnie to the others. "I wish all of you well on tonight's journey."

Bonnie reiterated, "You have great energy. You *will* have an amazing night…I can feel it. Remember to breathe and let go, surrender. Smile, too." That last part she added with a loving and flirtatious smile of her own.

Esther said, "Yes, brother, you are strong and have really warm and loving energy. You have a lot of courage and inspire us. Thank you for being you," or something to that effect.

Moments later, I'd say my temporary goodbye and leave with a clasping hand gesture, heading back to my mat on the other side of the temple. That conversation left me inspired and hopeful: *Maybe I wasn't as lost as I felt. How on Earth was I inspiring others?* I thought bewilderedly. It felt good to be encouraged by others. We were all in this boat together.

It ended up being another hour, possibly longer, before Vismay and Nicole arrived to begin round two. It felt like a strategic delay, implicitly suggesting that we arrive early to get our intention in order, to be focused and grounded.

Prepared and ready to do this again, we lined up to drink this powerful psychedelic healing medicine for the second consecutive night. Night two would prove to be an entirely different experience for me. I felt so much more aware of my surroundings from the word go. It was time to dig in, to give this everything I could.

I had consumed magic mushrooms and smoked a little pot here and there, but nothing like this ayahuasca healing ritual—this was something completely different. It was cosmic, otherworldly. It's not surprising that many report dramatic healing benefits from this out-of-the-box modality.

At the second drink, I recalled the need to consciously watch my breath while surrendering to what was coming up. To not give up, but to give in, and *trust*; to relinquish control of the outcome while holding firmly to my intentions the best I could. This night, I fully intended to give a stronger effort in singing, engaging, and concentrating my focus on the loving, high vibrational sacred music. I had heard many times, "The healing is in the music." At first, these metaphysical notions and insinuations were completely lost on me. But again, I had decided to trust in this process, and do my best.

Still, I struggled with concentrating on the music, not being accustomed to singing in Spanish, Portuguese, or Hebrew. Many of the songs, however, were easier, four-line mantra songs that felt like they went on forever. Seemingly, the more I concentrated on this singular objective (singing), the less room my mind had to wander into negative and dubious thought patterns. Perhaps that is why they encouraged everyone to participate in the first place?

Sound of Light, or SOL Circle, is what they call medicine work that centers around ayahuasca and non-denominational music. The inspirational songs spanned every religion and spiritual tradition, mostly about peace and love, letting go. About nature, our true nature—about being a better person living more aligned with our truth, gratitude, and the simple life. Universe means "One Song," and all of the music indeed had a Universal feel and depth to it.

Oh shit, here we go again. Deep into my second glass of the night, I could feel the medicine getting stronger and the storm coming on as forecasted. This feeling of dread and helplessness was similar to that from the night prior; once again, my wheels were begging to come off! I focused my attention on my breath and on letting go—on surrendering, whatever that meant. The night prior, I was unable to hold off the cosmic vomit, engulfed and consumed by it instead; purging from the deepest depths of my soul. This night, I greeted those same powerful urges with deep, calm breaths. A small victory was won by staving off my violent impulses to vomit, instead burping and digesting this strange medicine. Like a handful of snakes within, the medicine permeated what felt like every cell.

Still, my thoughts came and went in a fierce manner. Much of my thinking remained negative: *What are you doing here? You'll never find what you are seeking! You are destined for a life of smallness! Sucker—did you just get duped into joining a cult!? You will never find the love you seek.* All sorts of mean self-talk challenged my will and commitment to healing and seeing this through.

Keeping focused on the music, I sang until I could sing no longer. Until the medicine brought me down to my mat. I kept breathing, trying not to overreact. A dreaded feeling, as though this night could go in a horrible direction, surfaced. But strangely, however, I managed to keep calm while observing all of the terrifying imagery in my mind's eye. The more I withstood this fierce storm, the more I started to believe in my ability to push forward, to reach higher, to bring forth that which I was seeking. Although nauseous and in pain, it wasn't like the night prior—it was as if I was invited to go deeper. As if something inside of me had awoken to accompany me on this journey. I grabbed tightly to a mantra of *I AM worthy of this, I AM worthy of this, I AM worthy of this* and, like a pit-bull, I wouldn't let go. *I want this, I want this, I want this!* This moment was terrifying. But the same degree to which I was scared, I was equally supported by this feeling and knowing best described as grace—this was absolutely exhilarating. It felt like life or death: clearly a crucible. And I wasn't going to yield and check out early. That was not an option, I had been through too much pain and heartache to give up now. I wouldn't budge an inch. I felt an edginess I hadn't felt since my competitive sports days. The line was clear and "holding this line" as if my life depended on it was the game I played that night. A surge of adrenaline accompanied me when realizing the importance of this moment. I demanded a sign, guidance, what I had come for—even getting pushy with "The Mother" or whatever this intelligence was. Many moments later, it happened—POOF—everything stopped. Pure peace, as if I entered a room, the base level of a kingdom of my mind: bliss, true bliss. This was what I had been searching for my entire lifetime. This was what reality felt like without the incessant mind chatter; to be fully immersed in the present moment. I was completely out of my body, beyond space and time. *I made it! I did it!* I thought without knowing where or what had just happened, but knowing that this, too, was part of this unorthodox healing ritual. From that point on, I surrendered completely to the music and had the most expansive experience of my life. My body buzzed and vibrated, journeying that night through the deepest depths, highs and lows of the human experience, fully supported by this medicine. Fits of tears were matched with fits of hysterical laughter, and I didn't care.

I felt like I had gone completely mad and yet this was the sanest, best feeling of my life.

A simple but novel concept hit me right in the face. *Nothing really matters!* We make such a big deal about life when nothing really matters. It felt like the big "cosmic joke" was played on me. What an unbearable degree of self-loathing and torment that I had inflicted upon myself and my loved ones, when nothing really mattered. I felt throughout that evening a myriad of repressed emotions bubbling up to the surface, one by one; these emotions were felt, honored, and let go. I surrendered control and just trusted there was a higher intelligence at work with all this. It was the most beautiful experience of my life, more real and more honest than anything I'd been through before.

This was my first time experiencing the "bliss-fuck crucifixion" of "ritualized surrender"—terms coined by Jamie Wheal, peak performance expert and author of *Stealing Fire*, a text that I came across a few years later that helps one to fully understand this experience, though strangely without even mentioning the word ayahuasca.

Others around me were deep in the medicine as well. Sebastian, another Brit, the slender and frail artist, was to my left, appearing to be the immersed in same experience; both of us bowed and prayed, but to what? The music played louder and louder, nearly everyone was engaged, pouring their hearts out in devotional exaltation, raising the group energy to incredible heights. But what was this experience? Whatever it was, it was the first true religious experience of my life, and God was love and truth and peace all in one; an infinite intelligence that is everywhere, connecting everything. I was completely engulfed in the most powerful feelings—this was total rapture!

It is funny, when I was going through this experience, none of this vocabulary was relevant. Previously, I had never given much thought to a religious experience. I would go to church and go through the motions, disengaged, to meet the expectations of my family and others. To be a good boy. This experience was not that.

Sebastian had the Jesus thing going on, very slender with long wavy hair, almost emaciated. He was on a twenty-day fast of only drinking coconut water. That seemed a bit extreme and intense. A kind and loving man, very humble, soft-spoken like many others I met at Florestral. He was traveling with his partner, Nila. After the ceremony, Sebastian had surges of enthusiasm, sharing creative inspiration and many song titles for an upcoming album, no different than a small child unable to conceal his excitement.

Nila was the first person I tried to explain the unexplainable to the following morning. As I foolishly grasped for language I did not possess, she calmly put her hand on my shoulder with a slight smile, without words reminding me to relax and breathe, to soak all of this in; reminding me to savor these moments of peace; reminding me I would have plenty of time to share and wrap my head around this transcendent experience. It was bizarre to communicate without talking, no words, just her body language in an almost telepathic manner.

During the midst of this peak experience, I had dialogue with a power within. It felt like it was part of me, but also separate from my being. An entity or higher intelligence, the plant medicine spirit or "The Mother" perhaps? I am not entirely sure. Whatever it was, this higher power gave me options: keep living my life as it was and I'd likely die in my 50s of heartbreak in poor health, all alone with an ornery family filled with anger and resentment in the midst of material riches—or, I could choose to stand, and, in doing so, choose to end the karmic cycles that had bound me to a life of smallness and conformity, lacking love and honest expression. I could choose to draw the line in the sand and heal. Everything was a choice from this instance on. This stand would require much more responsibility, a lifelong commitment to serving my brothers and sisters at a greater capacity, properly honoring my place in the world in relation to others and our natural world. This commitment required being of service to those who may need help working through the same challenges that I had been fortunate to work through. Unknowingly, that night, I made a soul's contract to live this life in its absolute fullness in service to humanity. Like a deal with the devil, but this deal was done with a benevolent force, an intelligence with only altruistic and loving intent.

Everything changed in an instant: I finally let go, trusting. I surrendered fully to what is.

I had never experienced anything like this in my entire life. Putting this into words doesn't do justice to the actual experience, this is no different than trying to describe a rainbow to a blind person. All of this otherworldly experience took place, of course, in my imagination, in my mind's eye or the "third eye." Sure, I had done some yoga before, and have heard others speak of chakras and this so-called extra eye, but I always balked at their existence with a tinge of jealous disbelief.

"Imagination is everything. It is the preview of life's coming attractions." Albert Einstein's words were never more fitting. That night, I had a preview of my life's coming attractions, and all of it was beautiful, full of grace and hope.

This transcendent experience was more real, in many senses, than the waking consciousness through which I live my life and am writing these words. A world of wonder and awe, indeed, lies just beyond our earthly senses. A world where the underlying guiding force is *love*. Everything connects in some way to everything else; we are truly interconnected, all part of this magnificent web of creation—we are all *one*.

At times throughout the evening, the singing and music became incredibly intense. Many would head out to the large bonfire, where people gathered in silence, taking in the fresh air and movement for an inviting break. We observed a night sky like none I have ever witnessed. Bursting with clarity and depth, shooting stars abounded—staring out to infinity. What a special gift! With the medicine in full effect, I understood why this place was called the "astral forest." All the while, I thought, *People won't fricking believe this! I don't give a shit, though. I'll share everything.*

The mental storm had long passed. I was now dancing in the meadows of my mind, completely free from any worry for the first time I could remember. This special night would continue. Why stop? Knowing much work still lay ahead, I was content with letting the good times roll, exploring further what this experience was all about.

It was late, probably around 2am. While in line awaiting the third glass of the night, I couldn't help but seek out Bonnie to once again give my thanks for the loving pep talk I received hours earlier. Like an angel, she wore all white, and had an all-knowing grin, as though she sensed exactly what I was experiencing. After hiding from this bliss for a lifetime, I was not going be bashful by dimming my light and pulling in the reins of this expansive exuberance bursting from my heart. I gave her a giant hug, showing her my deepest depths of gratitude and appreciation for those seemingly small gestures that proved to be instrumental to my healing experience and personal breakthrough. The minute we embraced felt like hours: feeling into her heart, the beauty and depth of a goddess. Tears of joy welled up and I was overcome by this intense feeling of gratitude for Bonnie. Her kindness had a profound impact on my life. She, and her band of British beauties, had the courage to seek me out, providing the comfort and assurance that I desperately needed at that time. I am forever grateful and always striving to pay that kindness forward whenever I can.

Shortly after that epic hug, the lights were turned off and nearly everyone soon fell fast asleep; the guitar, drums, and other instruments were put away. By this time the night prior, I was passed out in deep slumber like I'd been hit by a truck. Vismay, a former DJ in Israel before finding his calling to work with the sacred plant medicine ayahuasca, would stay true to form. For the next many hours before the sun would rise, we were all graced by the grooviest introspective music mix I had ever heard. Journeying music, deep and melodic, covered us like a loving blanket, leaving further impressions upon all of us who were still under the influence of this special medicine; our subconscious minds were being programmed lovingly to a higher frequency and vibration while we slept.

These prerecorded cosmic healing songs further aided my journey within, allowing for inner space travel, accessing parts of my psyche that were off-limits from my normal waking state of consciousness. That night I wouldn't sleep. I felt as though I had direct communication with a

Universal Supercomputer. From this place of profound peace, I objectively observed the inner workings of my mind, emotions and habits, with my inner critic (self-talk) completely offline. As if separate from my body, I started to inquire as to where I was going wrong in my pursuits of love and a deeper connection, my elusive life purpose. Safely, I rappelled deep within the rabbit hole of life where nothing was off limits; everything was in play and subject to scrutiny—*everything*.

I pondered my life like never before, asking a myriad of relevant questions that were all answered from an infinite intelligence and unlimited wellspring of love. Most answers came before the question was even asked. With novel insights abound, this clarity was exactly what I had come for: for once, to see things for what they really were, from an objective stance, was unbelievable. Every action that I envisioned yielded many probabilistic scenarios; it was is if I could now think with an added dimension.

For seemingly the first time, I clearly saw how all of my actions create ripples and aftereffects. I was given a firsthand experiential view of the workings of karma, cause and effect, the law of compensation, whatever you might call it—they are all the same. It felt as if I had tapped the main vein of source creation. This very notion is likely why ayahuasca and plant medicines/psychedelics are "the secret that can't be told"—poignant words from psychedelic pioneer, a forefather in inner space travel, Terence McKenna.

I could see clearly the many ways I was self-sabotaging my life, the many ways I was making myself sick by leaking energy. I could see the many places where I was not true to my word. All of this insight was handed to me in a safe and trustworthy container. It was a blessing to have the objective space to rehearse many of the conversations I would surely have with friends and family in time to come.

It is said that we humans can consciously process 120 bits of data. A normal conversation takes up 60 bits, leaving us attention to process, at most, two conversations at once. But with my doors of perception kicked wide open, my subconscious mind was fully engaged. It is thought that our subconscious minds are nearly infinite in computing and processing power. Without my ego to contend with, I gathered an immense amount of data and input from all my senses. The picture of Leonardo DiVinci with his arms stretched comes to mind. My memories and all perceptive impressions were now colored with a richness in detail previously unseen and/or unacknowledged. It was as if I could see everything from a different angle and viewpoint. It wasn't all pretty; in fact, much of these insights were disturbing, but, again, the experience was as honest as anything I had ever encountered and I viewed these insights from the safe place of an objective observer.

The memories that flooded my mind that night would often be accompanied with tears. At times I felt overwhelmed by sorrow and loss, knowing that many goodbyes were imminent; much would need be let go during the time of change that was surely to come from this transformation. It was sad. Many of my loved ones may never understand or accept these words or my new path, and yet, strangely, this heavy notion was perfectly okay. Understanding and acceptance gracefully replaced anger. Many conversations I had been avoiding were all of sudden clear and non-threatening; solutions came forth where worry and dread once resided.

My fear response that typically accompanied "going there" to challenging memories or confrontational notions was absent.

Self-inquiry cut like a laser. *What else am I hiding from?* This was my time to dig in and: "get while the gettin' was good!"

With unbridled access to the deep recesses of my mind, I consciously chose to sit with my inner child, assuring him that everything would be all right, that he was safe from this point forth. Going back to ultra-vivid and traumatic memories of my past, reliving them at a higher state of vibration, I felt safe and supported by this visionary medicine/ancient healing technology. As a grown man with proper objectivity and compassion, I felt empowered and enabled to completely re-contextualize the original traumatic experiences and memories from my past that for so long had been off-limits: this is truly the magic of entheogenic therapy. The term entheogen comes from the Greek en, meaning "in" or "within," theo, meaning "god" or "divine," and gen, meaning "creates" or "generates." Thus, the Greek translates as "generating or creating the divine within."

Using these plant medicines as healing technologies allows people to safely go within the nervous system where normally too much emotionally charged pain would prevent such an action. During this healing process, the medicine makes conscious the unconscious, accessing what is inaccessible during our normal waking state. That night, I felt an intuitive power come online, and it has been online since.

The ayahuasca experience felt like a lucid dreaming—wide awake and yet fully at the mercy of whatever lies behind the curtains of your subconscious mind. Nothing is off limits to this medicine, this is truth serum in a shot glass.

During this profound night of healing, all of my struggles back home lost their energetic charge long enough for me to clearly see a solution to remove myself from the struggles that I had created. As for my work and career back home, it was just a matter of time before I would close that chapter, deciding to move on from the new company that only months earlier had purchased my business, determining then I would leave the busy business world in the coming year for an extended travel journey. Everything would unfold with grace if I fully committed to meditation and yoga. If I did *my* part, I would be able to access more frequently and with greater ease the ever-elusive present moment. If I did *my* part, I could co-create the life of my dreams. All of this was a lot, but again, there was this overwhelming feeling of, *it will be okay—everything will be okay.*

The peace and comfort and the healing I was seeking did indeed come to me. But the real challenge would now lie ahead in integrating this back into my day-to-day life.

All of this bliss was nearly too good to be true. I expected challenging times and hard work in the days forthcoming, but fortunately I have never been scared of hard work.

It was abundantly clear to me that, at some point, my experience needed to be shared. All of it. Every detail. Too many people are hurting. In good conscience, there lies a duty to express myself honestly. It didn't stress me out the least bit, with tapping a wellspring of creative ideas, the answers and methods surely would come in divine timing. When the time was right, I would raise my hand and do what I knew I had to.

After this revelatory weekend, heaven and hell were not places we go when we die; they were states of mind we embody and experience on Earth, in the here and now. The vehicle that takes you to either destination is simply your thoughts which we govern with our will. High vibrational thoughts—love, peace, truth, gratitude, and honesty, centered around our true nature—take us higher. Lower vibrational thoughts—worry, doubt, jealousy, lack, gossip—will take us directly to a hellish reality.

Everything is choice; we choose in every given moment to experience heaven or hell.

The egalitarianism I experienced at Florestral was intoxicating. Surely it aligns far closer to our evolutionary past as hunter-gatherers than the modern world we live in back home does. My own identity, my narrative and mental constructs, weren't important or relevant. This medicine strips you down to your truest essence, but with a loving hug that provides the space necessary to rearrange your life to align with your soul's calling/higher purpose. There was a sense of affiliation and belonging that I had never felt before in my life; love with no conditions or expectations, a group of like minds that all love for the sake of loving.

At Florestral, I wasn't the important business owner/Mr. Boss Man; I was just a dude trying to find relief, trying to make better sense of this human experience.

During my healing retreat, I truly felt love for the first time, an unconditional love so powerful I was changed forever. Once you see and feel something that intense, that honest and pure, there is no pretending it didn't happen or doesn't exist. This supportive healing container facilitated an environment for a peak experience where I could see the best possible version of myself through my own eyes.

The biggest part of this healing ritual with ayahuasca is you have the safe space to go within, a supported container to truly feel the emotions that are often repressed in our busy world. This methodology of healing is difficult to grasp because of our cultural biases and our conditioning as to how healing is supposed to take place. Another factor that made this healing ritual a lasting blessing was the incredible relationships that were forged. Going through an experience like ayahuasca as a group required trust, courage, and faith. Everyone stripped off any bullshit pretenses, creating optimal conditions for new friendships and lifelong bonds to form organically.

Days after this profound healing experience, I approached Vismay and Nicole separately. I shared my plight, what I was up against back home. Vismay was brief in his responses to me, listening to my exuberance and enthusiasm with as much patience as he could expend.

Surely, he has these conversations often and has nearly mastered the art of holding space, listening intently. He kept repeating, "Everything you are looking for is in the music; the healing is in the music," and encouraging me to continue to listen to the sacred music upon returning home, where I could easily find the loving tunes on SoundCloud.

My conversation with Nicole was very different. I expressed my concern for my diminishing libido and zest for my life circumstances back home. She lovingly informed me with a deep sense of compassion that my sacral chakra had been cleansed by the loving music and that I might expect healing to unfold in the months and years to come. She encouraged patience. I had always held myself to an unfair and excessive standards when it came to sex. Growing up addicted to pornography warped my view of what sex really is. Constant comparison to others, like my older brother Ben's stud-muffin-stallion claims of seven times in one night, didn't help my perception. That it is a lot of sex! And, whether true or not, his boast had me competing, feeling inadequate, lagging behind, myself having only achieved three, maybe four times during debauchery-filled nights.

I was missing the point while stuck in self-abuse; all of this misdirected obsession with sex would only serve to cause immense pain, to distract me from the spiritual and emotional aspects of this sacred act, where our deepest healing can be found. My failures with human intimacy were the basis for an overwhelming existential distress; prior to my healing with ayahuasca, I was unable to make my way through all the rampant, confusing mixed messages that inundate our warped sexual energy world.

After this intense and profound healing experience, I started to dream in color. Vivid dreams at night while I slept as soundly as ever. It was strange, but weeks after this experience I had my first wet dream since my teenage years. My mind had been overtaken by erotic thoughts while I rested and recharged in deep slumber, tag-teamed by Janine, the porn star and a gorgeous female accomplice. I obsessed about Janine in my youth and would welcome this feels-too-real erotic tryst. Perhaps that lightning bolt that shot through my energy centers cleared emotional blockages; I've felt like a horny teenager (with wisdom) ever since. This shouldn't be surprising; our sexual energy is channeled in two directions: we create miracles—the babies our women birth—and we also channel our sexual energy into thought and creative expression. We are creators of children and ideas/things. Often, our creative powers are lost on our species; we ignore how much we can control our sexual energy and its miraculous power. Perhaps our systems are designed for this oversight, as what this truly means won't resonate with most people.

After this retreat, I could feel the difference between a grateful thought and a fearful one; I discerned the inner joyous sensations from positive thoughts and an equivalent heaviness from negative thoughts. To actually, literally feel the power of your "Thought Vibrations" is something one can never forget. Still, many years later, I have never consciously engaged in a negative/demeaning thought about myself. Surely, in the times to come I would be challenged again, but I now refuse to give in to despair or negativity. Not on my watch. I can't begin to express my appreciation to know firsthand how powerful our thoughts can really be, from this point forth, I adopted a scientific approach to living: testing this, testing that, finding my way in this new world.

Four days later, we drank ayahuasca again. Another night of strangers gathering, consciously choosing to subject ourselves to the possible psychological horrors in the name of getting better. It was a lovely experience filled with intense joy, but frankly, I felt contented, unwilling to dive any deeper for another mind-blowing experience. I had seen what I needed to see, while knowing I had the clarity that I came for and more than enough insight bitten off; plenty to chew on upon my return home. Much more challenging work now lay ahead when I would need to integrate these teachings, folding these lessons back into my day-to-day life in the big city.

I often wondered what it would be like to be a child that lived at a retreat center where almost every weekend a new group of people arrived and departed. Surely, this was challenging for them, but Nicole and Vismay's children all seemed well-adjusted. The three children had so much life and vitality. The oldest was Luyaya. She was then a 12-year-old who spoke at least three languages, someone worldly and mature for her age. She had been drinking ayahuasca (smaller/micro doses) for five years, since the age of seven. It was part of her family and culture. Ayahuasca was, to her, not a big deal at all, simply a ritual to engage responsibly with family. Luyaya served her family as a second mom while Nicole had attended to much of the organization of the retreat space, while also serving the medicine with

Vismay. Neyam and Ereya were the other surprisingly well-adjusted children.

Vismay, the soft-spoken and tender leader of this forest tribe and family, spent much time mixing music and working on his craft as a shaman/musician/healer. We would see him around from time to time, mostly during meal time. He put forth a lot of energy during the ceremonies. The man rips the guitar and sings with the most fiery inspiration while channeling the medicine; it is truly a sight to see, some of the most beautiful music one will ever hear.

Having led nearly one thousand ceremonies over his past 15 years, it is truly remarkable work they are doing in the astral forest. Nicole and Vismay have hearts of gold, with unwavering devotion to heal those who have been unable to find relief in our faulty Western medicine mental-health paradigm; a paradigm that only placates symptoms while mostly ignoring the root of the mental afflictions that plague our modern world. Vismay speaks of the "Newmanity," a world where we love our neighbors as ourselves and love our natural world as if we are a part of it.

As much as I was excited about this "Newmanity," I knew that an incredible amount of work lied ahead. But after this initial retreat experience, something had changed and since then I have lived life with the wind at my back.

6

ANYTHING CAN HAPPEN

"Don't ask what the world needs. Ask what makes you come alive, and go do it. Because what the world needs is people who have come alive."

— HOWARD THURMAN, CIVIL RIGHTS ACTIVIST

JANUARY 2015

Flying home from Costa Rica after this incredible revelatory healing experience, I pondered: *What is crazier, following my heart and shaking things up, trusting in my direct experience and my inner ability and power to forge a new path—or continuing to live with this crippling fear, subscribing to the collective vision that appears to have lost its way and gone mad?* Any questioning along these lines had been previously off-limits. The dissonant pain in my heart would have been too much to bear when broaching taboo notions like truth and freedom. It was easier to keep my head down and to go along with the herd. It was much, much safer that way.

Self-help guru and TEDTalk legend Brené Brown writes in her book Daring Greatly, "Curiosity is a shit starter, but that's okay, sometimes we have to rumble with the story to find the truth." Boy oh boy, her words are spot-on. Much rumbling lay just around the bend for me. Everything was now in play and everything would need to be examined thoroughly and honestly from this point forth.

My waking reality had just been challenged by the strongest power I had ever encountered. Like a crystal vase thrown into the heavens and then falling down to crash on the sidewalk, my world was completely shattered, never to be the same. This time of brokenness was different than all previous turmoil, however. I had experienced such profound and loving peace and clarity that the 10,000 pieces that would need to be picked up would be a welcome challenge. This was an honest pursuit, accompanied with a lengthy moment without ego, just enough to temporarily overrule the fearful tendencies that previously governed my being. The peace I'd found helped me see more clearly how I needed to rearrange my life based on my truest values, intentions, and longings.

After my healing retreat, I pondered the notion of freedom more intensely: *What did it mean to be free? For a country that prides itself on freedom, I sure as hell don't feel free. Why is this so?* I knew that I was in a self-imposed prison with only myself to blame. The bars of this prison were my fears, and the warden was my past. *Do I stay in a life where I am miserable and "stuck," or do I bet it all on myself and take leap into the unknown?*

Duh.

Upon returning home to Chicago, I'd craft a viable plan to execute a bold escape from the all-consuming rat race, making way for world travels and a truth-seeking journey of a lifetime.

While feeling the "pink cloud" or "afterglow" of my experience with ayahuasca, a euphoric and blissful state that knows few limits consumed me. It felt like anything was possible, as if anything could happen. I hadn't felt that since I was a small child. I now suspected this feeling was omnipresent and might be "normal" for the healthy and emotionally balanced. *Is this what it feels like to be whole?* My inquisition into my inner world remained relentless, not letting up. Although painful at times, we all know the truth can hurt. This notion of seeking guidance from within myself was too novel and exciting to ignore, no matter the temporary pain it dug up.

Now was my time: Light had just touched my heart for the first time, creating space for inquiry where none previously existed—a lasting glimpse of what may be possible for myself and our troubled world.

This flight returning home from Costa Rica was likely the most memorable flight of my life. With pen and paper in hand, I journaled compulsively, drafting a comprehensive escape plan from the only life I had ever known. An escape from the grip of crippling fear. An escape from the tyrannical mind that wouldn't relent. A great escape from a life of smallness that knew so little of its own truth. Effortlessly, like never before, I felt creative bursts of insight and inspiration. Embodying this childlike imagination, I felt safe-guarded with patience and discernment and an air of wisdom from a former life's many trials and tribulations.

For the first time in my life, I had the courage and foresight to question the herd. To challenge the establishment and the society that raised me. To exercise the freedom afforded to me as citizen of United States. More so, to exercise the freedom afforded to me as child of the infinite, born to and from this Universal experience. My motive behind all this questioning was sound and pure: justice, peace, love, and well, yes, the preservation of my own sanity.

Everything had changed after that original healing experience. I could now see the truth behind my actions. I could now discern whether my actions were rooted in love or fear. Before, I mostly went to church to please and appease my parents, even doing so in my twenties and early thirties. I tried to have a deeper relationship with Christianity, but that story just didn't resonate with me. When I did attend church, I felt good afterward—the guilt, the sexual shame temporarily at bay: I was a good boy, adhering to social norms of the culture that raised me. Begrudgingly, I'd even, at times, put a $5, or maybe a $10 or $20, in the basket.

To then have my first authentic religious experience while under the influence of a plant medicine? Crazy. I know! Understanding whatever this mystically transformative experience was quickly became my life's major quest. Everything I had been taught needed to be scrutinized, examined against my life's new measuring stick. Absolutely everything. William James, the father of modern-day psychology, writes in his classic, *The Varieties of Religious Experience: A Study In Human Nature* that mystical experiences share four common traits: Ineffability, Noetic Quality, Transiency, and Passivity. Because the term "mystical" doesn't always fit in the scientific model, "peak" is often used synonymously in the waters in which we will swim in the remaining chapters of this book; it is all the same, this is just semantics.

In one weekend, I became a believer: a true believer. Not one that talks a good game, boasting and blowing, blabbering about this and that, but one who acts in accordance with what he believes to be true. Ninety percent of my addictive tendencies and my desires to drink excessively were thrown up, some dry-heaved, in what felt like a sort of cosmic burping. Ayahuasca was a strange but effective medicine.

Why did I have to go *Costa Rica* to heal? Why couldn't I have done that at home? I swam upstream against ferocious water: why did this seemingly sure-bet healing process seem like a huge risk? Why did I have to seek refuge in secrecy? These medicines clearly have been withheld in the U.S. for reasons I was surely going to figure out. Before all of this, the fact that psychedelics have been suppressed should have been an obvious clue to their value. I knew I wasn't the only one who had been duped by our nation's broken mental health paradigm while the "fat cats" at the top swam in corporate earnings. *How many others were begging for this kind of liberation? How many others were stuck in addiction, abusing themselves, quietly pretending everything was okay? How many others were crippled by depression and PTSD? How could I be of service to this modern world that has lost its way, where success is determined by the ownership of shiny things rather than one's character and influence for good over their networked circles?*

We all know that we have a broken mental health paradigm:

Suicide rates are up in ages 8 to 80.

Depression is soaring.

PTSD affects 8% of the population at a given time.

Crippling anxiety is rampant.

Addiction rates are up and our country is on fire right now with the opioid crisis.

And there are an estimated 40 million adult survivors of childhood sexual abuse, and it is thought that as high as 90% won't ever say a word, instead taking that deep, dark secret to the grave. We got problems...#truth.

I now had the courage to ask tough questions without my world falling apart. Even the questions that didn't have clear answers.

For the life of me, I couldn't let go of the notion "love thy neighbor." How have we forgotten to love our neighbors? How have we forgotten something this essential? With all the blabbering righteousness talk we see in society, so few live a life that factors in this most elementary notion. ...Maybe all this collective sickness is because we aren't loving our neighbor?

In the next couple of days, I returned to work armed with an inquisitive spirit and childlike curiosity. Fitting back in, playing the game of life with a smile on my face; each day, putting on my suit and tie, going through the motions, trying my best to be fully engaged in my loveless work in corporate America. I knew, however, that my work was a means to an end. This notion motivated me greatly. I gave myself one year to untangle myself from the mess that I had created in Chicago. This timeframe served as a guard rail, protecting me as I became more rooted in this pursuit of freedom. Looking back, all this provided a necessary speed bump that would slow down my eagerness and overzealousness; this kept me safe as I wrapped my head around this incredible "What-The-Fuck-Just-Happened" inaugural visit to Costa Rica.

In accordance with my Nintendo youth, I had finally found the real-life "reset button."

Paradoxically, it is the not caring by many of our culture's standards, that provides the solution for how to be present and engaged. We care so much about the non-essential, things that distract and pull us further away from our truth, from the love in front of us in each moment. So much precious time, energy, and attention is wasted placating our fears and disharmony. We are systematically distracted by a constant barrage of noise which keeps us from feeling and reaching this elusive state, from embodying the infinite within.

My whole life, I wanted something for nothing. I wanted a whole-hearted love but wasn't willing to heal my heart. I wasn't willing to address the pain and let go. To put in the effort required seeking and insisting on more out of life than I could get for free, wallowing in entitled victimhood. I didn't know how to do this; the medicine showed me how. I could see ahead through my own eyes now, and would trust in my ability to create and bring forth that which my heart desires.

Much later, I came across this profoundly relevant caption in *Getting Grit* by Carolyn Adam Miller: "Compelling research in the field of positive psychology: Pioneers of this emerging field have found that happiness is a precursor to success, not success to happiness. We don't become happy after we succeed at something, but rather we succeed precisely because we are happy first." Like many truths, these words were lost on me for the first 30-odd years of my life. It seemed the more I accomplished, the emptier I felt. It doesn't matter how much you attain; if you aren't happy first then your efforts are all for naught. That said, this isn't entirely true: the best way to figure out what works for you in life is to try things out, narrowing the field of possibility with each life experience. My spending thirteen years in corporate America was useful in that it fervently showed me that this work was not for me. Once I got over the bitterness, I could see this more clearly. My pending travel journey would really be about cultivating this happiness from within. Staring myself in the mirror each day, learning to be okay with me, warts and all. Before leaving on extended travels, I demanded that my calling be made known; during inner dialogue with my Creator, exclaiming just how serious I was about making a difference.

I was prepared to do whatever it took for the long and potentially lonely ride back home to Self, knowing that the stakes were higher than ever before. True love exists. This was something I finally knew, since I felt that powerful love within while in Costa Rica. But I also knew that the only way this love can be actualized, and in time realized in its fullest expression, is through the long, arduous, and daunting journey into the heart. The remaining pages are more of my odyssey into my heart and the heart of humanity.

In the following chapters I'll be sharing all the information I've compiled from my long journey down Esoteria Lane. My original idea for this book was to document a travel journey and all the amazing places I went, the incredible people I met, and my spiritual insights at every turn. Once I began writing this book, however, my focus started to shift toward you the reader. *Worth the Fight* became more than a book solely about my spiritual insights, love interests, and romantic endeavors, my many interpersonal dramas with family and friends. I still share much of that, but hopefully only to the extent to which it provides what I feel to be valuable context.

This book showcases the incredible healing tools I have come across on my journey: the psychedelics/plant medicines, meditation, breathwork, and the many other agents of change and what they could potentially mean for individuals struggling with mental health. As a global family, we got some big problems; no one will deny this for a second. Although not a panacea, I believe in these alternative modalities as disruptive healing technologies, and strategies that have been bestowed to team Earth in general and you the reader to make Bullshit, Inc. more honest. Bullshit Inc., AKA, the forces that are behind our collective sickness and ignorance, appearing due for a sort of well-timed, natural checks and balance.

Not everyone who undergoes this sort of awakening is compelled to quit their job and travel the world. This just happened to be my path. My circumstances allowed for this time of strategic withdrawal, a special time for me to dive into the innermost parts of myself, knowing that eventually all the insight revealed will be shared with you. My travel journey, an intentional time to jump in the deep end of life, a practical exercise of stripping myself of most of my creature comforts and, in doing so, testing my willingness and resolve to see just how much I wanted my dreams to come true.

This time away gave me much-needed freedom from the mess that I had created. It was me and my backpack—17 countries in 18 months. Ralph Waldo Emerson wrote "The desire for gold is not for gold. It is for the means of freedom and benefit." These profound and fitting words embody my reason for leaving with only a backpack for indefinite travel. It was time to claim this freedom and benefit!

7

UNHARNESSED

"Happiness is a choice and so is courage."

— ALEX SEYMOUR, PSYCHEDELIC MARINE

Ayahuasca: The Secret That Can't Be Told

Years back, while watching Avatar, the cinematic wonder directed by James Cameron, I found myself blown away. This prophetic film really resonated with me, enough that I watched the near-three-hour movie on consecutive days. Tears streamed down my face just as prevalently during round two. Avatar left me enamored by its hopeful message of unity, loving nature, and respecting the wisdom of other cultures. Michelle Rodriguez gracefully starred in this Hollywood hit, although, she was incredible, some might even say that her work in the far too many Fast and Furious, Vin Diesel racecar shoot-'em-up movies was her best. But to me, without question, her best and most important work was in *The Reality of Truth.* This documentary investigates the link between plant medicines, religious traditions, and spirituality. It's another provocative and controversial fact-finding mission that really makes one think hard about the rightful place of plant medicines in our overconnected world where struggles with PTSD, depression, addiction, anxiety, suicide and many other mental health afflictions abound.

In this groundbreaking documentary, Michelle Rodriguez, with a group of 10 others, embarks on a healing journey to Peru to drink ayahuasca and San Pedro under the guidance of Deepak Chopra. Yes, the lovable Deepak, arguably the most trusted, popular, and renowned guru on planet Earth, gives the thumbs-up to psychedelics as medicines for the afflicted (or serious seekers) who are stymied by our limited Western mental health paradigm. In this provocative film, Michelle bravely opens up about her painful loss of her lover, her partner in crime Paul Walker, who had died in a car accident years prior; her existential struggles, coming to grips with the pain and all the repressed emotions that she held tightly to since her youth. She hits the heart with her honesty and edginess, fully embracing her most authentic expression. Michelle and many others liken this healing experience with ayahuasca to receiving 10 to 20 years of therapy in a weekend, recommending that others partake if at a dead end with conventional approaches. When I came across *The Reality of Truth*, I started to better connect the dots on my own personal healing journey finding inspiration from the brave work done by those who have gone ahead. The provocative film even goes as far as suggesting that Jesus may have used "magic mushrooms" (psilocybin) to perform his miracles, finding in the Bible this mysterious mushroom called "the manna." Who knows? That was a really long time ago.

In this chapter, I hope to leave you with everything you would need if you plan on embarking on your own healing journey with ayahuasca. Or, at least, enough information where you might be able to relay the basics about this unconventional healing medicine from the Amazon Rainforest to a struggling friend or family member, imparting the relevant notions to consider when engaging this plant medicine that dutifully heals on the mind, body, and soul/spirit levels.

Maybe this doesn't deserve mentioning, but I'd like to remind you I am no certified expert. I am not a shaman or medicine man. I am not a qualified medical professional with initials after my name, so by no means is this medical advice. What follows is simply compiled knowledge shared from a guy who chose to step outside what is socially/medically accepted because of the dire need to heal my near-broken heart. I believe in ayahuasca as a powerful healing modality, but it is no panacea and, again, this medicine is not for everyone. After spending nearly four years trying to wrap my head around my own healing shifts and transformation, I've come up with material that has been relevant to everything I've experienced myself or seen in others. All the resources and important notions I've compiled to ponder when engaging this unconventional healing plant medicine follow.

What Is Ayahuasca?

Ayahuasca is a psychedelic tea known as the "vine of the soul" made from a combination of plants native to the Amazon basin: ayahuasca vine and the chacruna leaves. For thousands of years, the indigenous have used this plant mixture as a religious sacrament. The active ingredient is DMT(N,N-dimethyltryptamine), which has been labeled the "spirit molecule." It is said that we have surges of DMT when we die. DMT is a schedule-one controlled substance in the U.S. and is illegal. In 2006, however, the U.S. Supreme Court affirmed the right of the Brazil-based UDV Church to use ayahuasca as a sacrament.

Because of the legal status of DMT in the U.S., many fly to Central and South America to experience this powerful healing ritual and medicine. Costa Rica and Peru are two countries where I have drank ayahuasca. There are churches throughout the U.S. which can legally serve ayahuasca as a sacrament, too. And, of course, there are many underground circles that are purported to becoming more and more popular in big cities all over the world, including in the United States, which have shamans traveling to share the medicine and wisdom of the jungle.

This may be a bit sinister, but I believe ayahuasca is illegal (along with many other psychedelics) because people get better and no one makes money. There! I said "it," that troubled notion so many feel but are unwilling to accept or do anything about. Psychedelic healing is poorly aligned with the Western healing model; these alternative medicines aggressively target the root of the trauma, which allows for letting go—once the trauma has been let go, there is no need to take a regiment of pills that, at times, have harsh side effects. Currently, we have whole entire industries (Big Pharma) that revolve around people taking pills daily, including antidepressants/SSRIs: we are the Prozac Nation. One in four Americans are currently taking psychiatric medication. Often, pills that barely beat the placebo test and have a reputation of numbing out emotions, highs and lows, are used as a tool to hide from the underlying root cause instead of treating it.

Who Is Drinking This Bitter Brew Medicine?

Ayahuasca is one of the strongest available natural medicines for trauma. And in 2019, we don't have to look too far to find people struggling with PTSD—In the remaining pages of this book I reference PTSD often, Post Traumatic Stress Disorder a condition that affects 8% of our population at any given time. In no way do I look at PTSD as a disorder or disease. It is merely unprocessed emotional stress that can be felt, honored and let go. Just as in my healing journey, this holds true for our war veterans and our world that struggles too much with emotional challenges related to trauma. Ayahuasca has a special affinity for those suffering from trauma: whether it's war, childhood, or sexual trauma. On my journey, traveling to and from Costa Rica and Peru, a common thread among 99% of those I've met is that at the root of their dismay lies a hurt, an unresolved trauma, that robs the one who suffers of peace of mind.

War veterans have had astounding success with the ayahuasca intervention, this no better detailed than in *From Shock to Awe*, a compelling documentary that follows two U.S. veteran families on their respective healing journeys. These veterans kicked their war-chest-medicine-cabinets full of pharmaceuticals for the natural medicines (and MDMA, more in Chapter 10) cannabis and ayahuasca. Twenty-two U.S. veterans fall to suicide *each day. From Shock to Awe* is a hopeful documentary that provides a desperately needed lifeline for our U.S. war veterans who struggle with mental health, as well as for anyone who suffers from PTSD. Our brave veterans lead by example to show the kind of healing that is possible. Historically, whenever a new technology or tool is presented, it is often the courageous warriors of the society who venture out to explore the unexplored. This example is no different. With the dire state of our veterans' mental health (much more in later chapters on this important topic), it is a shame that these medicines are withheld to those who really need healing, those who are all out of options at the end of life's road: sick, scared, confused, and in pain.

In addition to those struggling with PTSD, depression, anxiety, and other afflictions of the mind, many high-profile figures are speaking up about their own healing journeys with the sacred plant medicine ayahuasca. Successful entrepreneur, angel investor, author, and podcaster Tim Ferriss speaks openly about his struggles with bipolar and suicidal ideation and how psychedelics, specifically ayahuasca, provided deep healing that have contributed to his well-being and successful productive nature in dutifully serving others. (https://tim.blog/2015/09/14/are-psychedelic-drugs-the-next-medical-breakthrough/) Ferriss has been a staunch financial supporter of psychedelic research, donating significant financial resources, and, more importantly, retelling the story of what is possible. On Tim's world-famous *The Tim Ferriss Show* (300,000,000 downloads—that is a lot of zeroes!), a business podcast dedicated toward lifestyle design and peak human performance, he discusses at length the "life hacks" his inspired guests from all walks of life use to excel in their field but, more importantly, he shares front and center the work of esteemed psychedelic influencers: Dr. James Fadiman, Dr. Gabor Mate, Dr. Dan Engle, Michael Pollan, Dr. Rick Doblin, Dr. Dennis McKenna, and many others. His commitment to psychedelic research and reframing how the world views these misunderstood medicines is as impressive as it is admirable.

Aubrey Marcus, another podcast all-star, host of the *Aubrey Marcus Show*, is an excellent resource for anything motivational or health/psychedelic/ayahuasca related. Aubrey is a fearless pioneer who shares loud and proud how impactful his healing ceremonies have been. An ambassador of the sacred plant medicines, Aubrey can also be found as a frequent guest on the mega-popular *The Joe Rogan Experience*. While I don't believe Joe Rogan has ever drank ayahuasca, he is a networked powerhouse who thinks magic mushrooms/psilocybin have the potential to heal our planet and he serves as a faithful advocate for the potential of psychedelics and cannabis as viable healing modalities, hosting an array of guests, truly telling the full spectrum of what is possible. Rogan's podcast brings together people from all walks of life with his humorous charm and commitment to transparency.

Tim, Aubrey, Joe: a three-headed monster that gracefully serves as a pace car for the movement of psychedelics as medicines by open-sourcing everything one needs to have a successful healing journey. They foster our populace in the direction of transparency, objectivity, and sanity. All three luminaries aren't shy about the risk/reward profile of ayahuasca (and other psychedelics), leading with the utmost importance of safety and self-education when embarking on a journey of experiential spirituality. Together, along with many others, they are part of a movement that is retelling the story about what is possible.

Pre and Post-Ayahuasca

The rule of thumb is to pull back on salt, red meats, sugar, alcohol, drugs, and sex a week or so before ceremony, though the specifics differ depending on whom you ask. The principle behind withdrawing from these foods/behaviors is to come into the ceremony as clean as you can. The medicine works more effectively when one honors a restriction diet for the time leading up to these important and powerful healing encounters.

In my personal experience, I found that the more and longer I abstained from the above, the stronger the healing experience was. For me, even going so far as not eating at all on days of ceremony was beneficial. I'll talk more about fasting in later chapters.

In addition to providing you with diet and activity recommendations, your retreat should first screen you and ask you health questions and, after doing so, give you their personalized recommendations. If they aren't providing this foundational presence, you might think twice about whether this a good fit for your healing.

As for post-ayahuasca, the entire next chapter will be devoted to integration and the most powerful integrative tool, "the secret sauce": meditation. Personally, I am a big believer in the importance of integration and that these psychedelic medicine experiences don't mean shit if you can't ground these insights and concretely make your world and the world of those in your circle of influence better; this medicine is not about getting high—it is about loving ourselves and our neighbors more fiercely. It is about getting yourself right, healthy and fit for service to a world that needs you present and engaged.

In many people I've come across, ayahuasca has helped with losing weight. After the healing ceremony, the medicine forces us to take inventory of the food we eat on a daily basis. It helps us to cultivate the awareness that we are what we eat. An awareness of what our bodies need to feel strong and healthy. Please do not use ayahuasca as a weight loss strategy; if one did, I suspect they'd be in for a rude awakening. After first embarking on the medicine path, my diet has been radically transformed and my health has improved significantly.

What Are Potential Dangers?

Usually dangers are tucked away, limited to a sentence or two in the back of the book. Not in this book. Let's put these front and center and be sure we thoroughly understand the potential risks of engaging in ayahuasca or any other plant medicine or psychedelic. There are significant risks associated with those who are on antidepressants/ SSRIs: toxic, potentially lethal effects. Both ayahuasca and SSRIs work on the serotonergic system, and this potentially lethal contraindication can't be dismissed. You should NOT be taking ayahuasca while on psychiatric prescription medication. Those with more serious mental health challenges, or a family history of mania/bipolar or schizophrenia, are also not good candidates for healing with ayahuasca and psychedelics, as these medicines can exacerbate instability from these afflictions.

With the surge in ayahuasca tourism in Peru, Brazil, and Costa Rica, there is an increase in charlatans as well—fakes, with ill motives, unprepared to serve as proper guides for those looking to heal outside of the Western medicine paradigm. If you are interested in this healing modality: **do your own research! Lots of it!** Approach finding a shaman as you would finding a surgeon or medical specialist, or in making any other major life decision. The ayahuasca healing ritual is essentially a form of spiritual brain surgery that should not be taken lightly. This cannot be stressed enough. I recommend finding a reputable place where you can get a firsthand recommendation of the integrity of those holding healing space.

There are some predictable potential psychological problems for the unprepared seeker looking to address mental health challenges. In all the material I've reviewed, no better warnings exist than those from *Stealing Fire*, the ultimate guidebook to radically upgrading your life with altered states of consciousness, written by Steven Kotler and Jamie Wheal. I've expanded upon their top four predictable pitfalls and do so because I've taken their expansive experience to heart, utilizing these sacred medicines as a powerful healing technology that ought to be respected with the deepest of reverence.

4 Potentially Mind Saving Warnings

"Don't be a bliss junkie": Do the Work! Sorry, there is no substitute for doing the work. Life is hard. We can't be on all the time. We need the contrast of sober moments—a waking state, a baseline reality—to best understand the altered states. My wise friend Atticus once said, "Contrast is clarity!"

"It is not about you": We are all in the boat together. We are all *one*; a collective global family inhabiting this planet. Ego-inflation is the most obvious and predictable danger that comes from engaging these powerful plant medicines. Surround yourself with friends, family, and trusted allies who aren't afraid to call you on your bullshit. Having support from your community is invaluable on the path less traveled.

"It is not about now": Have patience. Good things take time to unfold. It is imperative to find and own your lines. It takes time to process the healing, to become self-aware of your life and how these powerful experiences fit into the day to day. We can only find these lines during and through a daily practice of some sort; obedience to your higher power, to something greater than yourself, checking in each day, an essential time to connect to the powerful emotions felt during the healing ceremony. There's no need to rush off to the next ceremony. These healing impressions can be accessed any time through our nervous systems after the original transformational experience; like the traumatic memories that people heal from, these healing memories are stored in a similar manner.

"Don't dive too deep": Easy, Tiger! Pace yourself. What is the hurry? Any big rush to have this human experience

all figured out is likely a symptom of our "instant oatmeal" quick-fix society. Enjoy the journey; life's ride, the day to day, magic is experienced between the lines each day. What good is diving too deep if you can't bring back any of the information to make your life better for you and your loved ones?

These four warnings are essential to be cognizant of when embarking on your own healing journey with the sacred plant medicine. For good measure, I'll include a bonus fifth maxim: "Hold the Gold." Keep your healing experience close to your chest for a time. These wise words are from Dan Engle, MD, a board-certified physician in psychiatry and neurology and a renowned expert in protocol for healing with ayahuasca: "Keep that experience really close and private. When it feels right to share, share it with people who are very sensitive to the fact that you just went on a strong life-altering journey, and who are going to be supportive of that. So many people, when they have a big experience, want to go share it, and sometimes the response they get isn't always supportive. That alters the healing that they just received." I couldn't agree more with Dr. Dan's spot-on assessment. On my personal healing journey, it took many months before I felt assured in sharing with friends and family; it didn't feel right to share something that I didn't yet understand myself, having needed more time to wrap my head around the transcendent experience. Everyone's path, however, is different. These are just some "best practice" notions to be mindful when engaging these disruptive healing technologies.

Ayahuasca: The Essence of This Powerful Plant Teacher

In Michael Pollan's book *How to Change Your Mind: What the New Science of Psychedelics Teaches Us About Consciousness, Dying, Addiction, Depression, and Transcendence,* Pollan eloquently surmises why this unconventional healing modality is so misunderstood. "Psychedelic therapy seems to be operating on a frontier between spirituality and science that is as provocative as it is uncomfortable." No words are more true as I do my best to dance with science and spirit while describing the core essence of this sacred plant medicine healing ritual.

During my travels in Central and South America, I never once heard the term "intervention" used to sum up the psychedelic experience or the ayahuasca plant medicine healing ritual. This was an odd realization, because that is really what this experience is—an intervention against addictive behaviors and toxic habits, a depressed mind or mind suffering from post-traumatic stress resulting from war, childhood, or sexual trauma. In many ways, it is an intervention against our egoistic tendencies that keep us from looking at our lives in an honest light and objective manner.

The term "intervention" has a certain unsavory connotation in our society: we can all picture frustrated family members surrounding in a confrontational manner the one whose behavior is in question. One by one, everyone shares his or her hurts, just how so-and-so's behavior has negatively impacted their lives. The "intervention" spoken about in this book is very different. It is an intervention between you and your creator—healing on a spiritual plane. Ayahuasca aggressively targets the root of the trauma like a laser-guided missile. There's no dancing on the surface, placating symptoms, pretending that there aren't demons to slay, while the root cause goes unaddressed, like many of the pharmaceuticals currently prescribed. This is otherworldly, no-nonsense medicine that cuts right through the bullshit. This intuitive medicine goes directly to "that thing" that we spend so much time hiding from, forcing us to face what needs to be faced.

These "plant teachers" have a sort of ancient wisdom, or they give us access to a part of ourselves that is omnipresent and all-knowing. Either way, you come out of these healing experiences changed, most often for the better, although we all know that sometimes you have to go backward for a bit in order to move forward. Like with any intervention, this healing can get messy—from the outside it may look like a breakdown, which may be a quite accurate way of describing what happens while engaging this powerful medicine. Breakdown or spiritual awakening, it doesn't really matter; these are just semantics, two ways to describe the same thing. Death/rebirth is often used to describe this experience. This way of looking at it is quite accurate. What makes the ayahuasca healing ritual is the safe container in which the healing takes place. This container shields the outside world and allows the participant the time and space to go within to safely and fully address his or her existential challenges or mental health afflictions. It is not a fun experience. Getting ripped apart into thousands of pieces is not fun. But doing so under the guidance of trusted supervision, that of an experienced shaman or medicine person, yields extraordinary levels of healing and often a feeling of transcendence and novel spiritual insight, creative problem solving that serves to dis-integrate unhealthy and toxic behaviors.

Often those seeking relief from emotional challenges report natal regression, which means going back to their birth trauma, going back to the early years of childhood development, often healing preverbal wounds. Participants report fractal geometric shapes, snakes, visionary dreams. These dreams are merely guides and shouldn't be taken as literal but as another way to glean insight into what lies in one's subconscious mind. At times, this notion gets lost on people and can be destabilizing when integrating the healing experience into the day to day, normal waking reality. That is why this path should only be pursued by those with mental health challenges or may be reserved for the ardent and fully committed seeker of truth. All others need not apply and should steer clear.

In my case, I knew that I would be sharing loud and proud when the time was right. Too many people are hurting and I knew after my first weekend of ceremony that when the time was right I'd share my best with as little censorship as possible so others may make the most informed decision possible. I'd do my part in slowly breaking down the stigma and taboo of these wrongfully demonized medicines, paving the way for others to heal and for the healing of our planet.

Everyone has their own unique gifts to share and offer our world. Just as a butterfly flapping its wings in the southernmost tip of South America can cause an avalanche in Canada, we are all connected to the whole, part of an intricate web of creation. William James spoke of the noetic nature of the mystical or peak experience, to experientially feel and be made aware of the truth of our existence, is what underlies the incredible healing success of ayahuasca; after the ceremony, you just know that you are connected and part of creation as if you have been let in on a secret. It is in this knowing where we experience connection, where we experience wholeness, where we experience oneness—this knowing persists long after the healing takes place. And it is in this experiential knowing that you alter your habits and can realize ways to grow aligned with your soul's calling. After one pierces the veil of consciousness, every thought, word, and action matters: we all play a much larger role in the collective narrative than most would care to accept or acknowledge, and the idea of abusing yourself with drugs and alcohol isn't nearly as appealing after healing in this manner.

Likely the concept of intervention was not discussed on this healing path because the term "intervention" denotes that something is wrong, that something is in need of fixing. As humans we have this thing called an "ego," the part of our psyche famous for denying that we are part of the whole, and that at times we need help from outside influences. When I initially embarked on this journey, I was in denial of just how much my actions were to blame for the disharmony I found in my life, for the circumstances and dramas I was tethered to. Because that is all I had ever known, there was no way to see clearly just how much I needed to intervene against my unhealthy patterns and how much I was contributing to all the disharmony in my life prior to healing with ayahuasca and psilocybin.

These trusted power plant teachers help us look at ourselves in an objective light by dismantling our default mode network (DMN), aka our "ego." Researchers believe the DMN is responsible for higher-order activities like self-reflection, mental projection, time travel past or future, and telling stories. It is the autobiographical mind that ruminates and creates our sense of self. Activity in this region reduces during a psychedelic experience, which results in the loss of self, or the merging in one—oneness.

At times, the unavoidable truths confronted are scary. Hemingway succinctly surmises: "The world breaks everyone." That said, taking a proactive approach, a "let's get this over with" mentality has been an unsuspectingly productive orientation for my own personal healing and transformation. My wellness strategy is to aggressively target the root of the problem, no placating the inevitable by dancing around the symptoms, pretending things aren't as bad as they really are. Life is too short. And denial is always a failed strategy. We must be real with ourselves, to admit that we are struggling and can't do this alone. This is not weakness; paradoxically, this vulnerability is far more powerful and productive than many will ever realize. In our "always on" world, leaning on others by admitting our hurts is discouraged. Culturally, we have conspired against vulnerability. It doesn't align with our collective capitalistic values and the brutish narrative about our human history.

We all have been fed a load of bad bologna about what we *really* are, our evolutionary roots. Darwin's "survival of the fittest" narrative is only partially true. Dr. Chris Ryan writes in his groundbreaking bestseller *Sex at Dawn: The Prehistoric Origins of Modern Sexuality* about how humans share 98% of the same DNA with aggressive chimpanzees. These chimps live in a patriarchal society defined by fierce competition. But, interestingly enough, humans also share 98% of our DNA with the bonobo, another great ape that lives in a matriarchal society defined by cooperation, not competition. So, it appears, as humans we have genetically evolved to have equal dispositions for both competition and cooperation.

The ayahuasca healing ritual is very feminine and since engaging this plant spirit I am far more empathetic, caring, and cooperative with others. This medicine, again, affectionately called "The Mother" or "The Grandmother," does not always give you what you want, but what you need. Both women and men have a balance of masculine and feminine energies. Personally, I can attest to the fact that I was not in touch with my feminine energies. I had shallow life goals and would run over anything and anyone in order to achieve them. This notion was definitely part of my inability to embrace change, contributing to my strong masculine ego and rigidity and leaving me out of touch with my inner bonobo. I couldn't cry. I couldn't be vulnerable. This inability to feel into my feminine energies left me largely unable to admit my mistakes, to be wrong. When one can't admit they are at fault, how does one error-correct and grow? How does one heal? My inability to be vulnerable made it nearly impossible to receive help, to cooperate with intimate partners and those close to me, leaving me void of the external help I needed. Ayahuasca showed this all to me, alongside many other lessons, seen through my own eyes, allowing for novel insight that can be trusted and then implemented. None of this, however, is a quick fix. This plant spirit demands that you "do the work." Unfortunately, there appears to be no way around this notion. While traveling with a backpack for nearly two years, I indeed looked for shortcuts, but found none: Do the work! Whatever that means to you.

This plant medicine teacher is truth serum in a shot glass. Her spirit, the impression that she leaves on those who brave her lessons, aligns closely with our highest self and deepest truth. This visionary medicine cuts through all the bullshit, often leaving those brave souls with an action plan on how to further heal and ultimately find peace and love through connecting deeper with our inherent truth and serving our networked circles of influence. This is why it is so unbelievably effective in healing people that have found no prior success when trying the standard Western healing modalities in place. The plant spirit of ayahuasca shows us where we are going wrong, where we are acting and behaving out of alignment with our highest values and truth.

Ayahuasca Science

Ayahuasca has far more anecdotal reports of its effects than hard science studying it. Still, modern science is coming to better understand this powerful alternative healing modality.

A recent scientific study shows a 64% decrease in depressive symptoms after one week. (https://www.biorxiv.org/content/early/2017/01/27/103531)

Researchers from University College London (UCL) and the University of Exeter in the U.K. analyzed data from a global drug survey with nearly 100,000 people worldwide and found over 500 ayahuasca users. This group reported higher well-being, along with less problematic alcohol and drug use, over the previous 12 months than others surveyed.

"These findings lend some support to the notion that ayahuasca could be an important and powerful tool in treating depression and alcohol use disorders," lead author Dr. Will Lawn, from UCL, said in a statement. "Recent research has demonstrated ayahuasca's potential as a psychiatric medicine, and our current study provides further evidence that it may be a safe and promising treatment."

Ayahuasca Ancient Science

Much has been made about science's role in the revolutionary way that we look at healing with ayahuasca. But the reality is that human beings have been tinkering with psychedelic healing for thousands of years. Some anthropologists believe ayahuasca has been used in healing rituals for 4,000 years: that is A LOT of trial and error, figuring out what works and what doesn't work. There is no replacement for experiential science. For doing. And while there is much mystery as to how this power plant teacher ayahuasca works, the reality is, there is equally as much mystery in our human existence. What are we all doing here on this massive rock called

Earth that is hurling through mostly empty space in our Universe? A Universe that scientists believe has 2 trillion galaxies. It is believed that just our galaxy, The Milky Way, has at least 100 billion stars in it, although that figure may be far greater. Ayahuasca connects us to this mystery, and how this unconventional medicine works is a mystery to embrace rather than reject.

Ayahuasca and Possibility

I smile when I listen to Frank Sinatra's "Come Fly With Me," Old Frank sang about a one-man-band in Peru—a shaman and his flute or drum. I think that the song was about a psychedelic trip. Perhaps a transformative healing journey helped him be a successful world-beater in his day, obviously sharing the taboo/esoteric would have been met with fierce resistance in his day, clashing with the Judeo-Christian values of his time. Who really knows? Regardless of its inspiration, it's a great tune that makes you think.

During my first ayahuasca retreat, Vismay's parting words were: "It's The Matrix—ayahuasca is The Matrix—the red pill." In the movie The Matrix, Neo, played by Keanu Reeves, stumbles down the rabbit hole and comes out in a self-aware world (Matrix) with an ability to essentially program his neocortex at will. The ability to program at will, to learn anything new, was Neo's "superpower." Flow research, which we will talk more in later chapters, purports that subjects in flow learn up to 430% faster, they have elevated creativity as high as 400-700%, and are at times 500% more *productive*; this cutting-edge flow science is an invitation to upgrade whatever station in life you now reside, and complements the medicine work with ayahuasca with much shared neurochemistry. Modern science has learned more about the brain in the last 10 years, than the previous 2,000 years. Robin Carhart-Harris, a leading neuroscientist and psychedelic researcher at the Imperial College of London, says, "The ego is really just a network and things like psychedelics, flow and meditation, compromise those connections, they literally disintegrate the network." This disintegration of the default mode network (ego) paves the way for health and healing and is why the "death and rebirth" example is so widely used to describe the ayahuasca healing ritual.

Buckle up: it is gonna be some ride in the years to come!

CHAPTER

8

ROAD HOME

*"A present or being present is '**pre**'-sent. Giving thought and attention about something ahead of time, that is a present or having presence."*

— AMY GRANT (MY FRIEND, NOT THE SINGER)

Personal Account

I had tried everything to find relief from my mind's incessant chatter. Twice. And then I found meditation. *What could it hurt in trying this out?* I thought, beaten and battered from an unrelenting mind. *Worst-case scenario, I sit on a cushion and just think. That isn't so bad, is it?*

Upon returning from my maiden voyage and healing journey of a lifetime, I was determined to figure this whole meditation thing out. I engaged this inner-peace practice as if my life depended on it. In retrospect, it may very well have. At that time, I had been meditating off and on for the past few years. While I wasn't sure why or how it worked, when I meditated I felt relief and everything in my life seemed to have more order. This practice of non-reactivity making my hectic, go-go schedule more manageable.

During one of my plant medicine ceremonies with ayahuasca it was abundantly clear to me that I had to meditate every work day first thing in the morning for the entire year of 2015. There was an entirely different level that I suspected would come once fully contented in this daily practice. So I got up early each day, often before sunrise, to sit and following my breath. If Abe Lincoln had six hours to cut down a tree, he would spend four hours sharpening the ax and two hours hacking away at the arbor. Meditation is a powerful sharpening tool of the mind, our will, and the habits that ultimately run our lives. Scientific research reports that meditation can help foster self-awareness, empathy, compassion and increased feelings of overall well-being. Everything we all want more of in our lives.

I knew at the end of the year I would be leaving on a travel journey of a lifetime, and in order to safely make my way through the inevitable challenges that lay ahead, I would need a sharper ax—a less reactive version of myself. So, I went to work. I spent countless hours on the meditation cushion. Strangely, in time, not that long even, I was feeling so much love, joy, and inner peace from this once-esoteric, now-mainstream daily practice.

But before this bliss and inner peace, there was a shitload of the meanest, most manipulative self-talk one might ever imagine. I became aware of the most disobedient and toxic "monkey mind" one might ever know, saying things to myself that I would never say to even my worst enemies. Each day was (still is, at times) a showdown with the omnipresent negative chatter and self-talk: *Why bother even trying? You will fail and probably end up locked up in a padded room. This is all crazy. Your loser track record speaks for itself. Self-reliance? HA.* This chatter was louder than ever, as it felt as though I had awakened my senses and was far more sensitive after my healing journeys with ayahuasca. But to the degree to which I was agitated, I was supported by this increased intuitive power, that same one I described in Chapter 5, the one that is beyond words and best described as grace. The feeling and inner power lies within us all, and it is realized when we see through the hazy stench of Bullshit, Inc.

During this practice I became determined to understand: Where do those voices, the inner critics, come from? What control (if any) do I have over those voices/mental impressions? Do I have flawed wiring? Is there anything we can do anything about these swirling thoughts? Why are people so scared to be present, often avoiding still moments like the plague in our always-connected world? What is so terrible about our normal waking state of reality that we must constantly distract ourselves?

Over the past four years, I've been motivated by these central questions. Every day, when going into the stillness of my mind, I have pondered these notions, approaching meditation in a scientific manner, doing my best with where I am at during any given day—practicing life, not overreacting to any findings but just sitting with what is.

In this chapter, I am going to cover the meditations that I have done personally. Early on, I found that guided meditations and letting go mantra/meditations worked great for me, which is part of the reason why my own personal experience is limited in terms of various forms of meditation. I always recommend people to take a scientific approach—find what works through trial and error, by doing, trusting what resonates and letting go of what doesn't. It is in the doing where the magic happens. If you haven't found a practice that resonates, keep looking, trying, and dabbling till you do.

Making the time each day to confront our truth is powerful, and making this time satiates our evolutionary craving for ritual; typically, prioritizing time each day at the same time lends for better results: first thing in the morning, before bed, at lunch, and so on. The specific time isn't important. It's the consistency that counts. But remember that there has to be an "acceptable loss," meaning, if you miss a day here and there, do not take yourself too seriously. Do not beat yourself up! Meditation is a means to practice life and, being realistic, some days we just don't have it, or our priorities, or lack thereof, get the best of us. Find what works for you and do that.

Lighting a candle or incense, or putting a small dab of your favorite essential oil under your nose, are tools that make this practice more intentional. Really, that is what we are doing when looking within. We are exercising our "intention" muscles: our ability to command and corral our wandering minds by directing focus toward a task for a given moment in time. In a world where the onslaught of data and constant choices bombard our "psyches," is there a more important muscle to train if well-being is our desired state?

Before I started meditating, I had really shitty values, and, sadly, I didn't truly believe in anything. Sure, I would have said I did, but those would have been ungrounded words that weren't rooted in action or substance. This hard truth was the underlying reason why I struggled finding peace of mind. I talked a good game, completely unaware how dangerous my loose words were and how my errant speech affected my well-being.

My inability to set and hold intention was an obvious symptom of a greater problem. It is only in fully committing to this peace practice that I've become a believer in human potential and all that is possible for our world. Progressing in my meditation practice has been a slow burn that has been a test of my faith. To commit to this inner peace non-reactivity training with no expectation of anything in return is a powerful form of self-love.

I feel this chapter on meditation is the most important chapter in this book. It certainly isn't the sexiest and won't be the most entertaining—how adventurous can sitting on a cushion and follow your breath be?—but it is still the most important.

What qualifications do I have to write a chapter about meditation? Again, none, really, except for the fact that I have practiced intently for about three hours per day for the last four years. Every day I sit in stillness, connecting to my heart's whispers, that still voice inside, intently seeking ways to be of better service to my fellow earthlings, using the gift of meditation as a tool to bring light into the world. My practice has required that amount of time; I've had a lot of karma to burn (see Chapter 2 if you've forgotten exactly how much). This probably isn't a normal devotion to inner peace, my creator within, but what is normal anyways? I've known many who claim to get much out of their meditation practice in as little as 10 minutes per day. We all are different. There is no right or wrong answer for any given person—life can be really hard, we just do our best.

Who Is Meditating?

Nearly every influencer or person worth admiring that I have come across these past four years has some sort of meditation practice. Tim Ferriss, a modern-day Napoleon Hill, one of the greatest interviewers of our time, says 99% of those he interviewed on his podcast have some sort of meditation practice.

Now we see and hear about this peace practice nearly everywhere. Meditation has gone mainstream: Katy Perry, Jerry Seinfeld, Lady Gaga, Ray Dalio, and Arianna Huffington all swear by their daily peace practice. Yoga, an active form of meditation, has exploded. Go to any Main Street in America and you will see a handful of yoga studios offering diverse styles and instructions of the 5,000-year-old practice. Yoga and meditation have changed my life by quieting my mind and transforming my physical body.

Again, this is practical meditation advice about what has worked for me, someone who didn't have his first mindful moment until the pain of my waking reality became too much to handle, when I was never further from well-being and peace of mind. If you want a more comprehensive book about meditation from a guy whose practice involves a more robust resume, try Sam Harris' bestseller *Waking Up*:

Spirituality Without Religion. Harris is a leading neuroscientist who also has a lifelong meditation practice, having trained with the best of the best in Nepal and India. He has done the work and he, too, is a proponent for psychedelics as medicines, even going as far as saying he would be disappointed if his own daughters didn't dabble, at least to know what the psychedelic experience is about.

I typically don't care much about Bible quotes and such, having taken a secular and scientific approach towards this path, but since I suspect a disproportionate amount of those struggling with mental health are doing so as a result of sexual shame that derived from or around the church's dogmatic teachings that tie sexuality and a fiery hell in the same breath. Or the sexual abuse pandemic (1 in 5 of us), our global sickness started many millennium ago when the Roman Catholic Church thought it was a good idea to have its clergy abstain from sex. Yep, that is right, Pope Siricius, the year 385 and the cult of Christianity, a divine order that has led to billions being subjected to abuse of deviant priests commissioned to safely care for our vulnerable children and youth. I shake my head as I write these words. Back to meditation, peace, and, yes, forgiveness, which is surely needed for the church's sick perpetrators.

Below are some biblical quotes that support meditation as a peace practice and way to heal by cultivating self-love.

- The kingdom of God is within you. Luke 17:21
- Seek ye first the kingdom within and good things shall be added unto thee. Matthew 6:33
- You are God. John 10:34

And Oprah, known as a modern-day Jesus and saint-like figure in our world, breaks down the consciousness that lies within with an unmatched grace. "I was like you are. I thought Jesus came and died on the cross. Jesus' being here wasn't about his death and dying on the cross, but it really was about him coming to show us how to do it." Oprah's words put me at ease early on in my meditation practice while I pushed forward through the resistance. She is a trusted ally for team Earth, one who has walked the talk; she knows soul, she knows pain, and is a living example of triumph over despair. She expands further, "[Jesus came] to show us the Christ-consciousness that he had and that consciousness abides in all of us. That's what I got. That's what I got." Powerful words of encouragement from the Big O.

With all this Jesus stuff and history book stuff, who really knows? That was a long time ago and I mistrust a 200-year telephone game, let alone one of 2,000 years. Onward.

Infinite power comes from true peace. Yes, it is a puzzling paradox and counterintuitive notion. Proof: Gandhi led the Indian Independence movement against British rule by employing nonviolent civil disobedience and freed a whole country from tyranny and injustice. Leading with peace, Gandhi has inspired a world by leaving a roadmap of the way, of how sustainable change can be brought forth. Having nothing but the rags he called clothes and a sharp mind, this frail man changed our landscape by inspiring movements for civil rights and freedom across our world. A short time after Gandhi made his mark on the world, a man named Martin Luther King Jr. would emulate this orientation of peace while leading the civil rights movement of the 1960s. Dr. King observed, "Non-violent resistance is passive physically, but very active spiritually." The power of peace is a strange paradox, but it makes sense. Only in a state of peace can we see the way forward unencumbered by the agendas of external influences.

It is 2019. We all know that our abundant planet provides plenty for us all. Meditation is all about peace, starting and creating change within the individual. Many of our esteemed scientists believe that peace on our planet is a mere math equation. When we hit a critical mass of fully committed meditators, our global family will realize this peace and unity: The "Newmanity" coined by my teacher and shaman Vismay and mentioned in Chapter 5. YES, our global family coming together, making this human experience and human experiment work—bring on the Star Wars! In the meantime, meditation is a special tool for self-inquiry and examination, promoting higher levels of self-awareness and overall well-being. And with all this peace talk, it doesn't hurt anyone to believe in all that is possible.

Letting Go

For the past four years, my go-to meditation has been a "letting go" meditation. When I first started this practice, I was jaded, cynical, and hurt from a lifetime of dogmatic certitudes, so naturally I chose a secular approach; just follow the breath and mantra into the present moment. In the practice of letting go, I create space for my light to shine by clearing energetic space or thought energy. Yes, this is a form of addition by subtraction. Again, this is a counterintuitive view, but one that relies on the foundational truth that inherently we all come from love, that our truest nature is love. Our world, from the time we are youngsters, conditions the love right out of us; we are blocked from seeing our truth, our fullest essence. It is by this practice of self-love that we reconnect with our light, but only those who are willing to push through the societal conditioning will realize what has always been there.

The best part about this practice is that it is free and right underneath our noses. And it is just that, a practice with only one requirement: to show up and just do it.

Why Do Most People Fail?

"It is too hard." "I've got too much going on!" "This just isn't for me." We make all sorts of excuses. We sabotage our own growth when buying into our limiting beliefs. Meditation can be quite painful for those who have spent a lifetime ignoring how they really feel. I know this pain. Believe me, I know about hiding from truth and what lies within.

We keep busy and do everything except for the thing we know we should be doing. This ignorance is a symptom of a time where we have forgotten how to love our neighbor, how to love ourselves. Push through the fear, the resistance—I promise you it is worth it.

Another reason people fail to adopt and maintain a meditation practice is they aren't willing to stick with it. It requires a discipline that many of us lack. The average American spends more than five hours on social media or in front of the television every day and if you asked them why they couldn't meditate, their response would likely be: "I am too busy!" We live in an "instant oatmeal" society that doesn't always align with what we are. Good things take time. Put in the work. Do your best. I've heard that if you say your mantra only one time during a meditation, that is still a successful meditation that moves the needle forward.

Habits take time to form. Research varies on this notion, suggesting it takes between 21 and 60 days for a habit to crystallize and then become an unconscious behavior. Remember that you are Neo and learning anything is your new superpower. For me, between days 30 and 40 of meditating every day, something clicked. It was at that moment that I said to myself, *I will do this every day, the rest of my life. If this were taken away from me, I would truly miss it.* That was a day of grace, knowing intuitively that this daily practice had crystallized into a daily habit.

It takes time for our brains to change. It was previously thought that our brains were fixed once we reached adulthood (early 20s). If you were an asshole out of college, you were thought to be an asshole for life. That is not true. In the 1990s, scientists began discovering just how "plastic" our brains really are, birthing the field of neuroplasticity: The brain's ability to reorganize itself by forming new neural connections throughout life. In *The Brain That Changes Itself: Stories of Personal Triumph from the Frontiers of Brain Science*, Norman Dodge, M.D., helps us understand the true power of positive thinking and gratitude, and how this orientation actually changes our brain. Further, according to brain expert Jim Kwik "people who meditate show more grey matter in certain regions of the brain, they show stronger connections between brain regions and show less brain related atrophy(aging). Scientific research(UCLA neuroimaging) supports that meditation helps one achieve a bigger, faster, and younger more connected brain."

Resistance and the "Monkey Mind"

Fear is the most basic hardwired survival mechanism we have. Fear has kept our ancestors alive, but now, at this stage of our evolution, fear is incorrectly processed. Nobody breaks down this abstract concept better than Seth Godin, one of the most prolific writers of our time, author of *Tribes*. "We have a bug in our operating system," Seth says. Humans have quickly evolved from hunter-gatherers who were exposed to nature's elements to humans who sit in at a desk all day, largely protected by our creature comforts. The fears that once protected us now serve as the very obstacles we are all looking to overcome and move beyond. So, essentially, those nagging voices in our minds, "the monkey mind" that won't sit still, are a product of our evolution. Knowing this, perhaps you will look at your mind's resistance in a different light and not be so fearful of engaging your "monkey mind" and inner critic that inevitably becomes more vocal as you work in earnest to adopt meditation as a daily practice, a healthy habit that underlies the creation of all other habits.

Fun fact about evolution: It takes 25,000 years for humans to adopt an evolutionary change. Ten thousand years ago (Premodern Agriculture/Farming), all of humanity lived in hunter-gatherer societies. So, in many respects, our basic hardware is not compatible with the demands of our modern world.

The encouraging news is that we aren't bound to or stuck with those voices, and with practice, we can hack our biology and upgrade our hardware to utilize a myriad of life-accelerating software. In time, while practicing meditation, you begin to see which thoughts align with your heart and which thoughts are fearful projections. In a way, we start to consciously manipulate the voice inside our heads. Neuroscientists have discovered that experienced meditators have a less reactive fear response. Their amygdala actually shrinks. It appears as though the peace practice is a tool that can be used to "hack" our fight-or-flight response, giving us a subtle increase in processing time between external (and internal) stimuli and providing more opportunity to consciously respond instead of unconsciously reacting. And we all know that responding is better than reflexively reacting for the long-term sustainability of our healthy relationships; we don't have to regret a conscious response. We can avoid excessive rumination about the could-haves and should-haves of life. Think of your mom or dad, or your boss or colleague; people say the darnedest of things. How beneficial would having even the slightest bit more ability to respond rather than react help your overall well-being?

Mindfulness and Meditation

Mindfulness can change your life for the better, but it isn't meditation. Meditation is a practice of mindfulness, but mindfulness is not meditation. Meditation requires ritual and structured intention. Mindfulness is a powerful tool and shift in the way we look at life, and how we relate to our day-to-day external stimuli. By taking time to be aware of our surroundings, to consciously make an effort to be engaged in the present moment, our lives can become richer. While mindfulness has many benefits, it isn't going to change your brain like a consistent meditation practice. The magic of meditation is the neurogenesis that happens when the committed and ardent practitioner pushes through and establishes a habitual practice. Our brain begins to grow new neurons, and the neurons in place strengthen their already-established connections. *This* is the process that changes our inner hardware.

Gratitude is a foundational tenant of mindfulness. Fear and gratitude can't occupy the same space, and when we are grateful something really special is happening in our brain.

My mindful gratitude practice looks like this: A sincere and genuine thank you for every new day; for all of the challenges, adversity, and obstacles life has thrown my way; for my physical body and my good health, for all the blessings in my life—I actually count them, or write them down; five deep conscious breaths before eating any meal, taking time to be thankful for the food and the nourishment that sustains me; and keying my mind to a state of thanks and appreciation before bed. These are simple ways to shift our awareness in a subtle manner that, in time, yield life-changing results. Like everything else, being mindful and grateful is a practice: we do our best!

Scientific research is showing with fMRI brain scans the tremendous overlap in brain activity in those that are having "peak" or "mystical" experiences and the brain scans of experienced meditators. This is a fascinating insight, likely underlying why so many who heal their trauma with psychedelic medicines eventually gravitate toward a meditation practice. These brains scans seem to suggest that in time, with intentional practice, we can access more readily those altered states with just the power of our minds.

Let's Practice Meditation Together!

I know you're super busy, but let's take some time to do a short letting go meditation together anyway.

Get comfy, sit upright, spine straight but not too straight, shoulders relaxed. Our mantra is I AM while on the in breath, LETTING GO on the out breath. The mantra is said in the quiet of your own mind, and is optional, too. You can just follow your breath. That works, too.

Before the practice begins, I set an intention that aligns with my heart's desire. Then I take a moment to create a container. Not a physical container, but a spiritual one: essentially, fair expectations and ground rules for the pending practice. Thoughts will come and thoughts will go during this practice. Just do your best with where you are at right now. When you find yourself engaged in a thought, come back to the breath, back to the mantra and the present moment, without judgment. Practicing this nonjudgmental orientation maybe the most important notion in this entire book. During this practice, we are the observer of our thoughts, mere witnesses to our wandering thoughts. It matters not if there are ten or 1,000 thoughts during the 20-minute meditation session. If 20 minutes is too long, try

10 minutes or even 5 minutes; the important thing is to just do it. All that does matter is coming back to the breath and mantra, letting go of all thoughts.

Let's set a timer and begin.

I AM while breathing in, LETTING GO on the outbreath.

I AM, letting go.

Just do your best. And don't judge. That is the secret.

In this simple letting go meditation is a practice of non-reactivity, a practice of peace. This peace helps you walk through the world in a more untethered state to external stimuli, or to the world of form that Eckhart Tolle speaks about in *The Power of Now*.

At the end of the day, this is just a practice: we can only do our best!

There are countless forms of meditation. There are thousands of research papers you can find online that support the benefits of meditation. On my journey, it was believing in the scientific benefits that helped me push through the initial resistance of my own mind. The belief in science led me to spirit, and in time I would see they are one and the same.

Again, there are many ways to engage this peace practice. The most important thing is to just do it. Commit and take the time each day to bathe in stillness, to engage a practice of self-care and self-love. If the plane is going down, we must grab the oxygen mask and put it on ourselves first before helping others. This is no different. By taking this time, we can show up as our most authentic selves. In a fast-paced world bursting with data, we can be still in order to sort the inspiration from the information.

Additional Recommended Resources

- For all things meditation and hard science: *Altered Traits: Science Reveals How Meditation Changes Your Mind, Brain, and Body.* Daniel Goldman & Richard J. Davidson

- The meditation app Headspace is a great tool. People rave about its simplicity. This app will keep you diligent with your daily practice.

- Sam Harris' Waking Up app is inspiring many to engage meditation.

- Muse wearable meditation technology monitors your brain waves, tracking your progress, informing you when you are present.

9

HOLD THE LINE

"The middle is messy, but it's where the magic happens."

— BRENE BROWN

In the middle of my travel journey I came across an ultra-compelling video. This wasn't your typical YouTube content. The surface impressions were nothing extraordinary, just two guys having a heart-to-heart conversation while walking through a beautiful park in what looked to be Northern California. This powerful video, featuring two of my heroes, and its heavy content moved me deeply—a visceral shift within grabbed my attention. These men were breaking down the "what and why" of the psychedelic experience in a calm and grounded manner. "*Acting* on the goodness, truth, and beauty that you apprehend while *there*, and then trying to live up your damnedest to be that example and inspiration when we are back *here*. And if you skip that step, it is on your mortal soul the next time you go back to the wishing well," Jamie Wheal shared with Jason Silva during this candid YouTube conversation. Wheal, of course, was speaking about the inspiration we receive while in altered states of consciousness and the importance of grounding this thought energy, harnessing this force by directing it toward a goal or desired outcome. Wheal and Silva are superstars of this movement toward a more sane mental health paradigm and planet, advocates and ambassadors that walk this path with grace and integrity as examples to follow. Anyone who misses the key message here is indeed just getting high with friends. That is okay, too, at times part of the healing process and your prerogative, but it might be on your mortal soul, like Wheal says, if we aren't integrating those insights.

We all know a life without purpose and meaning is a life that isn't worth living; the wear and tear, the endless struggle we confront during this human experience becomes too much. I believe we all came to this plane with an assignment, yep, all seven billion of us currently here have their own unique calling, dharma, gift to share with the world. Figure it out, be brave, we need you—go do it! You don't have to be anything, but you have to be *something*.

Slow and steady wins the race. You are a tortoise in our world where we aggrandize the hare. We are constantly bombarded with imagery, societal programming that says that we aren't enough. That we need to be richer, faster, smarter, stronger; we live lives inundated with six-pack abs and get-rich-quick schemes, find your soulmate in a hot tub overlooking the Swiss Alps if you do this, and so on. Those are most often only distractions from the work at hand. There is no way around it—every living organism in the animal kingdom has to work for its food or it will perish. Why should humans we be any different? We did, after all, come from the dirt, and there we all return.

My outlook about these misunderstood healing compounds might differ with the ayahuasca and psychedelic camp, though I am not sure. What makes sense to me, is that psychedelics are not about the medicine or your healing adventure, but about what you are doing to make the world better. This can easily get lost on the unprepared psychedelic traveler of inner space looking to heal from trauma. How are you using these powerful tools to be healthier, happier, and stronger for yourself and your networked circles of influence? Anything else is just talk; action and initiative are the *only* things that can bring love into our lives and the lives of those we care about.

But before we can make the world better, we need to heal ourselves. In order to be fit for service, we must be fit ourselves. To integrate means to make whole. You just had the most incredible, mind-blowing psychedelic healing adventure or went deep during a 10-day Vipassana meditation retreat. Now what? It's time to fold those lessons back into our day to day, or those lessons will have meant nothing at all. Buddhist scholar Jack Kornfield writes in his book *After the Ecstasy, the Laundry* about the pangs of coming back down from ecstatic bliss, the challenges of grounding these revelatory experiences and putting them in service of something bigger than ourselves. Whole-hearted, holy-man spiritual rocker Trevor Hall says it best: "you can't rush your healing; darkness has its teachings."

One of the biggest challenges to the seeker is making sense of what you see and experience "out there" and how it applies to your day-to-day life. Glimpsing eternity in an hour and then going back to your shitty desk job? Exactly.

It is no wonder these medicines have been suppressed and demonized.

There is no better integration tool than that of meditation: taking time on a daily basis to check back in, to reconnect to our truth, our higher self. A slow march toward healing, toward our dreams, toward the realization of that "glimpse."

Since my first ayahuasca healing journey, I have talked to many hundreds of people who have had similar healing journeys. Commonalities among them are an unwillingness to settle for Bullshit, Inc., and a deep-rooted hurt or pain that drives them—most often childhood sexual trauma is the culprit, and many struggle with DTD (developmental trauma disorder), a condition coined by Bessel Van Der Kolk, MD, in his groundbreaking book about trauma: *The Body Keeps the Score*. Van Der Kolk, a researcher and the founder of the Brookline Mass, believes that DTD is common in the 25% of people who have alcoholic parents. Al-Anon, is a loving support group for those who have family members struggling with alcohol and substance abuse, similar to alcoholics anonymous, the problem is that addicts can't connect in a healthy manner, leaving their loved ones, especially children, void of healthy connection. AKA, they have "attachment issues" or "daddy issues." Essentially, those unwilling to do their healing work are surely to pass on their shit and problems—their karma—to their children.

My first time returning home to integrate this healing experience was a great challenge. I felt like a fish out of water. There was so much to process, so much to factor when relating my incredible experiences to the day-to-day grind. What exactly happened to me in the jungles of Costa Rica? How does this healing really work?

Sure, we talked about integration after the ayahuasca ceremony, what we were to expect. But there is no way to fully prepare for returning to the space and time-bound body, and the challenges that might arise with this new level of awareness now that the doors of perception had been kicked wide open.

In many ways this book is a guidebook to help your life purpose move forward through integration, finding meaning and changing your personal story and narrative to one that aligns with what lies within. I believe that we are all co-creators with our higher power, god, Jesus, Buddha, Krishna, Allah, Source, Infinite Intelligence, Great Spirit, or whatever name you use: call it what you want!

I have made this trek to and from the jungle numerous times since first embarking on my healing journey. Each time it gets progressively easier to integrate the insights and teachings to my day to day, after much trial and error, I've found ways to maximize the healing experience.

Find Your Tribe

You have changed, but often, those around you stayed the same. You are now on a growth path, with a growth mindset, and the ones you love are standing still with a fixed mindset. I struggled greatly with this notion. It didn't take long to realize that I was sick because my entire life I had to be what I thought others wanted me to be instead of just being myself. I know, it's a pretty big realization to have in your 30s. We are herd animals. We are hardwired to follow along, to stay close to the others. Again, this part of our internal CPU served us and kept us safe until this point in our evolution. In our hunter-gatherer days, if we were kicked out of the tribe we were completely fucked; our likely fate was getting eaten by a large furry creature with razor-sharp teeth. This is no longer the case, but this hardwired fear is still present. It's still our predisposition to conform to the herd. But herein lies the problem: it appears as though the herd may have lost its way. Our environmental challenges—global warming, our mental health epidemic, obvious political discord, and social injustices—abound, and we forget the whole part about loving our neighbor.

It is no longer safe to conform to the herd. Our world needs brave souls willing to step outside and find ways to be of service to our global family in spite of what the overly judgmental herd might think. It is said that there are nearly a million conscious businesses globally working fiercely to create the change they want to see for the world. Being the change is the only way this process works on an individual and collective level.

The doing part of this path can be grueling at times. Microsoft giant Bill Gates points out this hard truth: "We always overestimate the change that will occur in the next two years and underestimate the change that will occur in the next ten. Don't let yourself be lulled into inaction." It is so easy to get discouraged and to give into despair, but it is despair that keeps us tethered to vicious cycles of abuse and unhealthy thought patterns. Keep going! Always further.

While compiling this book, I have never struggled better in my life. All of this is a labor of love—you are **worth the fight**!

Many find, and I agree, that community is more important than ever. Find your tribe, those who you can share openly and honestly without judgment; people you can trust and lean on during the inevitable challenging times to come.

The Line and Balancing Point

In probably the best blog post I've ever read, James Altucher describes "How to Be the Luckiest Guy on Earth" by doing something each day to benefit yourself: mentally, physically, emotionally and spiritually. This simplistic and relatable approach is a basis for achieving more balance in one's life. As humans, we tend to complicate things immensely by taking on too much. Again, we overestimate our abilities, which is often accompanied by talk instead of doing the right action our souls crave. Without some sort of daily practice, how do you really know what actions serve you and your greater purpose? You don't. And you can't truly know if you're at the whim of your external environment, but in taking time each day to do something physically active, reading a little, engaging your friends and looking within, these simple and seemingly benign undertakings create a reliable foundation to build on: a point of reference for our ever-distracted lives. Is balance the holy grail? Own your daily practice and you might see for yourself.

Our bodies are the vessels that carry our soul and spirit. In order for us to be the best versions of ourselves, we must be strong. We must build healthy habits that help us to own our days.

Aubrey Marcus is the master of integration, clearly owning many consecutive days in order to compile his bestseller *Own the Day, Own Your Life: Optimized Practices for Waking, Working, Learning, Eating, Training, Playing, Sleeping and Sex*. This near four-hundred-page bible of optimized health complements in the most comprehensive of manners nearly all that is needed to know when embarking on a serious growth path. Aubrey, a brother on the path, owns and runs ONNIT, an extremely successful supplement company. He demonstrates his immense knowledge with rigorously researched scientific data that will make you think twice about optimal health. Leading by example, Aubrey is showing the world a different kind of entrepreneurship while remaining a faithful advocate of the therapeutic benefits of ayahuasca and psychedelics as medicines. His book is a must-read for anyone serious about being the best version of themselves. Bravo Aubrey—great work!

Many of my friends work as nurses and are convinced that all the patients really need for balanced health is to go outside for walks, while eating daily veggies and upping their water intake. That simple. Why do so many people struggle with these rudimentary concepts? The indifference of man to himself is one of the great mysteries of our species. We all know what we need to do, but so many of us get caught up on the doing part.

While walking our Earth, breaking bread, and learning about what has worked for others on a similar path, there are three books that have been a near constant: Eckhart Tolle's *Power of Now*, Miguel Ruiz's *Four Agreements* and Napoleon Hill's *Think and Grow Rich*.

Eckhart Tolle provides the most comprehensive spiritual view of the maze we call life. Eloquently, prophetically, he lays out why we are where we are in his books that have sold many millions of copies: *The Power of Now* (and *The New Earth*), tells a new story about the plight of the 21st-century man and woman.

Miguel Ruiz's *Four Agreements* are spiritual teachings presented in the most uncomplicated of manners: Be impeccable with your word; don't make assumptions; don't take things personally; always do your best! For people struggling with emotional challenges, there is likely a breakdown in adhering to these straightforward commands. This handy 100-page book is a great place to start when rewriting your code and personal constitution.

Likely, you got into trouble and are seeking relief because your inner constitution was void of truth and order. Your system in place was insufficient, not meeting your needs at the soul level, failing to provide the peace of mind you've been searching for. This process of transformation is not an easy one and requires patience and fortitude. We don't undo a lifetime of Bullshit Inc., programming in one weekend of ceremony or by meditating for a couple of months. This is a lifetime commitment to living and being the best version of yourself.

Sometimes I wonder if Napoleon Hill's *Think and Grow Rich* might replace the Bible as our seminal text if the good people of the United States were given the opportunity to vote for a new and more modern standard, one that factors in science and shames the dogmatic certitudes that no longer serves the evolution of our people. A new standard that doesn't blaspheme the mystery of our existence. When someone is right, someone else has to be wrong. This creates separation that is poorly aligned with natural and universal law, and might just be what perpetuates war and the immense suffering we feel here on Earth. Sure, monotheistic religions served our people for millennia, but are they now archaic? Anything that discounts modern science (the organization of knowledge) is on the chopping block and under scrutiny, poised to be left behind in our rapidly changing world. But somehow the Church has snuck into the "Authoritarian Power" zone. We don't think to question just how much their unchecked evils and systematic pedophilia affect our global family. Turning a blind eye to this atrocity makes those who ignore these hard truths complicit, part of the problem.

Sure, we have the 10 commandments. But maybe 10 is too many for our attention span, which is now not much longer than a goldfish's. Or people are mistrustful of something that happened thousands of years ago—can we blame them? What we do know is that the followers, the obedient parishioners, have a horrible track record: hypocrisy, pedophilia/sex crimes, and scandal. #TRUTH

On my journey, there was nothing more important to me than having access to Napoleon Hill's lectures. This was strange as he had been dead for nearly 50 years at this point. No, I wasn't going crazy or hearing any more voices than usual. I was listening to old lectures from Napoleon Hill on my iPhone via Spotify. There was something about Hill's message that sucked me in, leaving me spellbound and enamored by his lectures. It was the fact that his teachings were corruption-proof. He was dead; he had no motives. Napoleon Hill spoke of the power of our sexual energy and leaves a roadmap in how to transmute this infinite power and direct it towards our heart's desires. He calls this process: Sex transmutation. And Hill's system of imaginary guides, although a bit woo-woo, really works, empowering his students to craft a container to safely express their creative powers and imagination.

Napoleon Hill was a man who walked the path of service, leading with grace in a modern world not that much different from the world we all maneuver through, a dignified man with a special lightness and orientation of humor and cheer, could speak right to me.

Napoleon Hill, an original Law of Attraction master, had a pragmatic, old-school vibe to his teachings that enticed me to commit more fully to spiritual practice. Hill had the privilege of interviewing over 500 of the most successful industrialists that built our country in the early 1900s. Under the tutelage and mentorship of Andrew Carnegie, the then-richest man in the world, he would put together our world's first practical philosophy on personal success. Of course, success is relative, but his neutral and all-encompassing stance is applicable to everyone with ambition looking to advance their station in life. "*Success* is the attainment of your *definite chief aim* without violating the rights of other people." This is a definition we can all agree on. Hill would gather that financial success rarely led to life satisfaction and fulfillment. By interviewing America's most influential people, he decoded peace of mind, working backward to what those who had it did to attain, and maintain, it. It has been said that he worked for 20 years with no pay to arrange this philosophy for our world. This was the man I entrusted to guide me on my path less traveled.

For hours and hours, I dutifully listened to Napoleon Hill's lectures on Spotify. *What a blessing technology can be!* I pondered while taking notes. His words had a way of making me see my own shortcomings. It was Napoleon Hill's leadership and humility that gave me much hope that I could someday attain the attributes necessary for me to do the work and be the man I envisioned. Akin to taking ground balls or spending extra time in the gym working diligently, practicing to be better, this philosophy of personal success is about practicing life to be a better person by putting in the work.

Many years back, I was turned on to Napoleon Hill's book *Outwitting the Devil.* Of course a friend I met at Florestral had reached out in perfect timing, saying, "This is totally for you. I know this will resonate with you!" Janel was right. Within minutes, I was engulfed into the audiobook's foreword. *Outwitting the Devil* was too controversial for its time (1938) and wasn't published until 2012 when we lived in a more tolerant time that was more accepting to Dr. Hill's views on organized religion and our education system. This book made the hairs on my arms stand up and dance; it was brash and bold, an "in-your-face" style, exactly what I needed. Again, the idea that Napoleon Hill's teachings were motive-proof is worth mentioning one more time in a world that lacks the ability to trust. I heard genuine enthusiasm in his voice and I could sense honesty and sincerity: all that made this philosophy on personal success music to my ears. I was rebuilding myself from the ground up so I could be the man that I envision. Hill's wisdom would be with me nearly every step of the way. I listened so intently that his teachings started to imprint my psyche and impact my conversations. I could sense his spirit or impression, the wisdom I had adopted over time with repetition of thought. A powerful question was asked during the book's foreword: "would you work your entire lifetime and do the right thing, even if you knew that you may never get credit for your work?" This hit me hard, and I have taken this as a personal challenge.

The Three Amigos

I could go on and on about all things integration, but will limit my sharing to three very important notions to consider when integrating a peak or psychedelic experience. While folding these powerful lessons back into your day to day, use these insights to level up your game and the lives of those in your networked circle of influence.

Engage Your Senses

Music/Sound. We are vibration. Universe means "one song." Remember, you are Neo from the Matrix; you chose wisely and took the red pill. Our every thought is programming us. This can be a good thing or a bad thing. Any given thought pushes us closer to our dreams or pulls us farther away. There is no better programming tool than music. Why do we gather for concerts and festivals? Our artists are the luminaries, the shining stars fostering the people in the direction of love. However, sometimes our artists are black holes who only serve to suck the love and light out of us: choose wisely your programming words, those artists you entrust.

Each chapter of *Worth the Fight*, and some chapter breaks are named with a song title that has been important to me on my journey. And often, relevant to the content of the given chapter. Most of these tunes are powerful affirmation songs that have a high resonance and words/messages/poetry that align with my truth. On my journey I have listened to these songs enough that I feel as if the words have been permanently imprinted in my mind, body, and spirit.

Vision Boards Work! That's right, grab a pile of some old magazines, a glue stick, and scissors and you are on your way. Engaging your goals in a visual manner multiple times daily has a way of creating magic, fast. You've heard the saying "keep the end in mind." Like a chisel, keeping your goal in sight slowly carves out any thoughts, words, or actions that are not aligned with that which you seek. This is Law of Attraction 101. It works, so be careful what you wish for!

Affirmations Work Too. Especially if you affirm that which you want while at an elevated emotional state, while engaging our senses. This is perhaps why the ayahuasca healing ritual is so profound: doors of perception swing wide open; all of our senses activate at the same time.

But yes, sometimes life sucks. I am not saying avoid your problems in a delusional manner. Just affirm more of that which you want: *I am loved. I am safe. I am worthy. I am abundant.* These are healthy words to adopt, good places to start, positive notions that we all aspire to bring more of into our lives. We become our thoughts. Whatever we think, we become. Be intentional and think things that align with your dreams!

Strategic Withdrawal

In chapter 7, Dr. Dan told us to "hold the gold," to not share our healing experiences before we are ready, as this premature sharing does indeed alter your overall desired result, the transformational process. I always recommend that people take some time to sit with that which they experienced, to honor the medicine diet or eat as clean as they can shortly after the psychedelic experience.

When I first returned from Costa Rica, I didn't drink alcohol for nearly 40 days. I hardly missed it at all while deep in the "pink-cloud" or "afterglow." This medicine supposedly stays with you for 30 days or so. This means there is no better time to dig in to start creating healthy habits than directly after the healing ceremony. Brain expert Jim Kwik says, "First we create our habits, then our habits create us." This maxim is so true. Science supports that psychedelics enhance neuroplasticity; this, then, is the optimal time for implementing insights, for learning new skills that align with our values and life objectives.

During my journey, I have at times pulled back from all external stimuli: sex, coffee/cacao/caffeine, psychedelics, alcohol, anything that provides a change of state. This is done only for the sake of contrast. I don't do this in some attempt to be abstinent; humans aren't wired for abstinence. Marc Lewis, PhD, and author of *The Biology of*

Desire: Why Addiction Is Not A Disease, breaks down why with cutting-edge brain science. Addictions are merely learned behaviors that manifest as failed habits, not diseases. When we think of something as a disease, we are disempowered to do anything about it. It is time to rethink addictions with the understanding that a powerful unprocessed emotion underlies all of our habits/addictions.

Take the time to pull back, to understand your vices and their effects on you. Strategically withdrawing will help you get the most out of your healing experience. At times on my journey, I've even found much value from pulling back from people, finding solace in brief stints of isolation and fasting from our busy world.

This also holds true for taking time to live on airplane mode if you can. Strategically shut out the world for a short time so you can "check in" and reconnect to your truth. These useful tricks help us to depattern and see ourselves in a more objective light.

I swear by these psychedelic healing medicines, but in order to truly know if I am walking this path in integrity, I stop all usage for at least 30 days each year. This time of forbearance is a safety valve for the over-zealous seeker, for the madman who lives in all of our hearts.

Journaling

I often hear from aspirants just how difficult it is for people to put pen to paper and journal their thoughts. Strong men who don't seem to be scared of anything end up stymied in fear when it comes time to take inventory of their thinking, unsure how to proceed. This is perplexing, but I get it. Journaling is a powerful tool that elicits a level of awareness that makes many feel uncomfortable—the truth can be scary! But why?

As humans, we think in feedback loops. Meaning, we have swirling thoughts that behave like solar flares shooting from the sun's surface. When we have a thought, it is that flash or flare we are momentarily aware of. Putting that thought on paper acknowledges that thinking and closes that loop, so that thought no longer flares up. When we close that loop, we create space for us to engage other flares, flashes of insight, thoughts that ruminate in the back of our minds. This process is tied closely to the creative process. Foremost teacher on creativity, Julia Cameron, sister of the cinematic wonder James Cameron, is a major proponent of "morning pages." Taking time, usually first thing, to jot down a page or two of thoughts and observations can be a life-changing practice. This is an active form of meditation, an approach Cameron swears by and promotes in her book *The Artist's Way*.

For me, typically I can remember 5 to 10 dreams from the night prior; this takes up at least half of a page. This has been a special practice for these past few years. Dream tracking has helped me glean insight on many of my personal challenges, getting a glimpse each morning of my subconscious thoughts from my deep sleep. Try it out. Buy a dream journal and place it next to your bed with the earnest intention to remember, and those dreams will likely start appearing in a few weeks.

Journaling is a vital part of integration. If we don't journal on top of our contemplative practices, we are likely to be confronted over and over with the same thoughts. Getting your thoughts out on paper is an active way to engage our mind's inventory.

The Information Age at Your Fingertips

Okay, you get a bonus fourth item, because sharing is caring: Informational podcasts. The value of being a fly on the wall with two of your heroes talking shop is priceless! Yesteryear, this would have been only accessible by watching shitty middle-of-the-night infomercials, ordering tapes for $49.99 and waiting 6 to 8 weeks for delivery; now these conversations have been open-sourced, given away as we have shifted toward this "gifting" model. Want to know what influences the people you admire? Listen to a couple of their podcasts and you will certainly find out.

- Anything psychedelics and peak performance: The Tim Ferriss Show and The Aubrey Marcus Show

- Anything sex: Tangentially Speaking with Chris Ryan, PhD

- Motivational podcast: Impact Theory with Tom Bilyeu

- All about brain science, memory, concentration, focus: Kwik Brain Podcast with Jim Kwik

- Life/Business/Philosophy: Seth Godin, Akimbo

- Anything spirituality: Sounds True, Insights at the Edge with Tami Simon

CHAPTER
10

LOVE IS MYSTICAL

"Psychedelics, used responsibly and with proper caution, would be for psychiatry what the microscope is for biology and medicine or the telescope is for astronomy."

— STAN GROF

In April 2017, the international psychedelic community gathered in the Oakland Convention Center for Psychedelic Science, an event which takes place every few years organized by MAPS, the Multidisciplinary Association of Psychedelics Studies. Still traveling with my backpack, I thought it prudent to attend in hopes of meeting with like minds, and of course I saw an obvious opportunity to further wrap my head around my own healing journey and learn more about these incredible tools of transformation. Still on the prowl for my calling, for that moment of clarity where I would know exactly where all of my energies could be directed, I engaged this incredible week of fascinating science.

MAPS' fearless leader, Rick Doblin, has been leading

the movement of psychedelics as medicines and a more sane approach towards mental health for our country since the 1980s. This man on a mission has a motor. His resolve and unwavering love for his country and fellow man (and woman) is truly inspiring! Who pushes forward for that long against the odds with no guarantees? "We are not the counterculture," Doblin told a reporter during the conference. "We are the culture." Doblin was referencing the baggage associated with these misunderstood healing tools that are entering the mainstream in perfect timing, when the mental health of our nation has never been more dire. MAPS has a cure for PTSD. Yes, that's right, a cure! Phase two results demonstrate MDMA's efficacy of nearly two-thirds of the participants completely shedding their diagnosis. Whether this cure makes it through clinical trials and is adopted by our Western medicine paradigm is another issue.

What would a cure for PTSD and in time, likely a cure for depression, do for our world's collective mental health?

While I write these words, MAPS is heading into phase three clinical trials with the FDA, and this once-demonized drug—ecstasy, or Molly—has been labeled as a "breakthrough therapy" by the FDA. The "breakthrough" designation means the FDA is working hand in hand with MAPS to get this medicine through clinical trials on an expedited basis, fully aware of the dire state of our country's mental health. The protocol involves both MDMA and assisted psychotherapy by a trained psychedelic therapist, and those with chronic conditions are taking this substance that has once been called a "love bomb" in pill form. This empathogen (heart-opener) raises your vibration and you feel really good. More important is the fight-or-flight responses are inhibited long enough that traumatic memories and the underlying emotions associated with those memories are kept at bay. After feeling what you normally can't while under the influence of this medicine, your traumatic memory then gets revised and then reconsolidated—all of this is done in the comfort and safety of an office, supervised by two professionally trained therapists. This medicine allows the patient to access the traumatic memory in a safe space and setting. They feel what has been long repressed, cry the tears, address "that thing," and move on with their lives. This allows for incredible healing and transformation, and is similar to the way ayahuasca and plant medicines/psychedelics work in general. Again, phase two clinical trials indicate that 67% of participants completely shed their diagnosis of chronic PTSD after one year. Three years removed, those people have actually experienced continual gradual growth. Having sustained a cure to their crippling afflictions, no more medication is needed as the protocol includes *only* three therapy sessions with MDMA. What is very exciting, what the data seems to suggest and anecdotal claims, including my own, support is the notion that these psychedelic healing sessions start a "healing process," as if they awaken the patient's "inner healer," and, in time, patients are free from taking prescription pills moving forward. Imagine that—a world where people don't need to take a pill every day, subjecting themselves to harsh and unpleasant side effects. Big Pharma hasn't done anything for our nation's mental health since the early 1990s: Prozac Nation, and the SSRIs we have barely work better than the placebo.

By 2021, possibly sooner, MDMA-assisted therapy is likely to be legal in the United States. This is a potentially massive game-changer, and its implication for our troubled times could be a timely godsend for our mental health care crisis, that finds us with unprecedented levels of PTSD, depression, suicide, anxiety, addiction, and many other afflictions of the mind, which I believe are symptomatic of the world in which we live and the values we collectively pursue. These medicines force those engaging them to view their past hurts and traumas, allowing the opportunity to access past memories stored in the nervous system, and making way for incredible transformations and healing to take place. All of this is facilitated in a controlled and well-thought-out manner.

Trauma is powerful. It only takes one traumatic experience to scar a child for life. One sexually frustrated priest who slips up, turns a blind eye to his vows and good conscience, giving in to his sexual desires, and a child's life is ruined—this is a sick and sad reality of our world. However, just as trauma is powerful, so are these powerful healing technologies. We are talking about fighting fire with fire. Dr. Peter Attia, a doctor with over one million patients (The Peter Attia Drive Podcast) and an advocate for psychedelic therapy, makes this poignant observation: "Sometimes you can't talk yourself out of something that you didn't talk yourself into." Meaning, since we didn't talk ourselves into the abuse, why should we think that talk therapy would be enough to work it out? These medicines cut through the bullshit, like a laser-guided missile, they target the root of the trauma: "that thing." No dancing around the symptoms pretending things aren't as bad as they are. You are taken right where you need to go to face what you need to see, what you need to feel.

"Psychedelics metabolize fear into appreciation," Rick Doblin eloquently says. Doblin, the unofficial leader of this psychedelic renaissance and movement towards psychedelics as legal medicines, is an ultra-impressive-saintly man. Doblin holds a PhD from Harvard in Drug Policy. He dreams of being a legal MDMA therapist, which will likely happen in the years to come.

Doblin gave a "psychedelic" state of the union on *The Aubrey Marcus Podcast*, painting an optimistic view of the year 2035 when this psychedelic prohibition might be over, and these compounds and plant medicines would then be legal for medical and recreational use. The stigma would be let go and the pesky stain scrubbed clean. We are all playing the long game. This collective shift will require patience, and with the sensitive nature of psychedelics, proper protocols must be followed. Much work lies ahead to properly undo the missteps from yesteryear; essentially, a rebrand of spirituality, that properly accounts for the modern flow science, the neuroscience of meditation, and the fascinating work being done to isolate how psychedelic compounds affect the brain must occur. Bullshit, Inc. best beware: a long-overdue check and balance is coming. The march of this movement is slow and steady in an effort to ensure its success and avoid the moral panic of yesteryear.

Plugging Pollan

Michael Pollan's book *How to Change Your Mind: What the New Science of Psychedelics Teaches Us About Consciousness, Dying, Addiction, Depression, and Transcendence* is a breath of objective, skeptical, and wise air. It's a well-timed breath, too, just in time for this movement toward a more honest mental health paradigm. With 7 NY Times Bestsellers to his credit, he was writing extensively about our food system with previous works being: Omnivore's Dilemma, In Defense of Food, Botany of Desire. In 2015, Pollan wrote a piece for the New Yorker called "The Trip Treatment," and this ultimately perked his curiosity to dive deeper into these misunderstood medicines and the burgeoning psychedelic renaissance. Pollan, a respected elder in our society, is a man with a track record of doing great work as an investigative journalist. As a professor of journalism at UC-Berkeley and Harvard, he approaches the land of Esoteria as a skeptic, willing to fully immerse himself in the land of psychedelia. He does an incredible job telling the story of how we got to this point: a clear mental health epidemic, science screaming we have a solution, a maybe-cure, and a collective people that are confused, not knowing what to believe, who to trust. Pollan, at the age of 55 years young, puts himself in the laboratory and shares his underground journeys with psilocybin, LSD, 5-MeO-DMT (senorum toad venom), and ayahuasca.

Much of what we have been led to believe about psychedelics is wrong and misleading, the harmful effects exaggerated. Pollan writes in-depth about the fascinating history of our world's first attempt to integrate these psychedelics and plant medicines to Western medicine in the 1950s through the 1970s. Clearly the most impactful psychedelic book in 2018, and maybe ever, about this topic, it is impeccably researched and presented from the perspective of a true journalist who maintains an air of skepticism even after his many trips and healing journeys. One point stood out above all the rest: during the 1960s and '70s, we struggled with these seemingly miracle compounds. The world was not ready for all the transformational healing that took place. Nothing like that had ever been experienced on a mass scale. Our youth were engaging in a rite of passage that the elders in our society could not relate to. This created massive dissonance, a threat to established power structures. Now, in 2019, we find ourselves in a very different time. Many of those who are in power and our regulators have experienced these medicines and compounds for themselves. They get it. They see just how much our dire mental health may be endangering our democracy. People with repressed trauma and garbled-up nervous systems have a horribly difficult time expressing themselves honestly. What was threatening to the culture in years past is now mixed in our day to day, and very much alive within our culture: yoga/meditation, open sexuality, environmentalism/activism. Pollan observes there wasn't a strong enough container in place during the '60s and '70s. Now it appears a container may be in place. But, of course, time will tell how this all shakes out.

I believe in these medicines and this movement to a more sane mental health paradigm, healing first the hearts and minds of our struggling U.S. war veterans, letting our soldiers and veterans have access to the healing they desperately deserve, leading with grace and courage, showing everyone else what is possible. That has always been the order of operations. Our brave warriors go first to show others that this path is safe, that there is nothing to fear. With their leadership, we can do what is right. And, in time, we can reshape how *everyone* looks at these medicines.

Pollan gives anyone interested in how to change their minds a mine full of golden data points that will help the reader formulate their own opinions on how best to heal, really everything that the would-be psychedelic explorer would need to know or anyone interested in the fascinating science and story of these medicines. Coupled with this impeccable research is the notion that a man in his 50s safely engaged these medicines, leaving a guidebook behind in his wake. Bravo Michael! Thank you for your brave and honest account of how we have gotten to this point.

With science coming out from all over the world on psychedelic medicine, this may be the "good news" the masses have been waiting for. Health and healing, a cure for PTSD and a likely cure for depression. A nation of traumatized souls that can now breathe a sigh of relief, knowing that help is on the way. Not so fast, though— these medicines still need to finish the FDA process and undergo the presumed subsequent rescheduling that would follow; meaning, these medicines would have to be decriminalized.

We all know that hope is powerful. It keeps us moving. Just the belief that things are getting better can help us sustain as we continue to push into the unknown. Times are changing;

there is an army of brave souls that won't settle for Bullshit, Inc., those willing to stand in the face of injustices; 21st-century Rosa Parks' who have a conviction rooted in fiercely bringing back the spirit of brotherly love. So, if you're struggling, hang on. Help is on the way. As I've mentioned early and will continue to mention, psychedelics are not required. If you are looking for similar psychedelic healing but aren't comfortable with the risk profile of these medicines, try holotropic breathwork or the Wim Hof Method. You might save yourself the experience altogether and just adopt a meditation practice: it is the secret sauce with all this. Peace.

I am clearly an optimist. All that positive thinking training has left me with this disposition and orientation. The obvious question that ought be asked is, will the levy hold? Are we ready for a world with two-thirds less depression? Are we willing to thoroughly investigate and be honest with the structures/ systems in place that are not working?

Aubrey Marcus encourages people to "weaponize the power of belief." I love this! Use earnest intention to join Team Faith, to be part of the solution by finding creative ways to help others in need. We all know you don't have to look too far to find an opportunity to be of service by embracing brotherly love. Now is the time.

Our Hopeful Cultural Container

To meet the world where the world is at, we must have patience and compassion for those we are looking to serve. We must have awareness for the challenges of yesteryear and the world that we want to bring healing to. It feels to me that there is a sort of rebrand with this movement of "psychedelics as medicines," again a slow march toward a more sane mental health for our nation and world. In the '60s and '70s there was a moral panic as these previously unknown medicines were thrusted on the scene.

With the psychedelic experience, there is indeed a feeling of authority that arises after a direct experience, the middleman is cut out of the equation. This doesn't always bode well culturally; it can be threatening to the power structures in place. Perhaps this is why the logistical safeguards have played out as they have.

With the increase in microdosing, the natural container of ayahuasca and "white-coat" shamanism, we are seeing a cautious approach to this progressive change; three reasons why I believe this movement will have a different outcome than it did some fifty years ago.

Psychedelic pioneers Ram Daas and Terence McKenna attributed the failings of yesteryear's movement to "idealism" and a "lurking righteousness." Any unwillingness to meet the world where the world is at is, too, a projection of unhealed trauma, a sort of delusional grandiosity that isn't rooted in peace and understanding for the world and people you wish to serve. This is a fine line, but one that must be walked as these medicines make their return to mainstream acceptability in the years to come.

Microdosing Psychedelics

While I clearly have nothing against heavy doses of psychedelics, I tend to look at them as an intervention, a powerful tool for depatterning. There is a variance that comes with peak/mystical type experiences and integrating these experiences can be quite challenging. I get now why microdosing has gone mainstream. Many are opting for lower doses over the disruptive high dose psychedelic experience. While microdosing, one can maintain their routines and daily habits/practices with less variance; seekers can find much relief with a much lower risk profile. At the end of the day, we are all on our own journey and for some of us the slow and steady approach pays best.

Personally, while microdosing psychedelics, I noticed a very slight and subtle boost in my overall well-being. I felt more creative and able to push through the day easier. Over these past few years, I have microdosed psychedelics occasionally. When I came home from my travel journey, I struggled with my new work, struggled in maintaining life balance as I integrated back to the busy world I had been accustomed to. I adhered to a regimen of taking a sub-perceptual dose, meaning you don't have altered perception. This dose is typically a tenth or twentieth of a full one. For me, closer to one-fiftieth of a full dose was more than sufficient. Perhaps the placebo effect played a part? I am not sure. Microdosing complemented my daily practices nicely. I noticed a slight augmentation in awareness and had the subtlest supplemental feelings of joy, a 5% to 10% increase from my baseline at that time. Following the guidelines set forth by psychedelic researcher James Fadiman, author of the Psychedelic Explorers Guide, I microdosed every third or fourth day, per best practice guidelines. My personal experiences fell in line with an account from Ayelet

Waldman, an author, lawyer and mother of four, who wrote *A Really Good Day: How Microdosing Made a Mega Difference in My Mood, My Marriage, and My Life.*

Ayahuasca's All-Natural Built-In Container

As we discussed in chapter 7, ayahuasca has a natural container built into this process. Mother Nature gives her children exactly what they need to heal. And since it can be such a messy and challenging experience there is little potential for abuse; the ayahuasca healing ritual is not a social experience because of the obvious side effects of soul-level vomiting and shitting profusely. She demands that you do your work, that you live the medicine, starting a healing process that helps people let go of past hurts in order to make room for a new narrative that aligns closer to one of brotherly love.

Bill Bryson, the lovable scientist who writes books with obscure facts, tells us in *A Short History of Nearly Everything,* we have an incredible amount of untapped potential. Each of us has energy "enough to explode the force of thirty very large hydrogen bombs." I came across this encouraging news after a deep healing experience with ayahuasca in Costa Rica. It was just after my "death/rebirth" weekend on Valentine's Day, 2016, a time when I felt as if I had split the atom with my mind that yielded an explosion of loving thought energy. To experience firsthand a phenomenon like this was life-changing, to see the untapped potential in my heart while knowing that this same potential lies in the heart of every human gave me great hope. This life-changing moment happened because I was given the space to look within, to do my healing work. And this book is a product of knowing that much potential lies within. What this special container might mean for our world is reason to be excited as we shift to a more sane way of looking at how we heal. That we scrutinize the ways others choose to heal is beyond me. This stigma will slowly diminish as science brings forth incredible news about healing and transformation.

"White Coat" Shamanism

This term, coined by Michael Pollan, is quite fitting. MAPS and other psychedelic researchers strictly adhere to a protocol that will limit the opportunity for abuse. MDMA-assisted therapy and psilocybin-assisted therapy are structured so those looking to heal will have to do so through their psychedelic therapist: a trained professional qualified to hold space for people to heal. No going to the pharmacy and getting a vial of opioids or stimulants, then sharing with your friends like one would share Skittles. That old model, propagated by shifty and unethical pharmaceutical companies and their complicit drug-peddling doctors, hasn't worked. In fact, this model has set our great country on fire. In the time it took the average person to read this book, 65 Americans have died overdosing on opioids, and no jail time will be given to those responsible (70,000 deaths in 2017). Since the FDA has been an active participant in this process of helping MDMA-assisted therapy through the clinical trials, procedures are in place to mitigate the potential risks as this transformational therapy becomes available to the masses of people struggling with mental health. Thankfully, the FDA is pro-science and surely they are versed in the sad state of our nation's mental health. Currently, research is being conducted on a wide array of major issues that plague our people: depression, PTSD, anxiety, addiction, cigarette smoking, terminally-ill cancer patients, and even opioid addiction.

It appears that psilocybin might be the answer to many of the conditions our world struggles with. Psilocybin doesn't have the cultural stigma tied to it from the '60s and '70s like LSD does, although LSD is another powerful healing agent. Psilocybin has also been fast-tracked and labeled a "breakthrough therapy" by the FDA. Roland Griffiths, PhD., a professor of psychiatry and behavioral sciences at Johns Hopkins University, heads the lab that conducted the first contemporary FDA-approved clinical trial in the early 2000s is very encouraged by the efficacy of these misunderstood compounds.

Power of Belief

In 1954, Roger Bannister did the impossible—he ran a sub-four-minute mile. Thank you, Sir Roger, for showing us the power of belief. It had been 11 years since the mile record had last been broken and many people were beginning to think that a sub-four-minute mile was beyond the physical limits of humanity. But strangely, just two months after Bannister's record, his time was bested by Australia's John Landy. Within five years, two others accomplished this feat, and within ten years, a high school runner made the once-impossible happen, too. Last count, I believe, it's been done over 1,300 times now.

How is Bannister's athletic feat relevant to this psychedelic movement?

The beliefs that someone has around these medicines has a huge impact on the outcome of the healing. Years back, I was in the middle of a challenging part of a psychedelic journey. I was overcome with an intense feeling of paranoia, buying into my mind's fears about the healing process and the methodology I was engaging. With a conscious breath, it dawned on me that the fear I experienced was part of the collective unconscious, not rooted in any truth, but faulty rhetoric and propaganda. These same fears are what have kept many from engaging these medicines or having successful outcomes. Thankfully, I could smell the stench of Bullshit, Inc., and I was able to let go and resume my healing work. Had that happened 5 to 10 years earlier, before I knew what these medicines really were, I might have lost my shit and done some real damage to my mind. With every psychedelic journey, every psychedelic article and scientific finding about the efficacy of these misunderstood compounds, we are slowly rebranding what these experiences are and how this healing process really works. We are slowly undoing the wrongs, creating and reinforcing a healing container that will make way for many others to follow suit in the years to come—there will be more collective healing and letting go. If we really want a peaceful planet, we will need more than well-intentioned platitudes. We will need to take an honest look at the forces that perpetuate the madness that we now call normal. Institutions that no longer serve the evolution of our people will have to evolve or they will be let go.

Universal and natural law govern the same on an individual level as they do a collective one. Together, we can believe this better world into being.

As we are slowly breaking down the stigma, as we demonstrate that these medicines are not what people had previously thought they were by redefining the risk profile with objective data and more anecdotal claims, the would-be inner traveler's success rates will only improve. Still, these are powerful healing technologies that are disruptive and ought to be taken with extreme care. Further, these medicines are akin to big data for the mind, helping victims of trauma change the story they tell themselves about the lives they live. This is a tremendously important notion, as the people who advocate for these medicines are leading and loving by example, laying a framework for how to best utilize these medicines in service to a better world by helping those in need. We have a model of do-gooders who are walking the talk, bringing back the spirit of brotherly love. And we all know there are enough people struggling, hurting, stuck in their trauma. These medicines help people wake up to their interconnectedness, shifting values toward love, service, honesty, authentic connection, and peace. With enough people reformed, awakened to a life lived outside of their trauma, what is possible? Dare I say—world peace.

Addiction Makeover Showcase

Psychedelic pioneer Terence McKenna: "Alcoholism is not a disease it is a failure of self-image." This powerful quote really hits hard, cutting right through our beliefs that keep us tethered to substance abuse.

For most of my life, my "social" drinking problem was largely "off-limits" to explore. But by investigating the silent bravado that was killing me, by challenging the faux definition of manhood scripted by Bullshit, Inc. and the patriarchy, a societal code that promotes this cowardly hiding by systematically closing off connection to the most vital part of the human experience. I was raised in a world where vulnerability is looked at as weakness and any man displaying vulnerability got shamed. But how else do we truly connect without being open, honest—vulnerable—about how we really feel? Without vulnerability there can be no trust.

Drinking was, in my circles, just what you did and how you lived. Calling it "social" somehow made it more acceptable to rationalize this mental affliction and imbalance. This was a big part of my identity; it was who I was. Looking back now, I can't blame myself or any others, I had to go through all of that to see my actions clearly. Strangely, I am actually grateful for this time. I had a lot of fun (albeit shallow fun) and it took this immense amount of pain to gather enough perspective to challenge our false narrative about substance abuse. Alcohol and spirits have been an extraordinary teacher, still instructing lessons about balance: Modern Temperance 101. I still drink. I like the taste and like to remind my demons who is boss. These days, I hardly ever feel the need to consume more than a glass of wine or two.

I am no moralist; people will do what they want to do. Actually, I think moralism is a sickness: projections of a life not lived.

I had many incorrect assumptions and false beliefs about what addiction really is. I was duped into thinking: once an alcoholic, always an alcoholic. Again, that pesky disease model has been proven to be erroneous by modern brain science. That is a severely limited viewpoint that ignores our true potential to change and transform. Every addiction has an underlying memory and emotion that is tied to the unsavory habit one wishes to discharge. Science has proven that we can let go of any emotion by reframing the associated memory. This notion is explained in more depth in a groundbreaking book about fear by Akshay Nanivanti called *Fearvana*. Akshay, a former U.S. marine who runs across countries in obscure lands to share his message of hope and healing, compares our memories to a Wikipedia page in that every time we access our memory, we update the underlying emotion that is tied to the original memory. This process is called memory reconsolidation.

Magic Mushroom Healing

On my travel journey, I was blessed to have the opportunity to be selfish, to heal, to get right, to value my own healing and growth above all else so in time I would be fit for service. It is my prayer that these words and values may impart a similar orientation, as our individual healing and growth make this human experience so much more worth living.

While on the move with backpack in tow and more than ample time at my disposal, I healed my near-lifelong depression with magic mushrooms. To think, these little miracle fungi could balance what was long fractured and chaotic; a deeply troubled mind that knew no peace, a mind that played past hurts on continual repeat, making the one thing my soul craved nearly impossible: authentic connection. Currently, psilocybin is being used to treat end-of-life anxiety in terminally ill cancer patients with great success. Deeply troubled minds struggling with mortality are being given the opportunity to die a dignified death in peace.

In my instance, I couldn't wait for our federal government to legalize it. I had to go rogue, taking the initiative by traveling, following my inner guidance and trusting what I believed to be true above all else. Cognitive and spiritual liberty are serious notions that we shouldn't take lightly; these are liberties worth dying for, as one who lives without them isn't really living.

At first, I really didn't know what I was doing. This esoteric practice is quite taboo; magic mushrooms are illegal and have been long demonized, part of the counterculture and an unjust "war on drugs," which has been more of a war on minorities than anything else.

I was shocked and confused when first undergoing this process. It felt incredibly just and honest. Immediately, I asked myself. *Why would this be illegal?* (A millisecond later) *Oh (REALLY LONG PAUSE)—I get it.* These medicines create a level of consciousness, an awareness that is less subjected to the control of others. And if everyone had this medicine all at once, the levy probably would not hold. That is what happened in the '60s and '70s. Too much, too fast!

In good conscience, however, I feel a duty to share this aspect of my healing journey. For a stretch of six to nine months or so, I was engaging psilocybin at a dose of 1 to 2 grams. I took the approach of starting small and increasing the dosage over time, patiently and safely engaging this healing technology in the comforts of a safe environment where I could embark on solo journeys. I would turn off my phone, fully committing to an inner journey of self-discovery and healing, approaching these little fungi with the same reverence and intention that I would have for an ayahuasca ceremony.

At first, this was quite scary, but the degree to which I was scared was the same degree to which I felt supported by this seemingly miraculous and intuitive plant medicine.

I am no dummy; I knew I was playing with fire. For that reason, I would recommend if anyone is looking to heal in this manner to find a trusted guide/space-holder to keep watch while you journey. Years back, when initially engaging this medicine, I properly addressed the potential risks, fully realizing this was a calculated gamble, though worth taking. In a controlled environment, I safely navigated the inner workings of my mind. Immediately, I could not deny how good I was feeling. And with the scientific research demonstrating the efficacy when taken in a safe and supported environment with proper intention I could safely maneuver any potential obstacles. During these sessions, I would find flow, a deep, cathartic healing from rewriting my neuronal pathways—shedding my depression—further letting go of the pain in my heart from yesteryear's betrayals, from the childhood trauma that nearly killed me. Researchers best describe flow as the optimal state of consciousness, when we are at our absolute best and feel our best. "Time slows down. Self vanishes. Action and

Awareness merge. Welcome to Flow," says Steven Kotler, a peak performance expert and leading researcher at the Flow Genome Project, an organization that is reverse engineering this once elusive state with rigorous science from nearly every discipline and background.

On these magical healing journeys, music took on a completely different role, providing an unquantifiable level of comfort. I would feel an undeniable loving glow for weeks after each therapeutic session. There shortly came a time when I no longer desired this experience. I was done. My therapeutic regimen was over—an important portion of my healing work was complete. Around that same time, I "magically" started having the foresight to properly address many of my interpersonal relationship problems. Strangely, once those unspoken conversations came to life, I had no real desire to engage this alternative medicine and way of healing. Reflecting back, I often think was it the judgement from myself and relationships that was making me sick to begin with?

I am no doctor or scientist, but I have been nearly obsessed with understanding the "flow state" and the brain chemistry that underpins optimum states of consciousness. Here we go. In an elevated state, removed from external stimuli, I could see more clearly all that I ignored and the maladies in my life that I chose to accept under false pretenses. This was a liberating time in my life, a reckoning when I could see just how complicit I was in the disharmony and hardships I encountered in my life. I still have my shit, we all do, just now my problems have been reframed as growth opportunities and lessons. We are always teaching or being taught; there are no exceptions to this. Further, these mushrooms have been proven to promote neurogenesis, which is the growth of new neurons in the brain's prefrontal cortex, a region of the brain thought to process one's will-power, planning, complex cognitive behavior, personality expression, decision making, and moderating social behavior. This process effectively strengthens and reinforces the neuronal networks already in place. Ah, the wonders of science. Just like the fMRI shows a decrease in brain activity in the prefrontal cortex where the DMN (ego) is thought to reside, these mushrooms allow parts of the brain to make connections that it normally wouldn't be able to make. This phenomenon is called transient hypofrontality, the always on constantly critical part of our brain shuts down and goes offline, allowing for outside-of-the-box thinking and neuronal connections that normally aren't possible. This is where the healing takes place.

All the while, my anchor was, has been, and always will be, my daily meditation practice. Engaging psychedelics can be very dangerous without proper intention and commitment to doing the work in the day to day. The commitment to implementing the insight that comes from stepping outside of yourself demands some sort of daily check-in, or you may be in danger of flying too high. No free flights—tread lightly—do the work!

If one doesn't have the stomach or foresight to do the work, then they are effectively embarking on this journey with a sense of entitlement: "I want to get high" or "I want something for nothing." Both could potentially put you in a bad place. You have been warned of this foreseeable pitfall. This is a potentially addictive neurochemistry that must be respected and honored.

Again, I AM NOT A MEDICAL PROFESSIONAL and this is not medical advice. And I am by no means encouraging others to follow my path. I am just a guy who experienced some pretty incredible healing, who now feels a duty and obligation to share. While I believe many of the negative claims made about psychedelics to be exaggerated and unsupported by scientific data, the reality is these medicines and compounds are illegal now. Many of them are schedule one controlled substances that can get you locked up. Proceed with caution.

11

WORTH THE FIGHT

"In order to carry a positive action, we must develop here a positive vision."

— DALAI LAMA

AUGUST 2016

I'd found a secluded campsite that met my simple criterion of being remote and only reachable by 4x4. It would be me and the wilderness for some time. I needed some strategic withdrawal from the busy, go-go-go world. Time for me to wrap my head around all of the shifting and transformational growth I'd been through, looking within for guidance, to decipher what was true, what was real. This nature escape and getaway came at the most opportune timing, the midpoint in my 18-month healing journey.

Each morning I would bathe in an ice-cold bustling stream. I had been working with the cold for some time and was starting to get serious about the Wim Hof Breathing Method. The cold was a motherfucker but, as Wim Hof says, "The cold is a noble teacher."

Every third or fourth day, I would make a fire and play music as I pondered my life's next moves. Where was I blocking and resisting what is? How would things look for me in a perfect world? Probably the biggest question: how am I feeling so happy and liberated with no sex and very few viable romantic interests? This boggled my mind. It did not make sense; in fact, it was completely counterintuitive to my upbringing, programming, and conditioning. Before ayahuasca, I was an antsy mess if I went a couple of weeks without sex. Now it had been some time since I last had the touch of a beautiful woman and everything was, strangely, just fine. I was content to play life's "long game."

A couple days into my camping, I met Richard, the gun-slinging wannabe-cowboy who apparently had a "claim" on the land that I was camping on. Richard wore a silly 10-gallon hat that made him feel special. He was in his mid-seventies and sported a big belly. He had a nervousness to him and would spit compulsively, almost to mark his territory, no different than your dog peeing every 50 steps on a morning walk. I was taken aback by his brashness, but was amenable to his presence as his six-shooter was made visible in his holster. Richard approached with, "This is my claim, you know." There were no niceties from the approaching stranger.

"I am just here to camp." I showed him my empty hands as a reflex to seeing his gun. "I wasn't aware that this is your claim. This seemed like a good place to set up camp for a couple of weeks."

He listened with an aura of suspicion and then asked, "Where you from?"

"I am from Chicago, taking some time away from the big city to enjoy these mountains and some nature." I responded politely.

"You know there is gold here. I bought this claim 15 years ago and there is gold here."

I was interested, having never known anyone to own a miner's gold claim. This immediately brought in a sense of adventure associated with the gold rush movies of my youth. *Could this be my White Fang Jack London moment?* I thought in a playful, dreamy manner.

Richard softened his expression once he realized that I was a city boy who didn't give two shits about his gold. "There is gold out here. Them damn jackals stole my drills and equipment." He would open up in a short time and go on and on about all his problems. I've found this is an occupational hazard that comes with my new mental territory. He was angry and wanted vengeance; all he would get from me was compassion and a listening ear. I sensed that was all he really needed. It was like an unplanned wilderness therapy session. "You look like you're on one of them inner peace journeys, or somethin' like that."

I explained to him openly and honestly where I was at and why I would choose to spend a month in the wilderness by myself. "Yes, that is about right. What better place to find your center than these mountains?" I responded with a zen-like calm.

"I don't get it. Damn millennials," he muttered under his breath so as not to be overtly confronting.

I smiled and appeased this man. "Yep, it's a crazy time to be in the big cities. Lots of fear. This will be a needed getaway." I made him feel as though I was his guest and he was my host that was offering me a safe haven. I didn't need to do that, but I was in the habit of diffusing tension and appeasing others with words. As the peacemaker in my family and group of friends, I became quite good at this.

"Well, you have to be out of here in two weeks. That is state law." He said it in a total dickhead fashion, but I didn't take offense or react. I had Richard pegged. He meant no harm and would eventually end up enjoying much of our conversation over the next few weeks. He would pop in every fourth or fifth day to say hello.

I quickly realized that Richard liked to babble on and on. Instead of resisting this seeming universal truth, I looked at this as an opportunity to sharpen my listening skills. I needed much work in the arena of listening. Being present and holding space for others was on my radar as a skill that needed augmentation. I had come a long way from the "Me, Me, Me" entitlement mindset I once had, but there was a whole new world of presence that would be demanded from me. I suspected that active listening might be the most important skill I could work diligently to improve.

On and on Richard went, and I listened. I pictured a 6-year-old Richard, knowing that he was merely blabbing away and projecting his own traumatic life experience, needing to be heard and listened to. He gave me his life story and told me all about his numerous college degrees. Even in his advanced age, he was still taking college classes and was very proud of it. It seemed almost in a manner to fleece the system. If he never ended his education, then he wouldn't have to pay back his loans. He would laugh about the loans he racked up and how they would never be paid. All of this was a strange interaction, to be sure, but I was loving every minute. I offered to help him mine for gold, thinking that would have been a fun experience. He didn't take me up on my offer. I imagine he was likely paranoid I would somehow run off with his new mining equipment, or sell his mining secrets online. Who knows?

Richard would bring news from the outside world and would let me know everything he thought about our oft-turbulent times. He was a man full of opinions but no solutions, like so many we find in our present times. Richard was a total asshole, but I loved him for it—for just being himself with no apologies or shame, seemingly contented in the life he had chosen for himself, although old and alone.

Days later, he would return armed with relevant material. After our initial conversations, maybe he could now sense what I was up to by taking a step back from the busy world?

It was only a matter of time before he would broach a subject that mattered to me. "That Nixon was a drunk, you know. He was drinking a fifth a day while in the White House."

Finally, something of interest, I thought. "What? Really? How do you know this?" I asked intently with exuberance, my ears perked up.

"There was a book, a 'tell-all' that got into the nitty-gritty about all sorts of despicable behavior of that Nixon Administration. Actually, all sorts of books have come out about that tumultuous time." Richard was educated and knew his history; I would give him that much. My patience and listening had paid off.

"Wasn't that when the Controlled Substances Act was put in place?" With no cell service and access to Google, I had to rely on Richard.

"Exactly, Nixon put those laws in place because he hated the blacks and the hippies. It was about controlling and maintaining the power structures in place."

Now I was paying full attention. "That is not surprising to hear." Nothing at this point in my life would be surprising to hear. "I have always had an air of suspicion when it comes to our government."

"Yep, that Nixon was a drunk and he was running our country. He stamped out all of the peace-lovers like you."

I smiled. Being generalized as a peace-lover was humorous but also accurate; old Richard had me pegged.

We would talk more about Nixon and many other things. It was interesting timing to have the only man that I'd see over the next few weeks come with poignantly novel and relevant information. This Nixon book that he was extra spirited about, going on and on with all the shady, unethical, and problematic behavior of our most disgraced president and administration became a fascination to me. It seemed whenever I was ready to expand my mind and thinking, the appropriate information would make itself known, somehow or someway. Or, better said, when I would shut up and listen, I would learn more than when I was boasting and blowing and babbling about myself. We never learn when talking, only while listening.

How could someone run the White House and be drunk the entire time? I pondered this heavy and disturbing notion. Then I remember how functional I was at times when mired in self-abuse, and just how many functional alcoholics I know that managed to punch the clock and engage in loveless labor. But what really hit me was that someone who is deeply engaged in self-abuse knows no love for himself. The abusive behavior itself is a clear symptom of self-loathing and indifference to the human experience: it is no wonder why Nixon was so obtuse and insistent on keeping the war machine going. Nixon hated himself, which made him the perfect puppeteer to perpetuate the Industrial Military Complex's war machine that Eisenhower eloquently warned our world about just years earlier. If this is all true, then what a messy conundrum our collective people and country finds itself in. Poorly crafted and constructed paradigms never hold up against the scrutiny of time.

The course of humanity was changed when the Controlled Substances Act, from 1971, put all hallucinogens in a schedule one class. This class is for drugs that are highly addictive, with no therapeutic value, despite the thousands of scientific studies and reports that would contradict this new order. This throwing the baby out with the bathwater approach might have held back our country and world 50 years or more. Is it possible the ghost of Richard Nixon still presides as our world's moral and spiritual authority? Could this be why the masses are so apathetic? And why we are in the midst of a mental health care crisis? More precisely stated, we have a sick-care crisis, where nearly a quarter of our country suffers from psychiatric maladies and afflictions. All the while, Big Pharma pockets are lined with gold and bursting stock evaluations. This could be why we live in a time where we have never lived more out of alignment with what is inherently good and human, with our innate brotherly love values and virtues suppressed. To think our whole healthcare paradigm may be built on lies and deception? And since this is all we have ever known, we wouldn't think to question the underlying deception which birthed our sick-care paradigm.

Our jails are mostly black and Hispanic prisoners who have been convicted for nonviolent crime/drug possession as they were unable to resist their need for healing through illicit drug use, to receive relief from the injustices they've experienced. Next to slavery, our nation's completely ineffective "war on drugs" might be the most egregious civil rights violation we have ever seen.

Our prisons are full of mentally ill people that have had a difficult time adjusting to our nation's drug laws, which are still mostly intact from the Nixon Administration. In recent years, Norway, the oft-leader of European progressive policy, has decriminalized drug possession to make it a health issue instead of a crime. They are following the example of Portugal, which decriminalized drugs 15 years ago and has since witnessed all drug-related problems cut in half—massive reductions in drug overdoses; violent crimes;

and a much lighter load for their once-overpopulated prison system. Portugal's bold move in the early 2000s is what I believe to be quite possibly the greatest social experiment ever. This trend makes me hopeful as other countries are waking up to their own faults and restoring a more sane look at mental health.

All of this research would be done at a local library after I had a chance to corroborate much of my new friend Richard's story: the gunslinging, nervous-spitting, wannabe cowboy whom I would grow quite fond of. I appreciated our time together, thankful for our insightful conversations that led me to some stunning realizations. Of course, this is all public knowledge. However, I am afraid this public knowledge is too heavy to hold for the average American citizen, who is too busy to care, too indifferent to act on or acknowledge it.

"The Nixon campaign of 1968, and the Nixon White House after that, had two enemies: the antiwar left and black people. We knew we couldn't make it illegal to be either against the war or black, but by getting the public to associate the hippies with marijuana and the blacks with heroin, and then criminalizing both heavily, we could disrupt those communities. We could arrest their leaders, raid their homes, break up their meetings, and vilify them night after night on the evening news. Did we know we were lying about the drugs? Of course we did." Former Nixon advisor John Ehrlichman admitted with a guilty conscience. (https://www.cnn.com/2016/03/23/politics/john-ehrlichman-richard-nixon-drug-war-blacks-hippie/index.html)

He came clean, sharing openly his role in this most shameful time in our country's history. I imagined seeing our nation's flailing class system unfairly awry was a heavy burden to bear, with the knowing that it was all puppeteered by shifty political moves, by deceptive lies and governmental corruption. I can't blame John Ehrlichman for his inability to carry this; I know firsthand how it feels to have to unburden yourself in front of the world. The suffocating feeling of karma wrapping its hands around your being, slowly squeezing the life out of you. All the while, you know the truth will eventually be made known and all debts will need to be settled.

While stunned, I was mostly prepared for all of this. As a faithful student of the art of letting go, I would quickly come to grips with our nation's egregious past. This charged me up for only a short while before I would get on with my own healing. These words would need to wait a couple of years before being compiled in these pages.

We all know by now that humans do insane things when in groups and in each other's presence. Our propensity to gravitate toward destructive "groupthink" is a fatal flaw in our wiring. Just think about these atrocities: Jewish holocaust, American Slavery, Rwandan genocide—you get the point!

German philosopher Friedrich Nietzsche sums this up quite nicely: "In individuals, insanity is rare; but in groups, parties, nations and epochs, it is the rule."

This quote summarizes why I spent so much time by myself with a backpack: strategic withdrawal. I took my own advice, learning how to love myself so I could love others. A lone wolf working on crafting a spirit of self-reliance, looking to untether itself from its own checkered past and unprocessed emotions. My time away in nature would lend an opportunity for writing the early verses of my own personal Redemption Song, a song that would need to patiently wait a couple of years before being sung and shared in front of the world.

Something to Believe In

It was winter 2016; at last I had arrived in Poland—greeted with cold, raw air, and the countryside unspectacular. The large Inner Fire Retreat group I'd met hours earlier at the Prague airport and I made our way to a quaint hotel off the beaten path near the Polish/Czech border. This was going to be a special experience; I felt ready for the expansion that comes from an honest challenge. The other attendees were an inspired motley crew of seekers from all over the world.

Close to our hotel were majestic waterfalls and access to cold brooks; the waterfalls were spectacular but polar opposites to the warm falls I was more accustomed to in my Central and South American travels. These falls provided ample space and depth to fully submerge in ice-cold Polish spring waters. Exposure to cold, being fully immersed in the frigid, has a way of waking up your senses.

There were travelers from all of the world that came to test out this breathing method and to see in person if Wim was legit. At the retreat were around 75 international travelers and participants, mostly male; at tops, 20 percent of the attendees were brave women. We were broken into three large groups. I'd be a Snow Leopard for the next five days, alongside some very special and motivated participants. Together, we would push ourselves past our limits, using the breath and nature as a catalyst for positive change. Everyone had this in common: we were on a quest to be better; we were determined to live happier lives; we were willing to put in the work and expose ourselves to risk; we had accepted that what we were seeking was on the other side of our fear.

It was a great honor to meet Wim, "The Iceman," the phenomenal adventurer I had read about and the man whose voice I had heard on many podcasts and documentaries. *This is really cool! Shit... I am actually doing this instead of sitting on my couch in my undies, stuck in a nervous feedback loop of judgment.* I had this pristine and lucid moment of clarity upon meeting this Dutchman—an acknowledgment that action is all that matters, getting off my ass and following through with my words and speech.

Just a year earlier, back in Chicago, I was out with friends on a frigid November night after an Odesza concert, touting that I didn't need a coat because I already had control of my mind, regulating my body temperature with focus. I was joking and mostly full of shit, mocking that this mind/body control stuff was even a possibility. I had just come across Wim's compelling story: I was completely in awe of his accomplishments and astounding claims for what his method could mean for physical and mental health. And here I was, free, in Poland, ready to dive in and see for myself.

Wim was a humble and gracious man. He emanated gratitude and appreciation and was present to the notion that people would want to spend time with him. Wim took full advantage of this special occasion to meet and engage everyone on a personal level, to take time to get to know what we were seeking from this experience, to glean understanding as to why we decided to answer this obscure call to nature, and this challenge in the most formidable of environments.

The first time I saw Wim, he was bantering with other attendees, telling lighthearted jokes while doing the splits to show off his physical dexterity and flexibility. He was the man of the hour. Or, better stated, the man of the long weekend. Holding that honor was clearly a sacred duty for Wim. Although he had an obvious lightness to him, he was equally, if not more so, serious and solemn. It was an admirable combination of two polarized orientations. Likely it is the balancing of those two orientations that make him so magnetic to those looking for relief from the many emotional challenges that plague our modern world. And, of course, the obvious feats he has accomplished and his tireless commitment to sharing his message of hope with our planet help with people's attraction to him.

What he has accomplished in his 59 years speaks for itself: he holds more than twenty Guinness Book of World Records, all revolving around the power of his mind to accomplish supernatural feats with unmatched focus. His ultra-impressive feats include: nearly two hours submerged in an ice tank without lowering his core body temperature to dangerous levels; running a marathon above the polar circle while only wearing shorts and no shoes; and running a marathon in the Kalahari Desert with no water. Check this guy out! Google him!

It's mind-boggling. It appears as though he can transcend his mind entirely and consciously enter into a trance state that allows for supernatural feats accomplished through his subconscious mind.

I observed him with astonishment. I searched for clues. How does he do all this? I was looking for a deeper understanding into his supernatural abilities and his abnormal drive to make our world better. In conversation, Wim wasn't shy about his obsession with sharing his breathing method with our world. He was obsessed with the science behind his method, the vehicle that would drive his message of hope into so many different channels. It was clear that he had a one-track mind and was only focused on the essentials, that which brought this mission closer to being attained. It was inspiring to see a strong man rooted like an ancient redwood tree in his calling and purpose.

Wim and his Inner Fire Retreat presented an unwavering message that centers on health, happiness, and strength for everyone. His breathing method, which involves extensive cold exposure, is a culmination of various disciplines compiled over years and combined with cold, hard nature. The Wim Hof Method's three pillars: meditation, breathwork, and gradual cold exposure.

Wim has an ambitious vision of our planet with no sickness. He is committed to sharing his method in hopes of healing our planet—walking the talk and leading by example. He works with many prestigious universities in an effort to quantify some of the dramatic transformational healing taking place by his students. PTSD, depression, anxiety, autoimmune disease, even cancer, are all on his radar. It is his belief that all disease is caused by shallow breathing. I completely agree.

When we are in a state of stress, our breath shallows and shortens. The analogy often used to describe this is that of confronting a saber-tooth tiger. If our hunter-gather ancestors were threatened by this tiger, the stress responses or fight or flight would be activated in order to ensure survival. Now, however, we live in times where there are few pressing physical threats. In our modern world, we don't have to worry about animals coming out of the bushes; we don't have to worry about being attacked by that tiger. We now are confronted with a different kind of threat, one that is constantly lurking in the back of our minds. Potential threats like job security and how others perceive our social status ruminate just below our conscious minds. These probabilistic threats also include the prospect of war and our often-ignored environmental crisis. For many, our fight-or-flight response is always on. This leaves the stress chemicals cortisol and norepinephrine to oversaturate our brains.

Common instances of fight-or-flight responses these days include wearing the wrong purse to a party or perceiving threats to our financial security as irrational threats to our life and family. I believe our modern world and collective definitions of success are as poorly aligned with our evolutionary drivers as any time in the history of man. A man who has a million dollars in the bank might be thrusted into a deep depression or worse upon losing his job. This is a crippling fear, when no clear and present danger actually exists.

Wim drinks beer. He stays up late and talks loudly and passionately. To me, however, he is every bit a master or even grandmaster; his method has been built from real life experience—finding inner peace through action. Through doing! Naturally, guru talk follows one in Wim's position. Any and all guru talk was redirected to Xena, the faithful, rambunctious chocolate lab. As I've suspected, Wim was the first to say, "the guru lies within us all."

SacredDownload.wordpress.com, 12/14/16

Here is a posting from my travel blog:

So, there I was climbing a mountain in shorts during what seemed to be a pleasant winter day in Poland. Thinking, *this ain't so bad.* Everyone talked and joked around in a lighthearted manner. *A walk in the park with new friends,* I thought. As the large group moved in unison on the fresh-packed snow, giant snowflakes peacefully fell from the ominous sky. Maybe all this extreme cold talk won't come to fruition after all? During that moment, I had a brief thought of disappointment as we all prepared diligently for the fiercest of mother nature's elements. Would we miss out on the real challenge? Then, a minute or two after that moment, things turned for the worse—or better, depending on how you look at it. A long stretch of open path fully exposed us to strong winds while at the same time the snow picked up significantly. *Game time!* I thought as I went within to focus deeply on my breath. Temperatures quickly dropped, with windchill they were 10 to 15 degrees below zero, leaving no choice but to focus all energies on the breath. Strangely, for that last hour, I was able to maintain my core body temperature with relative ease. The knowing that an extended disruption in focus could lead to hypothermia or worse kept me dialed in like a laser. Hands were another thing, as they were difficult to keep warm. Tucking them in my pants on my forever warm ass proved strategic. No shame; I didn't care to lose a finger. We were all battling in our own way to keep focus on the breath and the task at hand. *FUCK THE COLD!*...There was definitely a moment or two where I thought, *what am I doing here? Seriously, you paid money to subject yourself to this?!* Those fleeting thoughts were heavily outweighed by the desire to put my focus to the test, the desire to push past the perceived limits of my mind, to step out of my comfort zone in every way imaginable. "You can do far more than you think you can!" was another theme of the long weekend. Many of the participants had dramatic breakthroughs, realizing an inner power they weren't previously aware of or able to access. In the previous weekend's retreat, a man showed up in a wheelchair in ill health, suffering from Lyme disease. A couple days into the retreat, he tossed the wheelchair in favor of his new realized inner power. Eventually he would lead his group to the top of the mountain on their hike while singing a song that went something like this: "Fuck the wheelchair, da da da, Fuck the wheelchair, da da da." While I didn't see this for myself, I did see many arrive with an apparent heavy weight on their shoulders, myself included, only to leave days later in a relaxed state of being, with the lightness that comes from letting go and transcending lower forms of thought. All of this comes down to the power of focus and one's belief.

I see Wim as an atypical spiritual master, a humble man who wades through the world with a simple but profound message: health, happiness, and strength for all. Wim was content with letting his accomplishments, and now science, speak on his behalf as to the power of the breath and his method.

As I reflect a couple days after the transformational retreat in Poland, I am super grateful for this experience. I made more loving connections of like minds, further shaping my perception of the world and my journey. I got to see life and spirituality from another side. **All roads lead to Rome.**

Wim is a true believer in all that is possible for our planet and global family.

As a large group, we all participated in a breathwork session that felt closer to holotropic breathing. It was surreal to be a part of this group of near 70 people—everyone fearlessly diving into their breath and psyche round after round, probably for an hour. This was intense, and all of this felt very much like an ayahuasca ceremony. Obscure noises and loud breathing, but with an added element of coaching and encouragement. "Breathe! Push through!" There were lots of rah-rahs by the retreat leaders. "You can do it! Believe in yourself!"

It worked, as I ended up having a profound psychedelic healing experience from the intense breathing and mind focus. No drugs or medicine would be present this time around. Just the breath. I had been waiting for a visionary experience without the aid of external medicines—this was an ultra-empowering notion to know that I indeed have access to altered states any time I wish to activate this healing technology with just the breath and focus.

All of us have receptors that attach to the external plant medicines or psychedelic compounds. We can all access these states of consciousness; most of us, however, only do so while we are sleeping. In our dream worlds, we often have profoundly psychedelic experiences, but we just write them off as "I was only dreaming." The psychedelic experience is in our DNA. Further, researchers believe that these altered states can serve value in de-patterning, which, from an evolutionary standpoint, may be beneficial for those looking to break free from negative thought patterns that impede growth and positive change, from the toxic habits that endanger our survival. Ronald Segal, a UCLA pharmacologist and author of *Intoxication*, writes "so potent is the urge to get out of our heads, that it functions as a fourth drive, a behavior shaping force as powerful as our first three drives: food, water and sex." This sums up the incessant urge that I felt to heal with psychedelics and with the power of the breath, especially knowing that "The only difference between a rut and a grave are the dimensions." Wise words from thought-leader Ellen Glasgow.

Wim, a pioneer who is revolutionizing medical textbooks, is no different than many that I've come across on my life's journey; he too was deeply affected by pain and despair. His wife, who suffered from depression, killed herself and left Wim with four children to care for with no money. Imagine that. How does one respond from life's betrayal when presented with such dire circumstances? Wim found solace, healing, and clarity in nature. He pushed himself to the brink to heal and surely did his own depatterning from the immense grief in order to be strong for his children. Self-preservation for himself and his family propelled him to go beyond the mind and perform supernatural feats.

For the past many years and especially on my travels, I have been astounded by the stories of courage and bravery that others have exhibited in the name of reclaiming what has been lost. There seems to be a common denominator: everyone was unwilling to let their trauma or challenges define them.

As you read these words, take a moment to think about the obstacles and challenges confronting you. They may potentially be your greatest teachers.

Ryan Holiday writes in his best seller about Stoicism, *The Obstacle Is the Way*, "The impediment to action advances action. What stands in the way becomes the way."

It was becoming more and more clear that the obstacles in my life would become the eventual way for me. I felt an immense obligation to give back and share the insight gleaned from looking my truth directly in the eye without relenting. I know what is inside of me is inside of everyone else, and that many others are struggling just the same to find healing, purpose, and fulfillment in our complex modern world. Spending so much time, effort, and energy on the "way" would eventually enable me to guide others in doing the same.

"Breathe, motherfucker!" This mantra and directive Wim would say often and loudly with a big grin, almost as if to intentionally mock the overzealous spiritual seeker. Wim serves as a check and balance to those who think they have it all figured out. While almost over the top, it hammered home the point that you are not special because of your spirituality or your practices. What is special is what you can do to help others in need with those insights gleaned from your spiritual practices and inner work. Not the inner work itself, who really gives a shit? So often, people use retreats and their spiritual practices to delay actions, to put off the inevitable. On my path, strategic procrastination has been an ally. Waiting till the time is right to strike takes patience and a level of acceptance to be real with where you are at right now, but still working diligently toward your goals. This orientation can be a dangerous endeavor for our hungry souls that yearn to actualize our potential. Rationalizing inaction is a sickness, a limiting belief that stymies our progress. Retreats are great, but they must be a transformational tool that is in service to one's purpose and overarching objectives.

For the year after this retreat, I was diligently dedicated to this practice and would voluntarily force hyperventilation nearly six times per week. Each morning I incorporated this powerful breathing method with a more gradual exposure to cold. I found this practice deeply cathartic and therapeutic. With pen and paper nearby, I would monitor my times and holds, gauging where I was at in a given day, appeasing my competitive spirit. I steadily dove deeper and deeper, holding longer and longer. When I first started my hold without oxygen in my lungs, my times were just over one minute. Now my longest holds are just under 3 minutes. This improvement happened by slowly progressing and improving my technique day by day. The pen and paper also serves as a means to jot down any novel insight uncovered during this intense breathwork practice while at an elevated state of consciousness: super-charged journaling with many fears that linger just below the line of normal awareness are made known when engaging this daily practice; it is akin to a mini ceremony.

With the Wim Hof Breathing Method, you get high on your own oxygen supply. You elevate your vibration. This powerful practice most certainly is not for everyone as it can be intimidating for those who have no interest in addressing fears, but it can be exhilarating for enthusiasts who value their truth. It is an intense practice that gets easier the more you commit yourself. When charging your body up with oxygen, you breathe life and vitality into the parts of your bodies that hold suppressed emotions. By way of the nervous system, we unburden ourselves of emotions held too tightly.

Science supports that this breathing method and cold exposure can increase norepinephrine and adrenaline as much as 300% in the body.

Afterward, you feel an increase in focus and clarity—a great way to start the day and another practice with no potential downside. And your breath is legal, with an unlimited supply that is free and just under your nose. This is a perfect practice for any who may be hesitant to explore psychedelic compounds and plant medicines.

My time with Wim in Poland at the Inner Fire Retreat yielded a completely different way to look at spirituality by expanding my perception and equipping me with another healing tool.

While traveling to Poland and visiting with Wim Hof, I was turned on to a life-changing notion, above and beyond the Wim Hof Breathing Method and the daily cold exposure: intermittent fasting. Intermittent fasting is eating only eight hours per day, whatever you please, however much you desire (within reason), and then shutting it down for 16 hours till the next day. It asks you to do your best, without being neurotic about times, as this isn't an exact science. This revolutionary approach to health and eating requires discipline at first, but once the habit is adopted it becomes quite easy to maintain. I have found this health hack to be practical and enriching. It provides an enormous boost in my energy levels and overall health and wellness. My mornings are mostly free of food; I see through the myth of breakfast created by Kellogg's and Post to sell more toxic, sugary cereals. I still love my pancakes and eggs, but now eat them later in the morning, "breaking" my fast many hours into the day.

Nearly everyone I met on my travels had high energy and flowing levels of enthusiasm that aren't common in the busy working world. Not surprisingly, very few of them eat breakfast. It appears that breakfast might get in the way of inspired healthy morning routines. Our hunter-gatherer ancestors did not have constant access to food; they would miss meals from time to time. There is immense science that suggests that our biology benefits from intermittent fasting.

In 2016, Yoshinori Ohsumi, a Japanese cell biologist, was awarded the Nobel Prize in Medicine for his discoveries on how cells recycle their content, a process known as autophagy, a Greek term for "self-eating." Autophagy kicks in at 12 hours of fasting and has tremendous effects on anti-aging, cardiovascular health, immunity, and overall health. Surely this is why nearly every religious and spiritual tradition incorporates forbearance of food as a staple practice. Ohsumi's discovery is a game changer for our world that struggles with obesity and many other health-related challenges.

In addition to intermittent fasting, extended fasting provides even more health benefits. While on my travels, I had the opportunity to do a 10-day water fast. It was quite profound, to say the least. After pushing through the first two days, I was home free. While I had originally planned to do this twice per year akin to Napoleon Hill's claims, I have settled with the intermittent fasting variety. The biggest benefit of an extended fast is you never look at food the same way again. My ability to exercise willpower was majorly leveled up during that challenge. You think ten days is long? Angus Barbieri, a twenty-seven-year-old Scottish man who weighed 450lbs, spent 382 days on a medically supervised fast, losing 276 pounds. That is insane—no food for over a year!

Again, I AM NOT A MEDICAL PROFESSIONAL. NONE OF THIS IS MEDICAL ADVICE. Please consult with your physician before considering whether a fast is right for you.

In addition to intermittent fasting, other non-psychedelic hacks that I came across on my travels include:

Yoga. Well, I started practicing yoga before my travels, but during my 18 months with a backpack I practiced this ancient mind/body art nearly every day. There is nothing that calms me down like 30 minutes on the mat. Yoga has transformed my physical body and is a cornerstone practice for my personal wellbeing since I took my yoga teacher training while in Guatemala on my travels. Yoga teacher training was intense and akin to 20 days of spiritual boot-camp—highly recommended!

Raw organic cacao: My favorite plant medicine on Earth. Yep, even more than ayahuasca and psychedelic mushrooms. This legal medicine has strong anti-depressant properties and the active ingredient, theobromine, which translates to "food of the gods". It also has the neurotransmitter anandamide, known as the "bliss molecule" and named after ananda, the Sanskrit word for joy or bliss. Anandamide is thought to increase creativity and lateral "outside the box" thinking. Try it out! I add this superfood cacao paste to a cup of hot (not boiling) water with a couple drops of vanilla. It is delicious and drinks like black coffee!

Dr. Hulda's Liver Cleanse/Gall-Bladder Flush has been a surprise blessing. Since returning home from travels, I try to do this cleanse monthly. It serves as a powerful reset that mirrors the physical effects of an ayahuasca ceremony, waist down. I'll usually have a full day of fasting during this strategic withdrawal from food and external toxins. As someone who drank heavily for most of my life, this is some needed self-care to detoxify our largest internal organ, the liver, and gall-bladder; this self-care practice feels like a power wash for your liver. I have attached a cheesy video (https://www.youtube.com/watch?v=xXTUVDRkZCA) detailing the instructions of this cleanse, or you can easily find more details online. Beware of what comes out of you, though. It is quite startling how the toxins accumulate in our bodies.

Sacred tobacco and rapé. In the same way that we butcher real chocolate, we butcher tobacco. Aubrey Marcus includes tobacco as one of his "power plants" and I agree. Mapacho and rapé (pronounced "ha-peh") are powerful cleansing tools that can level-up your meditation practice. This tobacco is nothing like our toxic and poisonous American cigarettes.

12

ANGEL BY THE WINGS

"Once a man, twice a child"

— **BOB MARLEY**

I made my way back to Casa Mariposa, "the house of butterflies" a hostel/guest house in the mountains of Costa Rica: consisting of a small dorm room with six beds and four or five private guest rooms/suites. A shared communal space is a great place to meet with like minds and international travelers. Strangers would instantly turn into friends, making dinner together and swapping life and travel stories. This place had special communal vibes; everyone sharing space with other inspired nature explorers and adventurers. This was exactly what I needed to feed my soul.

This place is one of a kind, as it attracts the most special kind of traveler and adventurer, one who dares to embark on this most arduous of mountain hikes. Strong, motivated, and driven are prerequisites to challenge the seemingly never-ending hike through the most beautiful cloud forest en route to base camp at around 10,000 feet.

At Casa Mariposa, a revolving door of travelers make their way to this cozy charming getaway. It was my kind of place: lights out at 9pm to respect the fact that the hikers typically awake at 3 or 4am to make their way up the mountain—no television or anything else that ties you to the outside world. Simple, small-town living: perfect for rest and relaxation.

There was always an extremely social vibe at Casa Mariposa. When there, you meet many special travelers, a full house of mostly 20- and 30-somethings enjoying this mountain getaway. "I am from Chicago too. But I live in New York right now," a six-foot-tall bright-eyed beauty named Monica said in typical small-world fashion. She overheard me talking about my former home base, and revealed she grew up a couple miles from where I had lived my last 15 years in the big city. She was volunteering at the guest house, helping out with odds and ends, probably in exchange for free room and board.

"Chicago was a special city. Lots of lessons for sure," I added as we sat in the homey common space in the guest house, sharing a brownie, swapping how-the-heck-did-you-end-up-here stories. Every conversation presented an opportunity to share and plant seeds of hope in the minds of those my path crossed. Monica had fair skin on the borderline of pale; she had a noticeable heaviness to her, a strange, but attractive, frumpiness. This made my inquisition easier. *What is it? What are you running from?* I wondered, always curious as to the drives of others; through understanding others, we inevitably understand ourselves better. Our initial conversation settled on yoga, psychedelics, and polyamory. We didn't take much time with surface small talk as she shared her love triangle in the first conversation we had.

"Do you want to practice yoga together?"

She nodded in agreement.

"I would LOVE to teach, I have been looking for opportunities to practice," I said with boyish excitement, enthusiastic at an obvious opportunity to get to know her better and work on my craft and teaching in the process.

"This will be fun, Mateo," she said in a light and playful manner.

Monica's childhood home was a block away from Angela's Burrito Style, my favorite Mexican restaurant and late-night burrito stop in all of Chicago. I'd always order a California burrito with avocado and French fries, smothered with their in-house red and green salsas. Typically, I have them put on pastor, a special kind of pork. It is a borderline religious experience for me, although I am mostly vegetarian It would be a greater regression and moral crime to turn my back on those special flavors, but I digress.

Monica was on a journey, too: she broke away from her day-to-day life, taking a couple of months for travel to complete her yoga teacher training. Monica, an artist and creative who worked with children, was fascinating for many reasons other than her obvious beauty and sex appeal. Monica had two committed intimate partners. Both male lovers. Both completely separate relationships that offered her emotional support, accompanied with a likely high dose of sexual touch and contact. This absolutely captivated me.

How does she do it? What are her challenges? How does she navigate through the judgmental waters in which she surely swims? I pondered these questions when we set out on a nature hike. Monica and I had a special day exploring the Cloud Forest and its many sapphire blue waterfalls.

Monica, a self-proclaimed "ethical slut." Was really a special and dynamic woman.

There was clearly a genuine mutual interest in our respective paths; Monica's open sexuality and my extensive experience with ayahuasca and other plant medicines would lend for insightful and spirited conversation. She was a month away from her first ayahuasca ceremony and would ask me many questions, inquiring about best practices and ways to prepare so she could get the most out of her healing ceremony—and for me, this was the first time I'd ever engaged someone who fully embraced the lifestyle of polyamory, effectively balancing two lovers: I was very curious how she came to this lifestyle choice and how she made this process work and, of course, wondering if there was maybe room for a third lover.

Her long legs were accentuated by the high cut jeans she wore; she buzzed with a youthful exuberance and had the whole "openness" thing down to perfection: an attractive quality and one I knew that I needed much work on— being open to the ways people live and open to the infinite opportunities that life presents.

Openness and non-judgment are closely intertwined: are there two more important attributes to embrace for someone looking to embody peace of mind? I think not!

One of the most important parts of my travels was to thoroughly examine every belief and honestly ask myself if I agreed with it. Does this make sense with what I value, with who I am now and the man I envision becoming? From there I could accept or disregard it, letting go or creating new beliefs or affirming beliefs already in place. The belief that we are wired to be monogamous and that being with one partner is somehow natural or ordained by divine law was at the top of the list of values I wanted to more thoroughly examine. Partnership, and my inability to connect, was the cause of nearly all my heartache. This was my time to challenge this notion and truly decide what made sense to me now.

More people struggle with shame and guilt from dogma than anything else. Polite society does a really good job ignoring what we are: our inner animal, our primal instincts.

Sexual energy that we don't give proper channels to finds its way out in unhealthy manners. And I don't have to state the obvious as to how much we are failing with this monogamy notion in the West. This conversation with Monica was just what I needed as I was starting to ask myself what a desired relationship should look like. Polyamory did seem like a lot of work, however. This was all healthy questioning that I had been too scared to honestly ponder and to acknowledge what I truly believed.

On our hike, we pondered life and its challenges as we traversed the Cloud Forest and hunted for the most majestic waterfalls. With childlike excitement, I couldn't help but to ask Monica which one of her lovers she liked more. Her laser-sharp response proved I touched a nerve: "Mateo, have I taught you nothing?!" Her expression softened into a half smile as she realized my naiveté. I admired this woman and gave her much credit for having the courage to live and love out in the open, for not letting the harsh judgements of our sick society that largely scorns such behavior get in her way. She didn't give a shit what others thought. I admire that about Monica. Or, she probably did give a shit, but wouldn't let it stop her from being who she was and loving who she wanted. In my eyes, she was a pioneer of sorts. Leading by example; parading her lifestyle, loving fearlessly—showing others what is possible.

Although satisfied with lots of loving, Monica had something really heavy on her heart. I could feel it. After all, she took time away from her busy life in New York to retreat, traveling to figure her shit out. The word "retreat" gets a bad rap from the egomaniac workaholic culture. The rest of us use it judiciously as a tool to gather perspective and objectivity to help garner more life balance, or as a time to depattern and shake things up.

My last supper at Casa Mariposa was quite memorable. As promised to my new travel compadres, I'd be making yucca pancakes for everyone, sharing this gluten free and vegan delight with my new friends. Weeks prior, while at Florestral for a visit, we went on a dramatic hunt with machetes and shovels to dig up some fresh yucca right from the earth. It was the closest I have ever been to experiencing what it was like to be a hunter-gatherer, setting out with other men to hunt wild game. Instead of game, though, we slogged back to the group with giant pieces of yucca root over our shoulders.

At Casa Mariposa, cooking for others was a good way to make friends and favorable impressions, sharing my gifts by way of jaw-dropping tasty treats. These culinary wonders were quite simple: peel back the yucca's bark-like outer skin and grate its insides. After this, you cook it like a pancake, no oil or flour needed. Top with savory or sweet toppings and you have a delicious meal.

Shortly after sharing my dinner with others, I overheard a couple of travelers inquiring about the Tuesday morning Organic Market at TinaMaste. One of the prized gatherings, close to Florestral, where each week the community comes together to sell goods and to socialize with one another. You just don't see spirited responses to those kind of gatherings back home in the U.S.; this place is akin to farmers market but much more communal, everyone making their best and most earnest effort to at least stop through the market to say hello and pick up fresh foods and goods for the coming week.

Immediately after overhearing the talk about the market, I chimed in, as if an authority of the Tuesday market and one who happened to be looking for a ride in that direction. After some conversation, I'd gladly accept a ride from Laurie and Sarah, guiding them to the market and parts of Costa Rica I was quite familiar with. The two ladies were a "mother-daughter combo," a "dynamic duo" I would end up befriending. This was a special opportunity for me to guide my new Canadian friends to a warm community offering that was sure to wow. They were kind, immediately accepting me as one of their own.

During the hour and a half drive through the mountains and valleys, majestic views were plentiful in every direction. Costa Rica is truly a magical country in so many ways. On our drive, I'd find Sarah and her mother as different as night and day. Sarah was a recent graduate of pharmacy school, taking some time to see the world and get her thoughts in order before embarking on the likely lifelong career as a pharmacist in Canada—her mother Laurie was a sweet and kind woman, a yoga teacher and health coach in her mid-50s with the fitness, spirit, and zesty enthusiasm of someone half her age.

I shared the abbreviated version of my story of why I find myself alone with a backpack in a foreign country. Both were inquisitive of my journey, asking many thoughtful questions as if to figure how something similar could be done in their respective lives: "How the heck did he just up and go?"

After some spirited banter, we all danced with serendipity: Of course, Laurie let it be known that she was looking to drink ayahuasca again, inspired from my brief sharing of my healing experiences. She had an experience a year or two earlier with a Peruvian shaman in Canada that was profound and very moving, providing tremendous healing and insight. Laurie felt like she was ready for more teachings. It just so happened that we were going to be driving by Florestral and they had a ceremony that was scheduled for the following day.

It was cute to see Laurie ask her daughter Sarah if it was okay to have a couple days of healing and introspection with "The Mother." Sarah obliged, hardly understanding that part of her mother, but eager to have a break, as she had been traveling for weeks with her mom. Sarah didn't get that part of her mom that was okay with drinking the strongest psychedelic on Earth with a bunch of strangers in a remote forest in a foreign country. I observed that dynamic with curiosity, scanning for judgmental micro-expressions, but found none. I could only sense loving grace and an earnest attempt at understanding from Sarah. She had great energy, a vibrancy—I was quickly becoming intrigued.

Hours later, Sarah and I were dropping her mom off at ayahuasca camp, leaving her with my trusted forest tribe that has been so instrumental in my personal healing. I assured Sarah that her mother would be fine and that she was in trusted and loving hands. When we dropped Laurie off, we took a tour of Florestral, swimming down by the amazing river. It was pretty cool to show off my remote forest getaway to Sarah, a novice who was completely green in terms of the esoteric and the occult, having only recently been exposed to that side of her mother.

An impromptu adventure with Sarah was just the excitement that I was seeking. And exactly why I suspended my around-the-world trip. Sarah was very fit. Much like her mother, she radiated a healthy, authentic loving glow. Armed with long, straight brown hair and a beautiful smile, she wore glasses and her clothes were unassuming hot weather attire. My first impressions were: Sarah is cute and sweet, this will be a lot of fun—let's see what will happen. Having already met her mom, I knew she comes from a good and loving place. Something about those Canadians was so kind, warm, and welcoming. On all my travels, I have never had a negative impression from our neighbors to the North, just a lot of hugs, smiles, and funny accents.

My time with Sarah had zero expectations; perhaps that would underlie our magical time together. Frankly, I was just grateful for the company and our time as strangers getting to know one another. We shared respective stories while in pursuit of waterfalls and sunsets. Sarah, despite the kind vibe I received from her, was a bit high strung and shocked to be in the presence of someone as carefree as me. In a short time, she became more comfortable with the stranger she just met a day earlier. We set out for one of the many waterfalls in Uvita, a small surf town just south of Dominical on the Pacific side of Costa Rica. Immediately I got to see another side of Sarah. Never in my life have I seen someone come alive so much while in the water. We laughed and played like kids—jumping off cliffs. I awkwardly tried to show off my diving skills with no care in the world. I admired Sarah and the majestic waterfall the same, both natural, take-your-breath-away wonders. Her eyes lit up with childlike excitement. If ever there existed a mermaid, Sarah would be just that upon dawning the water. I was smitten from that point on, enthralled by this unassuming beauty that came out of nowhere—waking up slowly to this happenstance encounter.

"Matt, thank you for hanging out with me," Sarah said with softness and appreciation. She was polite and well-mannered. "I am really glad that we are adventuring together," she added in a forward manner. I'd later find that

Sarah would just say what she was feeling, almost without a filter.

"I am thankful that I met you and your mother, this is fun, we will have fun together," I responded with a grateful disposition as we indulged in fresh fruit smoothies, seeking shade not more than a couple hundred feet from the Pacific. I showed her around Dominical, my stomping grounds, where I spent much time during these past few years. "This is why I travel, to meet amazing new people. This is the best way I can glean insight and learn about myself," I added to affirm my peaceful intention and friendly orientation.

We later set out to find lodging and were introduced to the "Womb Room" at a local hotel and yoga studio, no bigger than a closet. It was ultra-cozy and inexpensive—a room that was surely for lovers or close companions, as only a small bed fit within. When the proprietor asked if we would take the room, I paused and let Sarah decide. Any words out of my mouth would have been very creepy. Plus, I was testing to see her temperature and interest. After hesitation, she thought the better for us. Too small for newly met strangers. That was a moment of levity and humor that we laughed at for the many weeks to come. "The itsy, bitsy, teeny, weeny, womb room!" She would exclaim with a gracious smile every time we reminisced our awkward encounter at Danyasa.

Something I noticed early on with Sarah was a genuine pause that she had displayed during our conversations. She was engaging, open, and honest trying her best to fully understand and soak in everything. She was so thoughtful and actually meant it. This was still novel to me. It was inspiring. Such a presence invited an equal effort from me. For much of my journey, it has been remarkable to meet genuine people who truly care about others. While I have always cared, there was only so much attention I could give others when I often struggled to stay afloat myself. There was only so much bandwidth I had to offer, with both my heart and nervous system overloaded with painful memories of yesteryear. It has always been a challenge for me to engage below the surface. Attention and presence have been things I've had to practice, working patiently and diligently to improve each day, consciously challenging myself to be better. More present. More engaged. It is counterintuitive, but when we consciously engage with others, we don't lose energy, but become more enlivened, creating space for inspiration and insight. Some say that active listening may be the most important life skill to work on. We can't learn from others when we are always running our mouths.

We found a more suitable bed and breakfast. An old Colombian man who settled in Costa Rica after fleeing his once-corrupt country was a gracious and amiable host. This room had more space and was better suited for both Sarah and myself.

After making a healthy dinner that was washed down with a couple of cold beers on a sweat-dripping hot and humid night, we would set out for a walk on the beach. It was near pitch black, we had to use our headlamps to illuminate our path. We pondered life as we watched a strikingly brilliant and bright red upside-down crescent moon (yes, such thing does exist!) set over the south Pacific

Ocean. I have never seen anything that even remotely compared; this all was otherworldly.

As we sat on the beach, I asked probing questions in a patient manner with no real agenda, but knowing that I may be snuggling up with her in the hours to come. Knowing that there lay inside a mostly dormant animal that was begging to come out and play, Sarah's orientation was coy and that of the demure female, almost as if she acted out the standard narrative cue cards.

Nothing happened that night, which was just fine. I was, strangely, just grateful for her company, for the closeness and our newly budding friendship. Her boyfriend back in Canada was used as a loose boundary and buffer. I honored this and wouldn't push. It didn't feel right to rush. Clearly, I had changed and was content on getting to know her better. My values were still shifting. I could now see that patience and tenderness are essential for building trust.

Throughout my travels, whenever in the presence of a beautiful woman it felt like I was being schooled. Sure enough, that was exactly what was happening. I was being reconditioned so one day, I may love more fully, so I could connect on a deeper level with intimate partners.

For the months to come, I grew very close to Sarah. I saw her a handful of times as she anchored down in Dominical with her girlfriends who came to visit from Canada. It was an absolute joy to have her around.

In one gathering, Sarah and Laurie invited me to join them in a large Costa Rican residence, and I, of course, obliged. Our time together felt familial. I was able to help

Laurie with integrating her ayahuasca experience, making sense of her deep healing, generously sharing my wisdom and insight as I was a bit more versed with ayahuasca than she was. It was a blessing to have met this dynamic duo.

During our time at the house, we would have the most fun making meals and talking about life, entertaining deep philosophical conversations about life that bordered existential. We mostly kept it light. I was getting better at filtering and censoring, meeting whomever I was speaking with where they were at. While authenticity is important, so is respect. I was learning the value in not scaring the squirrel away, dancing with the notion of being open but not too open. Not having to have the last word was an epic godsend; I was getting better at just "being."

Sarah was on a break of sorts from her partner John, whom was back in Canada. They had hit a snag of some kind in their relationship. In order to glean clarity, she set out to the tropics to dive into nature to look for answers. They had been together for seven years or so, and I suspected Sarah was losing patience, waiting for a ring and proposal.

Sarah was the full package. I fell hard for her. Our effortless conversations and our mutual respect and affection for one another was exactly what I needed. I felt a spark!

This all felt like love—true love—intense feelings like none that I'd ever felt before. My definition of true love is when both parties are fully open and completely honest and vulnerable with one another, no hidden agendas or nonsense, no game playing. This rare and magical phenomenon is real connection in a society where everyone is wearing a mask and hiding their truth. To instead be completely present, to feel safe just being myself with no shame—that's true love. That closeness I experienced with Sarah was why I originally left Chicago, and why I gave up everything in favor of travels.

Although true, it was clear that pursuing a relationship wasn't going to work. Or at least not at that time. While in pursuit of my life's purpose, I could not offer her the shelter she was seeking. She had much work still to be done with her partner, John, who was almost common-law family; it was imperative that she face and listen to the music of her life and not bypass her own lessons. I could sense it; after many years of troubled relationships, a rebound is easy to sniff out and if we were going to have anything sustainable it would have to come at a different time in our respective lives. One particular night as we lay together, pondering life and love and the future, this reality would become obvious.

Both of our paths were so uncertain, clearly not aligned in harmony. With her head resting on my chest, my hands through her hair in a calming and gentle manner, I would propose in a different manner. "If you ever find yourself in a different time, different circumstances, in need of love, come find me. I will be there for you." This was a clear turning point for me to offer love with no expectation of anything in return. Loving merely for the sake of loving.

My diligence in practicing the art of love, on letting go, would pay its first major dividend in my life's journey. All of the "letting go" I had been doing, prepared me to safely dive in, to fully give everything I possibly could, with the trust that things would be okay. The hard truth was she had a partner and I hadn't yet found my calling; my journey was not sorted out. Much work lay ahead for us both. She had to confront her partner and the relationship challenges, and I knew in my bones that I had the most important next few months of my life as I was going to reintegrate back to life in the states. It was okay. It was all okay.

It was eerie. Something had changed, my trademark neediness and clinginess were mostly absent. The extreme insecurity, which manifests as "jealousy," a form of insanity and common affliction of the mind, that used to uncontrollably rear its ugly head time and time again, was mostly gone. Together, Sarah and I bussed from the picturesque mountain town to San Isidro where we would go our separate ways. Her partner, John, was begrudgingly visiting her in Costa Rica as he was put on notice that another suitor was in play and if he wanted a future with Sarah it would be in his best interest to get his ass down there ASAP.

This burst of light reminded me what was possible, reminded me what is a conscious choice in every moment, of every day. Plenty enough to set my heart on fire. Love isn't something to get—it is fundamentally what we are—we embody love by living our truth.

I've since given much thought to the notion of finding true love while in the pack; while closely crowded against one another, we conform to the rhythms of group. Under these circumstances, how would we ever know if what we felt aligned with our hearts or only with the group's directives and expectations? It is only when one is in the deep stillness of their heart that they can truly know their most honest longings. We are herd animals who follow, mirroring those around us. I can confidently say this reflection would have never happened while in the city immersed in my patterns of old. As a lone wolf; I had broken away from the pack and would figure this all out for myself and would have the gift of truly knowing that I went for it. So many will sit back, making this or that excuse; they will play the victim and indulge in their narratives as to the many reasons why their life isn't the one they wanted. Many of us effectively give away the best part of our existence to Bullshit, Inc., trusting what others have told us or what society deems acceptable. This is maddening defeatism for the human spirit that knows no boundaries and limitations. With matters of heart and with love, we all have to formulate our own conclusions and definitions. How do we do this when fearfully immersed in our habits? We often don't. And that is why the world is as it is.

Blindly trusting the herd with matters of the heart is consigning away your connection to the divine. In doing so, you sell out on the most noteworthy part of the human experience. It appears there is only one way to arrive at this knowing: through the treacherous inner landscapes of our own hearts. There is no way around this, and one can only navigate that treacherous inner journey from a place of stillness and peace.

I had no motive but to be present to the beauty right in front of me, to honor the sacredness of this moment, the here and now. The moment, all of these moments, were perfect. It could be no other way, just perfection, just truth of what was.

My trauma had been neutralized enough, the pain was mostly gone, that energy could now be transmuted and redirected toward love, toward what has always been there.

In Sarah's presence, my mind chatter had nearly stopped. There wasn't much thinking; insights were plentiful like never before. All of this felt like magic. It felt supernatural, when reality is, this is a normal state of being, just one that is largely shut off from our senses. This is liberty, defined as the state of being free within a society from oppressive restrictions imposed by authority on one's way of life, behavior, or political views.

How would I have ever known a feeling like this existed had I stayed put, unwilling to take a chance? My monkey mind has been tamed enough to allow for true presence, a level of intimacy that was unattainable before I left on my travels. Maybe I could have figured this all out at a Tantra workshop, saving 18 months and many thousands of dollars. Who really knows? This was my path. This was why I left everything behind. I had to see for myself. I would have never forgiven myself for missing this opportunity and I would have died a loveless coward.

Our brief romance left me with an incredible optimism. Sarah and I said our long goodbyes. We kissed and held each other. And we kissed some more. This was as raw and as real as any moment in my life to date—being able to connect, being okay with the moment as it was. That our respective lives had orchestrated this moment of time where our paths would collide was profound. We ended our almost-lovers' embrace with promises to see each other again. Tears flowed down our faces. It was a bittersweet, intense moment, a test.

It hurt to let go as she returned to Canada, to be with her partner, returning to her life hallmarked by stability. It felt honest, though. All I could think about was the joy I had from the privilege of loving her and spending that special time with her. Our mutual growth. The joy of feeling the deepest levels of emotional intimacy I had ever felt in my life. All of this left me with an earnest hope for what lay ahead, in pursuit of my life's truest calling and purpose—in pursuit of romance and the life I envisioned.

When it comes to love, we can trust no other man. With love, the stakes are too high to trust anything besides the deepest depths of your own heart. It is pure insanity to forget the most important part of our existence, our deepest, most hallowed reason for waking, for weathering the human experience. I was lost before. All of this was lost on me. I couldn't see it through the hazy trauma that dimmed and discolored my lens of reality. I was an obedient follower who would have died a prisoner with the keys in my pocket. Turning that key was the scariest fucking thing in my life, to walk out and leave the comforts of home, to see for myself, so I would truly know and never have to doubt my truth again.

Most everything you hear from others about love is total bullshit: toxic, limiting beliefs projected into the ether that erode the adventurous spirit of man. Growing up, I often heard the gospel of settling. Friends and family tried to persuade me to see things as they did. They encouraged me that maybe finding a 6 or 7 to marry and have children with would be prudent, given my age and social status. Again, these misguided projections and words are only spoken to help validate their own often-shitty decisions, missteps, and transgressions.

It was now all about trust and presence, holding space for another's heart to fully open, while sharing my own. This was exhilarating, as if I had just opened myself up to a whole other level of thinking and being.

Had I never left for my journey, I would have never fully touched the deepest depths of my heart or another's. Caverns that are as deep as the ocean floor, hidden gems that await discovery, would have remained unexplored.

I believe breaking away from the herd is a necessity for finding a higher form of love within. It is only when we are energetically free from the expectation of others that we can truly and objectively know what lies within. I had spent much of the past few years experimenting with psychedelics and altered states, only to find that authentic connection is the most powerful medicine in the known Universe.

WIDER CIRCLES

"We make a living by what we get, we make a life by what we give"

–WINSTON CHURCHILL

Oh fuck! This is it, I said into the mirror begrudgingly after a phone call that would forever change my life. I just got off the phone with a military man, former U.S. Marine Ryan LeCompte. Ryan was the founder of a veteran organization,

Veterans for Entheogenic Therapy, that called themselves VET. Years prior, Ryan and a group of U.S. veterans traveled down to Peru with CNN's Lisa Ling to drink ayahuasca and heal from war trauma and post-traumatic stress in front of the world. A bold and impressive move had me wowed and proud, intrigued about the long-term goals of this not-for-profit.

I was introduced to VET when Robert, a friend from grade school, informed me of this important work at the psychedelic conference weeks earlier.

Something about that initial conversation with Ryan resonated deep inside. He was direct and honest, and very enthusiastic to speak with another psychedelic enthusiast who believes in the healing power of these plant medicines. Clearly Ryan was in need of help too; it felt from our initial call that he was a lone wolf in this organization. I got the sense he was on an island doing this "god's work" solo.

From the get-go, I could tell that Ryan was the real deal, that his heart was in this healing work and that he was fully committed. It was inspiring to speak with someone who I sensed was not void of his calling and purpose.

Ryan was doing this work for the right reasons, for love, for honor, and the unwillingness to turn his back on his fellow veterans in need. He took an oath to protect and serve. He would take this commitment and service to an entirely different level. I had watched many videos of Ryan online, helping me formulate a stronger opinion of this compelling work. This little reconnaissance mission was an opportunity to do my homework, taking advantage of the Information

Age where nearly every interview is recorded, breadcrumbs, signposts if you will, left behind for those who seek objective information. Years back, we could claim ignorance for not knowing something—now we can only claim laziness.

"Yes, that was correct, we have nearly 500 low-income, some homeless, U.S. veterans on the VET waiting list." Ryan repeated himself, as I needed to hear this twice.

"Wow. How are you planning on getting these veterans treatment?" I inquired with sympathy and great surprise.

"We rely solely on donations from the public, $20 here, $100 there. It has been challenging to get real momentum. I've struggled with raising funds," Ryan added in his deep, voice. I was stuck on the fact that nearly 500 veterans were locked and loaded, ready for this transformational therapy that I knew experientially really worked. I couldn't let that number 500 go, no matter how hard I tried. The people had spoken. Our U.S. veterans that have fought bravely for our freedoms and liberties were hurting and in need—there was no need to try to convince me of something that I already experienced firsthand and knew in my bones to be true: ayahuasca is a powerful healing technology to treat PTSD, depression, and addiction.

"How many have you treated? I asked.

"We have had nearly 150 successful suicide interventions in these past three years. This has been a lot of work and our program has been ironing out the kinks. We are ready to expand and pick up the pace," Ryan replied in a stern militaristic manner. Everything was a mission for Ryan. He talked differently, directly, but he also had a soft and humorous side which allowed me to trust him more quickly. I'd later find out that Ryan lost his wife to divorce because of his over-commitment to this labor of love and his mission to eradicate veteran suicide. He was all in, in addition to running a veteran not-for-profit, he was also finishing up his Master's Degree at Naropa, a prestigious Buddhist university in Boulder, Colorado and working as a counselor for at-risk and troubled youth. A modern-day Jesus doing god's work.

"How are these veterans integrating back into their daily lives?" This was my biggest question, as I envisioned total chaos as G.I. Joe sipped down a potion that would unravel all the tumult that lay beneath his conscious awareness.

"We have a great relationship with a psychedelic church in Orlando, Florida called SoulQuest Church of MotherAyahuasca...They do a great job holding space and providing non-dogmatic healing for our vets. Once Humpty Dumpty gets broken open, VET helps with the integration. We help our veterans put the pieces back together after ego death by making sense of their healing experience and their trauma. This isn't a magic instant fix, but it has been working. We haven't lost any vets to suicide and all of them have stopped taking their prescription medication." Ryan really broke down his process for me, shedding light on how his organization works.

"Is this legal?" I interjected. "The Church, how are they doing this legally?"

Ryan responded quickly with enthusiasm. "They are protected by religious rights freedoms and have been using ayahuasca as a sacrament." He said something about a 2006

Supreme Court ruling, putting my concerns at ease.

"WOW! This is incredible work you are doing—thank you for your courage and commitment. This is truly incredible!" I responded with exuberance and excitement. *Holy shit! This needs to be heard. People need to know that this work is being done.* I thought and then paused.

"Veterans have a bias toward action. They don't need to be told what to do. They already know discipline. It is instilled in them during their service time—they just need relief from the trauma and we are providing this opportunity for healing," Ryan said proudly in an enthusiastic spirit. "We are finding that many of our vets are thriving now, having shed the victim script. Even taking on their own service projects."

"Amazing, this is all amazing!" I responded. I never had thought of this notion before. My experience had been one of seeing many people drifting through life, myself included, without a real sense of urgency and purpose. That can be part of this process while people are learning to let go, to forgive, taking time to process these sometimes far-out healing experiences. These veterans have been in it—they have been to a real-life Hell, seeing and doing horrific things; veterans embody a sense of vulnerability and urgency that I hadn't yet been exposed to, "I can't hang on, these pills are poisoning me—I can't hang on much longer!" Ryan summarized a typical plight of the U.S. veterans he had been working with for the three years prior.

All of this was awe-inspiring, expanding my perception of what might be possible with this misunderstood healing technology from the jungle—what this could mean for a massive grouping of our U.S. veterans.

During this conversation with Ryan, I confirmed my biases, further rooting in my belief that I could be of service. A major shift took place; I wasn't the lone nut anymore. This military man seemed just as crazy as I was about pushing the limits of what was possible.

I could help. I knew I could, and all of this was right up my alley—fitting perfectly with my aspirations to be of service to others; the prospect of advocating for our U.S. veterans in need, engaging a demographic I honestly knew very little about, was intriguing. My father served in the Navy in the 1950s and many of my friends' parents served in Vietnam—but as far as the recent wars, it was as if that reality has been shielded from my awareness—as if our economic structure and national agendas intentionally created a smoke screen to divert attention from such a huge matter in question that affects us all: the mental health of our U.S. veterans: our warriors, our protectors.

To find out that at least 22 U.S. veterans, and likely far, far more, fall to suicide each day was heavy. *This is real—how is this so that I have never even heard about this suicide tragedy and epidemic? Why is no one talking about this?* I pondered these deep questions unwilling to let go until I had some satisfactory answers.

This hit me hard, like a jab from Tyson right in the sternum. That night I rolled around the floor at my AirBNB in Grass Valley, California, in a desperate attempt to deny that I ever had this conversation with Mr. Military Man,

Ryan; to deny what I was feeling inside, how real this all had become in a near instant. I couldn't deny this, knowing from the deepest part of my being that this was exactly what I had been asking for and patiently awaiting: an opportunity to be of service to others who are struggling, to give back and share the abundant blessings and insight that I have been graced with—to accept an honorable and noble challenge, to direct all of my struggles to a mission greater than myself.

Only days earlier, I started the process of putting together a 501(c)(3) for adult survivors of child abuse and for U.S. veterans in need: Next Level Transformation, Inc. My original intent was to provide holistic healing/yoga retreats to those that needed healing. I didn't know what to do, but I knew that this was something that I believed in. So I started the process, trusting that everything would come together. I wasn't a U.S. veteran and working to be of service to them wouldn't have made that much sense if I went at this alone. There was much resistance in this process. It didn't flow easily and I had much doubt as I couldn't see this all playing out. "Matt, the-hippy-new-ager-bohemian, or whatever he is, what does he want from us veterans? What are his motives?" These obvious questions would surely be posed in everyone's minds of those I wished to help.

All of this changed with that exploratory phone call with Ryan. I can help now. I can be of service to people that are suffering now. I can act now. The wise words of Napoleon Hill rang through my head, "Start where you stand! This philosophy is meaningless without action!" All this self-help stuff is total bullshit if you don't apply it. If you don't act.

I prayed and meditated on this—and prayed some more. Asking for guidance, for clarity—for the courage to stand—for the strength to do what was right.

What sucked me in was the surprising notion that around 90% of those U.S. veterans that had been through the VET program were from broken homes, and the root issue was childhood sexual abuse and trauma, most often broken homes exposed to church abuse. How is it that so many of our U.S. veterans were also sexually abused in their youth? Adult survivors of childhood sexual trauma were always the demographic I intended to serve since I started this path. All of this head-scratching truth: this startling realization would invite questions and curiosity that I would further explore in the days and months to come. I'd even later read in Sebastian Junger's Tribe, that veterans who have fought in our two modern wars (Iraq and Afghanistan) are twice as likely to have reported sexual abuse in their youth than veterans of Vietnam that were picked at random with a draft lottery. The key word in the previous sentence is "reported," that number is likely higher as we've come to know not everyone can admit these shameful truths.

At first, I felt a lot of shame knowing that I didn't have the courage to ever ponder the harsh realities and true cost of war—this never even made it on my radar. It was too heavy, having an opinion of this weight was too much when pondering the depth of this mission; before my travels, it would have caused far too much dissonance and would have disrupted my ability to keep my head above water to earn. Really pondering war, even pondering our own mortality, takes an immense amount of courage. Many of us don't have the healthy nervous systems required for an honest inquiry into these realities.

With knowing this reality—what kind of man would I be if I turned my back on this? I knew that I could help, that I could be of service and utilize my extensive business and marketing skills to raise awareness and money for our veterans who struggle deeply with PTSD and suicide. While I had resented my past for so long, in an instant it became clear that I had been training myself for this moment, my entire life. Everything that came forth, was leading me to this moment in time—where I could step the fuck up and get in the game of life! All of this motivated and energized me like never before.

I felt immense gratitude and appreciation for sticking to this path while not knowing how everything would shake out. For not wavering or quitting—for this incessant belief in myself, the knowing that something bigger than me was in store in this lifetime.

It was month 17 of my 18-month travel journey. This was it—my calling. Be careful of what you ask for, as it surely will come if asked in a spirit of humble earnest.

This was my calling and it scared the shit out of me. I had to act in the face my fears and insecurities. This is it, now is the time, no more hiding. Ready or not, here I come. This was exactly what I had been asking for all along—an opportunity to be of service to others in need.

I felt immense pressure to be somebody, to have something to share with my network and circle of influence.

To have something to show for my lengthy travel journey. All of this aligned with my efforts and values; the not-for-profit side would be a great place to start. With service, helping others, I could help myself as I integrated back to my life post-travels. From the moment I took on this assignment and committed myself to this mission, my personal problems became menial and insignificant. Psychologists call it the "helper high," whatever it is, it really works.

Ryan and I agreed that we would take on human suffering together, starting with those who deserve love and care more than any other: our U.S. veterans in dire need, struggling with depression and combat-related trauma. Game on!

WRITING TO REACH YOU

"For it is in giving that we receive."

— SAINT FRANCIS OF ASSISI

The day my old friend Joe called me out of the blue to lift the spirits of his childhood friend (see chapter 3) subtly challenged me to investigate brotherly love and, unknowingly, provided an invitation to come alive and led to the transpiring of these events.

This book has really been a love story. Not a memoir/self-help/motivational/Shamanism book or however the reviewers will categorize it, but an unconventional love story about never giving up, pushing through obstacles and adversity. About believing in love and all that is possible.

In this lengthy chapter I experienced love for the first time, finally catching up to that feeling I felt a few years earlier in my second ayahuasca healing ceremony. That transcendent love that I felt while ingesting this powerful psychedelic brew; a blinding burst of light that finally came from experiencing the all-elusive, true emotional intimacy kind of love with a Canadian woman named Sarah. This phenomenon was previously impossible to realize with the pain that I carried in my heart. The unresolved childhood trauma that once garbled up my nervous system made this level of connection a foolish endeavor to pursue, let alone realize. The childhood trauma had me stymied, nearly convincing me that this life of mine wasn't *worth the fight*, that love wasn't worth pursuing at all cost, even death.

It was no coincidence that I found my calling shortly after experiencing this profound state of being with another open and vulnerable heart; there probably is some divine law we don't yet understand, a balancing of the karmic scales. These two notions, love and service, are one and the same, both equally leading to the same divine outcome: authentic connection. Our societal failure in grasping this most essential truth is why I believe we are failing so miserably at loving our neighbor.

Trust is the best proof that love exists some sage once said. We all know that in order to build trust, a track-record of positive *actions* must be presented over the course of time. If this is so, then our ability to know love must be tied to our *actions* towards ourselves, but more importantly our actions towards our brothers and sisters, and those we expend towards our natural world in which we are very much a part of. Talk is cheap. Cheap talk is a sickness, a projection of unhealed trauma from those that have been overfed the gospel of Bullshit, Inc.

David Dieda, the author of *The Way of the Superior Man*, asserts a hard-hitting truth that goes something like this: the degree to which we live aligned with our life purpose in service to others, our world, is the same degree to which we are able to love our chosen intimate partner or partners. I suspect this notion is a pinnacle understanding of supreme importance for the brave seeker of this love beyond words, an impartial and foundational law of love.

But how did I miss this? Why did it take so long to come across this teaching? This simple concept, one that was missed by me for so long, will likely fly over many people's heads, completely missing this hard truth. The values of the society in which I was raised didn't promote genuine service and giving to others as a means to actualizing love. Stripped of all our cultural bias and societal programming, we are merely humans inhabiting this planet together. No one is given an official guidebook on how to make sense of the existential plight we all must face. And it is in doing for others that we embody the truth of why we are here on this physical plane: to love.

So many of us lack clarity, hate our jobs, and anxiously sleepwalk through life, oblivious to just how beautiful the human experience can be. I can't tell you how many people I have come across that shamefully admit they know not their own "what and whys," their reason for being here, their soul's calling. This shines light on one of the core questions I sought to solve while traveling with a backpack for nearly two years: why are people so apathetic? We live in this incredibly abundant world with blessings everywhere and yet so many have checked out, have given up their fight.

You are *Worth the Fight!* And if this is foreign, possibly alien, might it be time to try this service thing out for yourself?

Everyone is talking about love, but so few actually love their neighbor. Why is this so? How is this our reality—that we boast and blow empty words while the masses around us struggle? Why is this okay? Have we have lost our way as a people? "Shut the fuck up and love thy neighbor!" says my hero Jamie Wheal.

During my healing journey, I had to challenge my definition of what it meant to be a man. The previous definition I adhered to nearly killed me, so I set out on travels to figure out for myself what was real. In doing so, I subjected myself to risk in order to heal, in order to satisfy my evolutionary drives and my deep desire for a proper initiation into manhood. The society that raised me failed to give me this essential of rite of passage; I had to go out and find what satiated my deepest yearnings. It was in this quest that I found that in order to have true love, we must *act*. For the attainment of this rare phenomenon we must serve our fellow man and woman, those in our circles of influence—no exceptions. Yes, this is a call-out.

We all can do better. I can do better.

This talk about service may only make sense to those who have an unencumbered heart. It would have flown over my head years back. Trauma breeds entitlement. This entitlement I have found works in two ways: 1) It creates victimhood, those that wallow in the past, excusing themselves from participating and being an active co-creator. They can't be present and engaged because of accepting their past hurts, prematurely, under a faulty guise of the healing that is possible. They can only be present to the extent that their unhealed trauma allows. An example is the homeless man shaking the cup mired in a haze of darkness so thick, he is listlessly unable to relate or participate in the collective good or someone who spends most of their days in front of the TV mired in inaction with a million clever excuses. 2) There are those who lead with their hurts, buffered by past trauma and the coping mechanisms that were developed to protect the unhealed pain, but this "protection" also cuts off the ability to authentically connect, leading to an unquenchable need for more consumption—drugs, material, sex, alcohol, power—never feeling contented, completely duped into living a life defined by a definition of success crafted to keep one running on the hamster wheel of life. Prime example: the "Wolf on Wall Street" who has it all on the outside, but knows so little peace of mind in the midst of material abundance.

Like I said in this book's introduction, I have really done nothing in my life with the exception of attaining a level of personal freedom and purpose that is quite uncommon for our world. Now I find myself rooted in my truth, in a state of rarefied air, to truly know my "what and why" for getting out of bed in the morning. Each day, I kick the covers off because I *get* the opportunity to live a life of service to something bigger than myself. I suspect that this is a result of accepting the uncertain nature and mystery of the human experience. Perhaps, this allows me to humbly embrace the infinite possibilities that lie around the bend, knowing that whatever tomorrow holds will be just perfect as it is— We live. We love. We lose. We die: LIFE. Below are some notions that worked for me and might be helpful for those seeking to find their calling, or greater life purpose.

If you are stuck and seeking that which you came for on this physical plane, I have to let you know that you are much closer to that realization than you might ever give yourself credit for. The fact that you are looking puts you on the path, ahead of many who would have put this book down by now. Everything that has delivered you to this juncture in your life is a lesson, preparing you for this very moment. There is no exception to this truth. If you are stuck and stymied, your past experiences do indeed serve you graciously, especially those tough times. They are hidden assets begging to be viewed as adversarial growth. This orientation narrows the field of infinite possibilities by eliminating possibilities that don't serve your happiness.

The author of *Tribes* (and many other NYT bestsellers), Seth Godin, challenges people to be "Meaningful Specifics" as opposed to "Wandering Generalities." When we are presented with the ocean of infinite possibility, eliminating options can be advantageous and make the infinite seem far less daunting. Everything, all experiences, have led you to this point in time. Everything has served for your personal growth and evolution. In every moment, we have the power of choice to look at the world in this manner. To be a student of life, we must embrace the lessons—*all* lessons— that come our way.

When broaching the essential topics of service and love, and finding your calling, there are three notions that stand out above the rest: vulnerability, open sharing, and defining what "success" means to you in relation to your life values and objectives.

Vulnerability

Brené Brown shares the gospel of the paradoxical power of vulnerability, teaching us, "Vulnerability is the birthplace of innovation, creativity and change," and I would take this even further. If this is true, why is this so hard for us, especially for men, to embrace? We would rather die than be vulnerable, than face our shit and admit how we really feel, especially in the presence of a strong female rooted in her truth. But why is this so? Could it be the patriarchal faux definition of what it means to be a man? We have been overfed a script that is inhumane and makes attaining what we desire the most impossible for too many. Terrence Real, the author of *I Don't Want To Talk About It*, argues that the masculine code is intrinsically destructive and I agree. This "code" doesn't allow for intimacy. This faulty script that scorns vulnerability keeps many from the very thing we want and desire the most: connection. Often we ignore this reality; the hazy stench of Bullshit, Inc., keeps us from seeing this clearly. But since a disproportionate amount of men are suffering from sexual shame, our hands are forced: either be vulnerable with your intimate partner or be cut off. When bypassing this essential step to intimacy, the connection we do have only serves to temporarily satiate egoistic desire, leaving the heart and soul empty, with a hunger which inevitably causes even greater problems.

We are cut off from true connection because we struggle to be vulnerable. Those we are trying to connect with can't trust us. And why would they? We don't have the courage to admit what we really feel, our truest motives, objectives, and desires. They won't open their hearts because our hearts are closed. Mirror neurons have been proven to exist— we are wired to have empathy and match the emotions of others. When we are real with others, they are real with us.

But how do we be "real" with others when we can't be real with ourselves? Like everything else, vulnerability is a practice. It's a process, a commitment to being better that starts with "I need help." I thought I would die with my deep, dark secret before ever admitting my truth, what happened, unburdening my heart of carrying this childhood trauma and immense pain by myself. The reward from being vulnerable has been infinite; practicing vulnerability has given me my life back.

We have to consciously make time for this by looking within, and, by doing so, examining what we really feel. For me, this has been a grave challenge, but its rewards are unmeasurable. A life without vulnerability is a life that isn't worth living. That is why our suicide numbers are off the charts. This lifeline is discouraged by the patriarchal code that defines manhood by repressing our feelings, discouraging us from asking for help or leaning on our loved ones in times of need.

Terrence Real says, "Authentic connection to self and others is the cure for what ails us." And, unfortunately, or fortunately (depends on how you look at it), the only way to access our authenticity is in stillness. This is the only way that we can distinguish whether what we experience is from our hearts or from the programming impressed upon us from external influences that aren't in the business of serving our well-being: yes, you guessed it, Bullshit, Inc. We should ask ourselves: why would the patriarch code subvert authentic connection? Those with broken hearts have broken spirits. People with broken spirits are much easier to manipulate and control. Be vulnerable and rise.

Open Sharing

Is there a more important notion than "open sharing" in a world largely defined by fear, pain, and discord? Is there anything more crucial to our world than loving loud and proud out in the open? Love is truth, and truth is love. You can't have one without the other. It's another one of those universal laws. Our global family is more connected than ever before; it is this interconnectedness, like a mycelium web, that gives me great hope and you the reader a tremendous opportunity. This intricate webbing has us able to transfer information in almost unimaginable ways. And since light is infinitely more powerful than dark, hearts will be inspired more readily when actionable truth is shared in our exponential social media world. A single post can hit the heart of millions of people; positively influencing others, spreading love like a wildfire.

Martin Luther King, JR. once said "Our lives began to end the day we become silent on things that matter." It is never too late to speak up and stand. It is never too late to say those words on your heart. On my journey, some of the most profound moments have come when pressing "send." Important blog posts or Facebook updates, putting myself out there in our judgmental, keeping-up-with-the-Joneses world. Often, my heart beat out of my chest as I pressed send, but there remained a conviction to lean into my fears and stand, knowing that my actions are closely watched by those I wish to serve.

Coming out of my psychedelic closet was a deeply profound and freeing experience. Sharing is caring. Your voice matters infinitely more than you might ever realize. Our democratic system is reliant on your honest expression— on all of our honest expressions. Democracies fail when a disproportionate amount of us eat our words. Gulp. Embrace your responsibility to find your gift and share it while you can. Tomorrow isn't promised. Legendary social media guru Gary V., a holy man disguised as a leading marketer, implores us all to "Do the work! Everyone wants to be successful, but no one wants to do the work." This is a hard truth from a man who leads by example, encouraging his following to be humble and of service. Once you find your gift, share it with the world. And yes, do the work! We need you, dear one.

Defining Success, Our Values

Our values drive our behavior. When we shift from the victim mentality to one of empowerment, the basis from which we operate is often called into question. When we struggle, it is because of poor values that don't serve our objectives and life goals. During the transformational process, one must slowly and patiently be mindful of crafting agreeable values that can serve as a measuring stick of your day-to-day habits. This can be a lengthy process that demands patience and a willingness to stick it out.

Are there any words truer than Tony Robbins' words? "Success without fulfillment is the ultimate failure." A power quote from a powerful man who has the designation of being the most esteemed life-coach on Earth. What makes this notion so powerful is it demands a sort of personal responsibility. If you're not happy or fulfilled, then do something about it. It is often the doing that can trip us up. It takes risk, effort, and sometimes rejection to keep moving forward. These outcomes demand a healthy and resilient nervous system. As one starts to incorporate some of the healing modalities outlined in this book, a stronger nervous system will be the result of a foundational daily practice.

As we talked about in chapter 8, we know that self-awareness can be cultivated with the practice of meditation. In time, we can see ourselves and our errors in a more objective light, and the lens in which we see our own reality changes. This can be of great importance in a world where politeness trumps honesty. Many of us are lost at sea to figure this all out on our own. Often, even the people we depend on won't speak up and tell us what we need to hear. Instead of belaboring this truth, we can work to craft a spirit of self-reliance.

Leadership expert Peter Drucker once said, "Tell me what you value and I might believe you. But show me your calendar and your bank statement, and I'll show you what you really value." It is only in our actions that truth resides. In what direction do we channel our energies? Time and money are two metrics that objectively tell our personal story. They don't lie. Having self-awareness and the ability to rely on oneself are cornerstone notions when crafting sustainable values. Let's pause, and close our eyes and take 3 long conscious breaths before asking: Would your calendar and bank statements prove you to be part of the solution or the problem?

13

LOVE OF THE GAME

"The market for something to believe in is infinite"

— SETH GODIN

lmost immediately after jumping on board with VET, I made the visit to Ryan at his home in Denver, Colorado. A time to meet in person, to break bread and strategize about our forthcoming work; our efforts to create awareness for the veteran plight and raise money to sponsor low-income U.S. veterans at the end of life's road. Ryan is a really impressive man, a single dad with two small boys, Trent and Tanner. I had much to learn from this man's path. He arrived at similar viewpoints about our world's mental health, but his way couldn't have been more different than mine.

Ryan was from a completely different world, a military brat, a third-generation serviceman—his grandfather was a Marine and his father serves in the Air Force. We were an odd couple from the start, but clearly we had a few important things in common: our love for our country; our willingness to do the right thing for our veterans; our understanding of these transformational healing medicines; and our knowledge of what this understanding could potentially mean for not only our veterans but also for the masses of the American populace who are stymied by depression, PTSD, anxiety, and addiction.

Ryan, a true patriot, bleeds red, white, and blue. I never met anyone like him on many accounts. He had southern roots and has a modern cowboy vibe to him. He is immensely proud of his service time in the Marine Infantry 0311—it was eye opening, and very foreign, to be around this masculine soldier energy. Again, to that point in my life, I hadn't known many who served our country, and in all honesty, I didn't give that outlook much thought.

Ryan wore his Wrangler jeans with a big belt buckle that screamed "AMERICA!" displaying an almost noisy sense of pride. He was loud and made howls and other bizarre noises and yelps—"Marine noises" I'd later call them, a byproduct of his military service. Ryan, big and burley, possessed zero shame for who and what he was.

I had found myself right in the middle of another fascinating social experiment: We were crafting a mastermind group that's sole purpose would be to bring forth healing for our veterans struggling with PTSD and mental health.

During that initial meeting in Colorado, we broke the ice by tossing around the football in the backyard, the beautiful snow-capped mountains in the distance of his small, ranch-style house. That time was for sniffing each other out, swapping our experiences with ayahuasca and what we saw for our world, the surely challenging times ahead. Talking shop. We bonded and found synergy quickly by making meals together, pondering heavy notions, almost immediately finding ourselves in productive, coffee-inspired conversations about the work that lay ahead. Both of us were in clear need of a trusted accountability partner on our pathless path, one that could help rev up the motor when lacking the fire and motivation to move forward, neither of us naive to the work that needed to be done.

Ryan's healing journey began when he walked in on Sergeant Leon, blue in the face. Dead. Hanging from a rope in the military barracks space they shared together. Imagine that. Leon, was a close friend of Ryan, and this traumatic moment would forever change Ryan's trajectory, setting him in motion on an almost unbelievable journey. From that point on, he started to question what was going on; connecting the dots: "Why are so many U.S. veterans and active military killing themselves? What is it?" Powerful questions in earnest fashion like those Ryan was asking have a way of setting in motion a strong physical counterpart.

For the next many years, Ryan committed to changing the way our nation and world looks at reintegrating war veterans back into society, post service. Ryan and his organization worked with our nation's most vulnerable, treatment-resistant U.S. veterans who have been unresponsive to standard care from the Veterans Administration (VA). Each and every veteran that had been through the VET program had been unresponsive to a minimum of six months of talk and pill therapy. Effectively, the VA and Western medicine could no longer offer them hope. To take this bold stance and hold the line out of the principle of doing what was right was inspiring for me. This made Ryan special, exactly the kind of man I wanted to go to battle with. Although a giant, Ryan had a soft side and a heart of gold.

Our values were congruent, our deepest motives for this mission's work aligned: peace.

"Veterans are the light at the tip of the candle, illuminating the way for the whole nation. If veterans can achieve awareness, transformation, understanding and peace, they can share with the rest of society the realities of war. And they can teach us how to make peace with ourselves and each other, so we never have to use violence to resolve conflicts again."

The above is an excerpt from Buddhist monk Thich Nhat Hanh's "True Love," an eloquent peaceful message summarizing VET's mission of healing our veterans in need, healing a part of our collective psyche that knows experientially the greatest darkness of the human condition. They know pain, carnage, despair, death, and the horrors of war; realities that the civilian world is largely cut off from. And it is in the reforming of the hearts and minds of our struggling warriors that we collectively can find our way through this darkness.

VET was where I planted my flag in the ground with unwavering conviction. I volunteered to work in the trenches to help clean up a massive suicide problem that appears to be an inconvenience for our bureaucratic Federal government and the American people at large. We all know that veteran suicide is total bullshit and is flat-out wrong; our troops go and serve and fight in foreign wars, then come home and we mostly pretend that this suicide epidemic isn't happening. Like a game of "hot potato," no one wants to hold this issue. I'll hold for now. Veteran suicide is messy and there are some highly charged taboo notions that surround this national tragedy: the Church that abuses our children; Big Pharma, the industry that provides pharmaceuticals that often have a skull and crossbones in their warning; and, yes, the Industrial Military Complex, or, more precisely, the true cost of war.

And to think, from 2004 to 2011, when the U.S. veteran suicide tragedy exploded, the Department of Defense increased its budget on pharmaceuticals 700%. (Statistics from *The Body Keeps the Score* by Bessel Van Der Kolk, MD) There is no proof that Big Pharma is to blame with the veteran suicide tragedy, but there is certainly a warranted and healthy air of suspicion that we should all impart as a result of the health crisis and blazing fire that is consuming our country as you read these words.

Many veterans are numbed down and dumbed down by a cocktail of pharmaceuticals that only serve the corporate balance sheet and line the pockets of the fat cats while there are natural medicines that work abound. Big Pharma, drug dealers in lab coats—above the law—wreak havoc on our nation with senseless greed. While writing this book, our U.S. opioid epidemic is blazing out of control, our country's collective psyche is on fire. We have nearly 6,000 drug overdoses per month! In 2017, there were a total of 70,000 overdoses—ughh! And it appears as though none of the corporate executives, those who set this fire, will face jail time for their immoral and unethical practices of peddling these highly addictive, and highly toxic, painkillers like candy.

Further reports, like this federal oversight report, make you question further this suicide tragedy and epidemic (https://www.cbsnews.com/news/feds-say-va-failed-to-spend-millions-allocated-for-suicide-prevention/). The VA only used $57,000 of $6.2 million that was allocated toward addressing veteran suicide. Actions speak volumes and are the best reflection of priorities. If our government is too bureaucratic or just doesn't care enough to do what is right, then we must step up as a people and do this grassroots by rallying around our veterans in need.

Vet Inaugural Real Talk

Just over the glass double doors, behind our audience, hung a fancy wood-framed portrait of Abe Lincoln, my hero, my most revered U.S. president. I thought to myself, *Abe would be proud of this work. He would be on board with this mission of hope and healing. This work, in many ways, is no different than that which he died for. Liberty for the people.* The liberty I speak of is different. We aren't freeing a people that are physically imposed upon. We are advocating for those who have no voice and little representation. For those who are imprisoned by war trauma. At its core, our mission is about freeing a marginalized grouping of people that have repressed cognitive and spiritual liberties, an inability to ask for the help, to be vulnerable to admit they are hurting. A massive group is confused, sick, scared, and in pain. Our U.S.

veterans have been left behind by our government and by our too-busy-to-care American people at large. We all have blood on our hands with this one; none of us get off scot-free. Without the proper means to heal them, the nearly 1.5 million (According to 2016 VA records) U.S. veterans who needlessly struggle with PTSD, depression and other mental health challenges are stymied by the faulty narrative.

Six months after originally coming across this powerful mission of hope and healing, that time where I was rolling around on the floor in Grass Valley, denying this impulse, my new colleague, my brother-in-arms Ryan LeCompte, with three other veterans, Cam, Dan, and Chris, would be on a big stage presenting our provocative and controversial message of hope and healing to the world. There was no path; this hadn't been done, or, at least, not like this. Every step demanded care and thought. We battled fear, paranoia, and limiting beliefs in the name of doing what is right for those who have fought and served, for those who are falling victim to our mostly insane way of approaching mental health.

We delivered our message and program that night. We shared our truth with no apologies. Effectively, the VET Inaugural Real Talk (https://youtu.be/QM_ILJ3jB-o) would serve as an SOS for our struggling U.S. veterans, an SOS for the civilian population that also struggles immensely with mental health. That night we bridged two worlds—the civilian and veteran worlds—that couldn't be further apart, coming together in the spirit of harmony to talk about solutions.

I never thought of myself as patriotic until that chilly Chicago fall night in October standing in front of my circle of influence, friends, and family—standing in front of the world delivering our message of hope. Our big night, the VET Inaugural Real Talk was hosted on October 18, 2017. Two days after my 38th birthday and three years since I sold my former business, setting in motion my freedom and eventual path less traveled. While immersed in the busy business world, I had set a goal to be a millionaire by this day. That goal was sadly an ignorant plea for more money and faux-status, completely void of purpose and meaning and anything that would remotely benefit others, a reflection of my poor values and pain in my heart. Of course this goal didn't sustain, being poorly aligned with my soul's calling. I heeded the warnings of sages imploring me to not make money my God.

This book is evidence my soul is not for sale. I left the money on the table and took the gamble on love. I took the gamble on truth, willing to play the long game, knowing that the money will come in time. If I played my part first, honored my truth first, and fully committed to service, money would never be an issue.

That night at the Union League Club of Chicago, at a swanky social club that I belonged to years earlier I shared the stage with real American heroes: three U.S. Marines and an Army Ranger openly shared their plight and how the VET program has helped them heal from war trauma. Standing up in front of many of my friends and family, and those who had showed up to support Team VET's efforts in service to our veterans in need, I indeed felt like a millionaire. It was deeply humbling and my greatest honor to date being part of something that matters, something bigger than myself.

Our veterans shared their struggles, service time, wins, losses, and the healing effects of the ayahuasca suicide intervention. They shed light to a vitally important part of life, realities as to the true cost of war, shielded from the civilian world. We enjoy our freedom, but are largely unaware of what underlies this freedom: the blood, the deception, the pain, the carnage, and heartache for families who will never get their loved ones back. This was "Shared public meaning" in action, a term discussed in Sebastian Junger's *Tribe*, the foremost expert on war and PTSD, homecoming and belonging, our collective peril that is result of a massive chasm between the civilian and veteran populations of our great country. Junger posits that the U.S. veteran suicide tragedy is more a result of the disconnected American people who are unable to welcome back our veterans; we have all created an alienated, isolated, and cold world that is not conducive for reintegration. Further, with a disproportionate amount of veterans having been subjected to sexual abuse in their youth, often times they never had resiliency skills before they enlisted in the service. So, naturally, they return to a world they never had figured out to begin with, void of a tribe and the community they experienced in war.

For Dan, Ryan, Chris, and Cam, this special night would be a deeply cathartic part of their healing process, an important time where these warriors could share their truth, putting words into action for the betterment of all those who were present. In an effort to best articulate the events that transpired that evening, I referenced the dictionary definition of "cathartic" to validate my choice of words and found:

Adjective, 1 providing psychological relief through the open expression of strong emotions; causing catharsis: *crying is a cathartic release.* 2 *Medicine* (chiefly of a drug) purgative.

Noun, 3 *Medicine* a purgative drug. From Greek *kathartikos*, from *katharsis* '**cleansing**' (see catharsis)

The VET Inaugural Real Talk was a ceremony for all of the parties involved. With shared public meaning of war, our veterans could heal and make better sense of their sacrifice. That night, our veterans were "living the medicine;" they were purging words and emotions that are all of ours to bear.

Commonalities of our VET Real Talk and an ayahuasca healing ceremony were blatantly on display. Instead of releasing and purging the healing medicine, we were all sharing openly and releasing pent-up thoughts and emotional energy to an audience of caring difference-makers.

Our veterans and the many millions who suffer from war trauma, PTSD, depression, and TBI, just want to be heard. They want their sacrifices and experiences to have meant something, to have been *worth the fight.* Worth the trials and tribulation.

In an anticlimactic manner, we delivered this important message of hope, and that was that. No big celebration, since this was the first of many important steps that lay ahead.

My dear friend Lorena from Costa Rica was in Chicago volunteering support. "Matt, why aren't you excited?" she asked in her typical jubilant and cheery spirit.

"I got nothing left," I said with a coy smile, knowing that we did it. I had given everything I could to this work and evening—many months of heart and soul. Paradoxically, the joy in this labor of love is now experienced every day, in every moment. I am fully aware of the transient nature of the human experience. Tomorrow isn't promised—live life each day to its fullest!

That night we set in motion something special. Where it will lead, no one knows.

Each day that I become more and more rooted on this path, I believe more and more in what is possible. I believe in our ability as a collective to turn this ship around, to find a way to live in harmony with our brothers and sisters while respecting and honoring the natural world in which we came from and are part of. To embrace diversity and bring forth a global community that is committed to solving problems by working together.

The day after our VET Inaugural Real Talk, I drove Ryan and Chris to the airport and posed a relevant notion. "Men, we did a great job last night. It was raw and it was real. We hit the heart. Thank you for playing a special part!" Ryan was in the passenger seat and Chris, a Purple Heart recipient with no legs, was in the backseat peering forth with interest. "Everyone left our presentation thinking, consciously or not, someone is fucking lying. Either these guys are full of shit, or we have been lied to by the powers that be." Ryan and Chris were in agreement while listening to my over-caffeinated, enthusiastic recap of our special night, both smiling at the thought, embodying that proud moment. The windows were down on my Jeep; it was a beautiful October day. All of this was heavy and moving. Gratitude filled my heart and emanated throughout my being. *It is nice to be home. I made it back. I can't fucking believe I made it back.* I pondered life, my return to my people with tears swelling in my eyes.

14

COMING OF AGE

"Why not go out on a limb? That's where the fruit is."

— MARK TWAIN

At a Chicago dinner with former colleagues during the middle of my travel journey (summer 2016), I made the fervent declaration to start writing this book. This wasn't a loud and boisterous announcement to the world, but a quiet understanding that I had an obligation to share everything as soon as possible. From this moment, the heat was on!

Drinks were ordered. We indulged in a bottle of nice red wine—my favorite and most redeeming alcoholic beverage, my medicine of old that remained a fixture, but in far more moderate a role. We toasted to old times and my safe return home. It didn't take long for my old colleague and business partner Gary to ask, "Now what is up with all this ayahuasca talk?" This was a typical response to my open sharing about my spiritual journeys.

"It is a powerful healing medicine like nothing else I have ever experienced." I was prepared to share more of my experiences to satisfy his inquiry.

As if Gary was uncomfortable and had heard enough he cut me off with a grin as if he had all the answers. "It's like a Coors Lite buzz, huh?"

I watched him fish for a smile or a laugh. I didn't know what else to do. There was a long, expressionless and rather uncomfortable pause. Then the first course came. We wouldn't broach the subject of ayahuasca or psychedelics for the rest of the night. Any further words on this subject were going to fall on uninterested and/or deaf ears—so, I just enjoyed the Italian wine, Chianti I think, and the "to die for" truffle pasta, so tasty! Food is best consumed when in a harmonious state of mind. Indigestion is an unsavory result when tension joins the dinner table—I learned that a long time ago when unhealthy and overweight with low energy levels. So, I let it go. I was just grateful to see my friends and this special dinner would reinforce my original reasons for leaving and traveling.

It was an eerie interaction over dinner. Nothing had changed while I was away. I was greeted with the same gossipy expressions, the same low vibrational bad jokes, and at one point my former colleagues both admitted this with a sense of defensive defeatism, as if they were jealous and couldn't comprehend my path. "This is just the way it is!" This sentiment was shared with agreeing nods and support. Their expressions said more: "You work and pay bills. Death and taxes. ...What else?"

Reflecting after the fact, it was clear they had it all figured out. Their cups were full to the brim with preconceived notions, leaving no room for anything else to enter. It wasn't a big deal. We enjoyed the most decadent of meals. It was nice to enjoy this comfort food in my old stomping grounds; I missed many parts of Chicago and Gilt Bar had been at the top of the list.

That night, we talked about what we used to talk about. Or, better stated, they talked about what we used to talk about: sex, money, and work. The old clients who were still wreaking havoc and drama with odd and needy requests. For most of the dinner, I listened patiently, just observing. The banter of old, to have this time, was nostalgic, leaving me with a deep knowing that I was on my way, moving along on my path. For much of the night, I just listened and patiently observed. I love these guys. We don't have anything in common anymore, but I still love them, and am grateful for the positive mark they have left on my life.

At dinner, I got a larger multidimensional view of my journey and what it was that I was actually doing. To see the lives of those that I previously spent the majority of my time with largely unchanged invited many questions. What is it that holds them in place? Are they happy? Is it possible that they are on a growth path that I can't see?

At that time, I still felt a lot of judgment when meeting up with friends and family, but was prepared to keep marching in the direction of my dreams. I knew this judgment was all in my head, and if it wasn't, who fucking cares what others think? I am exercising my freedoms and living my life on my own terms, I reminded myself almost as a mantra or affirmation. I am in the arena of life. I am doing my best.

That night I walked away from that scrumptious dinner overfed with a knowing that these words would make their way into a book someway and somehow. *Coors Lite? And Ayahuasca?* I smiled with an air of disbelief that two more opposing notions could be compared. The two experiences couldn't be more different. Thankfully, I practice letting go and fiercely believe in personal liberty. Everyone has the right to thinking that which they will no matter how obtuse and ignorant their beliefs might be. Those are the tenants that make our nation great and this human experience so exciting. The year earlier I realized the flaw in proselytizing and how much discomfort can come from the need to be right. Nothing truly matters; let go and move on.

After our hugs and kind words and promises about keeping in touch, and the intention of having this dinner gathering again, I pondered further what had just transpired. I was dumbfounded and curious as to why my words and healing experience appeared to be so threatening to others. *Why did it feel so taboo for me to share my experiences?* Even with old friends who really know me and trust me. *What was it they were scared of?*

Something about that night stood out like a sore thumb. What exactly it was wouldn't be clear until sometime later, but I eventually realized it was their speech. It was all fear-based and mostly negative; low vibrational words oozing lack, void of vibrancy, color, and life.

Our reality is a construct of our perceived limitations: this is the best and most practical definition of reality I've ever come across. I came across that definition in *What the Bleep Do We Know*, a groundbreaking book/documentary exploring consciousness and the power of our thoughts. This all-star cast of thought leaders and scientists break down how our thinking affects our lives, investigating once-taboo topics like consciousness: Our ability to think about our thinking.

How do we define our limitations? We define them with our thoughts, our words and the belief systems that we choose to accept. Our actions are mere projections of our thoughts; all of our outer world is just a reflection of what is within.

The sacred plant medicine ayahuasca showed me my truth, stripped of cultural bias and cultural agenda. In an experiential manner, I saw the social adaptations of our current medicine paradigm, and just how maligned these adaptations are with our inherent truth and evolutionary drivers. To see with my own eyes and to feel everything intuitively was beyond words, awakening senses that had been numbed and dormant for a near lifetime. The trauma in my heart made this realization nearly impossible to see. That is why I picked up a backpack and left. When we are fearful of looking within, fearful of being real with where we are at, we are a product of our limiting boundaries and are locked in by our external circumstances. We aren't our pasts, we aren't our emotions, but when we are afraid to confront our past and emotions, we become imprisoned by that which we hide from. My personal healing journey has largely been a check and balance against the erroneous misguidance of my fellow man, and yes, Bullshit, Inc. In order to heal, I had to cut out the middleman, going straight to the source by way of the direct experience. An experience that needs no translation, an experience that illuminates the exact role you play in your own healing and reality. At every moment, we are co-creating with a higher power. Call it what you want! I call this higher power: source energy, god, love, truth, infinite intelligence.

Play It Right

As my travel journey came to an end, I was in limbo as to my next steps. After initially engaging VET and therefore now equipped with my calling, the big question was where to live. In an honest and heartfelt conversation, Ryan encouraged me to see more clearly the value of coming home, the value of not running from my problems but staring them right in the eye, addressing them head-on. The value of reengaging my circle of influence, my friends, my family, all who lived side-by-side with me for many years prior. "Matt, if you are scared of returning to Chicago, then that is probably exactly where you need to be," Ryan said once. There was no sugar-coating with Ryan; I respected his forwardness immensely. These words hit me hard. *He is right. I had been warned extensively about the pitfalls of spiritual bypassing*, I thought. *What kind of man would I be if I couldn't go back and immerse myself, face my relationships and my fears?* As quick as can be, a clear answer to that question appeared. A coward.

Returning to Chicago to live was never my plan, but almost immediately I saw the seed of incredible opportunity.

These are my people. The ones I love. The ones I want to help, to be there for. The ones who stood by me when I struggled in front of the world. I felt a duty to be loyal, to return the love with my now-healed and nearly whole heart.

After being home in Chicago for many months engaging my new labor of love with VET and writing the first chapters of this book, I began to miss Sarah. We had some flirty email exchanges that persisted for some time, trying to spark up another shot at romance. How could I not go for that? Well, that was my take on it. If you ask her, she will likely say it was an attempt at maintaining a friendship with someone she once cared deeply about. Either way, these things happen. What has lasted for me is the impression that she made on my heart and the magic that I know is available when two hearts freely express their fullest expressions. Remembering her fueled and inspired my work, reminding me to reach higher, reminding me that anything is possible.

Bronnie Ware, an Australian nurse who worked for many years with people on their death bed wrote a book: *The Top Five Regrets of the Dying.* Those regrets: I wish I had the courage to live a life true to myself, not the life others expected of me; I wish I hadn't worked so hard; I wish I'd had the courage to express my feelings, I wish I had stayed in touch with my friends; I wish that I had let myself be happier. When coming across her work, shortly after returning from my travels I had a profound moment of clarity with the knowing that I won't have any of those regrets once the grim reaper comes my way. I went for it and as I result I get to live the life of my dreams in service to something bigger than myself.

When I Grow Up

Since beginning this path, I have led fiercely with forgiveness. I could see no other way. My family didn't understand me and many of my choices and I couldn't blame them. It hurt, but I was expecting this and was prepared to not overreact and take the bait, being fully committed to holding loosely this line of expectation while standing in peace. I firmly believe that we owe nothing to our families but our truth, period. There is so much nonsense that we accept as familial and cultural norms. Much of this nonsense keeps our own dreams and aspirations at bay. All we owe our families is our truth.

I was sympathetic to the fact that I shook everything up by willingly subjecting my life to a game of 52-card pickup. Effectively, I had thrown a deck of my life's playing cards into a swirling fan on its highest setting. Those cards splayed aggressively into the lives of my friends and family and world; there could be no denying this. All of this was a part of the transformational process, cleaning up the mess I had created. Making right many of my wrongs. Starting anew, building and designing my new life on a solid foundation.

For my entire lifetime, my father gave love in direct proportion to how obedient I was to his beliefs and ideals. That was his brand of love, that is likely how he learned to love, probably being the measurement and metric instilled to him by his parents. How could I resist this notion and reality? I couldn't, so, yes, I led with forgiveness. We all do our best; always, all of us, no exceptions, everyone. But realizing this was easier than acting on it. For some time, this reality was excruciatingly painful and caused a sort of existential crisis. To think my tie to my "tribe" had so many requirements and conditions really fucking hurt. My whole lifetime I had to be someone else, what I thought others wanted me to be. I couldn't just be me.

For a short while, I was cold and resentful. This was a tough one to let go, as it brought up much discomfort and questions with unclear answers. In time I came to realize that this brand of conditional love with which I was raised kept me safe. The herd, my tribe, protected me from external threats I was ill-equipped to deal with in my adolescence. My journey has been about my transition from adolescence to manhood in a society that doesn't properly initiate its youth. That brand of love that kept me safe was now obsolete, and a possible hindrance, for the life that I envisioned living.

My father didn't know what to think. I didn't care. That was a form of judgmental love that no longer resonated with me. Again, I held the line—we were going to get through this as a family. Effectively, "agree to disagree" became the modus operandi. I took a personal challenge to focus all of my attention on things that we did appreciate and share together. We highlighted what was common and shared, not our now-obvious differences in how we looked at the world. With both my parents aging, time is short. I quickly saw that any hard line void of compassion and forgiveness was merely more of my unhealed trauma that may need addressing. All of this was a grave challenge, but it has been infinitely rewarding to be there for both my parents at this stage of their lives. I only share these intimate family details in hopes that my experience might serve as a roadmap for others maneuvering these complicated familial waters. My parents did their absolute best raising me. We aren't gifted with a universally reliable handbook on how to parent, how to live. This is the human experience.

I forgave my dad for being absent and aloof during my childhood. I forgave my dad for raising me in a "just because" household where asking questions was discouraged. I forgave the abuse that happened to me in his home under his roof, unknowingly on his watch. For the pain that I was subjected to because of his sometimes indifference to life. This was so unbelievably freeing to be able to forgive and to truly understand that we are all doing our best. Playing the blame game only perpetuates the original madness further; the blame game is the easy way, but nothing gets resolved and no healing can take place.

My mother could see that I was bursting with life and enthusiasm and was all about it. She has always wielded a more non-judgmental brand of love; unconditional love, giving love without identifying too much with the outcomes, is more instinctively maternal. My mother gave me immense space to just be me. To let me fall on my face. She never crowded me while I was mired deeply in self-abuse. She simply loved and supported me to the best of her ability. I am deeply grateful for this love which served as an anchor during my healing process and journey.

My mother was impressed enough with my own transformational growth that she decided to give ayahuasca a shot. Yes, that is right, at 71 years young my mom went two full rounds with The Mother! A detailed account of this extraordinary experience is on my blog. To summarize it, she probably won't subject herself to that crucible again, hours' worth of intense purging in what must have felt like a marathon healing session. But still, she claims years later to be more in touch with her intuition and at a better overall state of well-being. And happy to have tried her best. That night marked a special opportunity to heal her own trauma, as she struggled off and on her whole life with depression likely stemming from the early years of childhood development when her father, my grandfather, was physically abusive with his family. Both of my mother's parents were alcoholics. There were even a few instances where my mother had to call the police for fear the domestic abuse may turn deadly. Imagine the horrors of that? During that private ceremony in April 2017, under the guidance of Nicole, my mother and I burned much karma, letting go of baggage that had been carried far, far too long.

My brother Ben, who we met early on in this narrative, ended up getting married again and settling down in Switzerland with his new bride Vera. He has slowed down his pace a bit, having two more children: my niece Tina and nephew Oliver. I am grateful for his openness to my alternative path, the support and encouragement along the way to follow my dreams and aspirations.

At times, against my better judgment, I have found myself trying to persuade and change those around me. To influence in an active manner with words instead of a passive manner leading with action. We all know words aren't worth shit in our present times. It took me a long time to understand this, but it's not about words...it's all about actions! Right action is all that ever has influenced anything honest and true in our world. Theologian Albert Schweitzer once said, "In influencing other people, example is not the main thing, it is the only thing." Words are too heavily associated with hypocrisy. Action—being the example—is the only thing that hits the heart of another. People are cynical and have mostly lost their faith and belief in their fellow man and what is possible. We have been too compliant, conforming to the authoritarian power structures in place that have little regard for the individual spirit of man. We all have had enough of the scandal, lies, deception, and hypocrisy: an endless reality of people saying one thing and doing another, especially our political and religious leaders.

In the years to come, I believe there will be a day when actively trying to persuade someone to your belief system will be viewed as a form of mental illness. Yes, dogmatic preaching, out in the distant future, might be in the Diagnostic and Statistical Manual of Mental Disorders (DSM), the mental disorder guidebook published by the American Psychiatric Association (APA). We will see. Life.

15

WE ARE THE PEOPLE

"We are gods. Our tools make us gods. In symbiosis with our technology, our powers are expanding exponentially and so, too, our possibilities."

— JASON SILVA

I remember being so grateful to feel grace during the midnight mass Christmas Eve church services in my youth and early years in adulthood. What a special feeling it was for the nearly five minutes we would sing Silent Night? Sleep in heavenly peace.... My eyes would swell up with appreciation for all the blessings in my life; in a time when I couldn't feel, I actually felt *something*, overwhelmed with gratitude for that moment. This church service was always deeply moving for me: singing as a community, candles lit, everyone engaged and present to this beauty. I sensed that this was an important time for all the parishioners gathering during this holy time of observance. I looked forward to that five minutes, the inevitable tears I would cry, the relief and release I would feel—the grace. That same feeling of grace is now very much a part of my daily life; this grace is foundational to the life that I have designed for myself. And I don't need a congregation to access peace of mind and the creator within. I don't need a religious institution to connect with my truth. This grace I speak of is available to us all—it is everywhere, it is ubiquitous, it is our divine right and inheritance. This holds true for everyone, no matter the despair we may feel. No matter the erroneous story and flawed personal narrative we tell ourselves about what this human experience really is.

Traditionally, the inspiration received from religious institutions has been metered as a means to control the masses. Religion holds to a top-down hierarchical model that relies on subjugating its obedient followers with subversive and sneaky tactics: guilt, shame, sex abuse of our innocent and vulnerable children, the confusion that comes from a set of beliefs that condones, some might even say encourages, hypocrisy.

I first found flow while engaging psychedelic medicines because I wanted to heal my depression and settle my constantly ruminating mind-chatter. You know, those endless hellish feedback loops? I wanted to be healthy, happy, and strong. I wanted what was promised to me: life, liberty and pursuit of happiness. I wanted the love and intimacy my soul yearned for. I stumbled down the rabbit hole. After many years, I've climbed out with a message to let others know that it is safe to follow suit if proper precaution and attention is paid and adhered to.

I originally found flow with psychedelic medicines: ayahuasca and psilocybin. This flow I speak of has saved my life by curing my addictive thought patterns. Again, flow states are best defined as optimal states of consciousness where you feel your best and perform your best, where action and awareness merge, creating a perfect storm for productivity, creativity, and learning.

Now, I access the "flow state" to varying degrees in a myriad of ways: yoga, meditation, writing, sex, breathwork, running/weight-lifting, cacao/coffee, fasting, Bulletproof bio-hacks, juice cleansing, the list could go on and on. Humbly, patiently, quietly, I've designed my new life that is built around the state and the ecstatic bliss that comes from flow.

But the truth is: "How much do we really know about true happiness? Burning creativity? Unbridled ecstasy? As children we are taught not to play with fire, not how to play with fire. On the flow path, we are drawn forward by fire; by powerful hedonic instincts; by our deep need for autonomy, mastery and purpose deeply fulfilled; by dizzyingly feel-good neurochemistry; by a spectrum of joy beyond common ken; by the undeniable presence of our most authentic selves; by a cognitive imperative to make meaning of experience; by the search engine that is evolution and its need for innovation; and by the simplest of truths: life is long, and we're all scared and, in flow, at least for a little while, we're not." These are compelling and spirited words from Steven Kotler's *The Rise of Superman: Decoding the Science of Ultimate Human Performance*. It's true, we are just finding out what is possible. We are just scratching the surface in our understanding of the science behind flow, meditation and psychedelic medicines.

These ecstatic experiences can be akin to life x 10,000. If you have cracks in your foundation, you will get an honest and objective view of them; ayahuasca and other plant medicines are likened to drinking inspiration directly from a firehose. In this book, I've warned the aspirant of potential risks. In earnest, I humbly ask you to heed those warnings and remember your "what and why" for embarking on this intentional journey.

This amplified pressure will either forcefully formulate a plan to fix them, or one will see the value of falling through the cracks and starting over, leaping, surrendering to the uncertainty of life—the great mystery of human existence. I was fully broken down on February 13, 2016. A high-speed train derailed off the tracks and it was likely the most meaningful experience of my life. All this is likened to Andy Dufrain in *Shawshank Redemption* swimming through a quarter-mile of shit and piss to reach true freedom and liberation—a quarter-mile of hell for a near lifetime of heaven.

John Lilly said it best: "Cosmic love is absolutely ruthless and highly indifferent: it teaches its lessons whether you like/dislike them or not." That sounds a lot like karma actualized, an experiential glimpse of what is.

As I write these words, I question where the ayahuasca healing ritual in particular and psychedelic experiences in general fit into my life moving forward. It is good to question everything. In good conscience, I must share this with the reader. These disruptive agents of change have been such a big part of my life. They brought forth so much healing and growth opportunities to find purpose in service to our troubled times by living a life aligned with my values and my highest commitments. I have found the strongest connection in doing my work and being open and honest, vulnerable with my close relationships and intimate partners. As Alan Watts famously said, "When you get the message, hang up the phone!" Wise words that signify the importance of holding closely your original intentions for engaging these powerful medicines.

These experiences have taught me in every moment, we *all* have the freedom of choice to co-create with the higher power that lies within, with or without ayahuasca. She is merely a "guide" that helps us see what is always there, what we can't see for ourselves, a tool to be used judiciously.

There is a tremendous amount of responsibility bestowed upon those who come to this revelatory insight— to live the change; to channel this co-creative power for the betterment of our loved ones and our planet; to embody the inspiration received, ultimately sharing it with the world. To make it count! To give back.

"I care not a whit about a man's religion, unless his dog is better for it." Abe Lincoln quipped long before Kotler/Wheal later expanded upon this quote in the groundbreaking book *Stealing Fire*. "And this goes double for Ecstasis."

Ecstasis, a term coined by the Ancient Greeks, is used by Kotler/Wheal to embody the ecstatic technologies our modern world uses to find relief from emotional challenges and the human condition. It is defined as "standing outside of oneself" or "filled with inspiration"

For good measure: "I care not a whit about a man's religion, unless his dog is better for it. And this goes double for ecstasis."

This powerful quote is a faithful reminder that no one really cares about your "altered state" experiences unless the world is better for it. Fundamentally, boasting about your religious or ecstatic experiences is an egregious act sorely lacking humility and properly grounded perspective. Your inner child and unhealed trauma scream to the world, "Look at me! Look at me!" No one cares, unless your world and circle is better for it. *Go* and make a world better—then, boast and blow about whatever you want. Send me a note. It always warms my heart to hear when people are creating positive change in our world.

Help yourself and others, then broadcast the goodness, truth, and beauty—unapologetically and unabashedly—for the entire world to see: is this how we turn the tide?

We are at an impasse right now. That can't be denied. A juncture in time that is pivotal to the survival of our species. We now find ourselves in a time of confusion, pain, and much discord. Fear is winning the battle over hope and faith—on many levels, we are a broken and divided global family. Despite this stark reality, there is no time to waste wallowing away in negativity, as there are enormously abundant opportunities that are just under our nose. As with every challenging time we have ever faced as a people, there lie tremendous opportunities to be of service, to be part of the solution. Collective healing is needed more than ever before; we are just now starting to feel what has been ignored for too long. The truth is a motherfucker and the forthcoming grieving process might be messy. Progressive change always is, just like it is on an individual level. This stage in our collective evolution likely won't be denied much longer as the masses are hurting while the chasm grows wider and wider.

Is this why Tim Ferriss' mission is "Creating a benevolent army of super learners who test the impossibles"? Tim serves as a pace car and role model, graciously giving away all the secrets of how to create the most positive impact on our world by seeking to serve those "who are also willing to test the assumptions and have the uncomfortable conversations this country has been dodging." Tim is empowering super-learners to go out and change the world, leading by example and candidly sharing his own struggles with mental health.

We must find forgiveness for our past by letting go: Much of our foundational understandings are built on inaccurate falsehoods void of science. Science can help us see this and properly error-correct in no place more pressing than our failing mental health paradigm whose very foundation is flawed and maligned with our most basic human rights— life, liberty and the pursuit of happiness. This is where I will stand and won't budge, and you shouldn't either. Our collective has been severely handicapped by the deception and injustice of yesteryear. Despite our prior transgressions as a people, there is no time for anger, only forgiveness, healing, and right action—leading by example and being the change that you want to see in the world. Largely, we have been sold a bag of bad goods—a human experience that is void of that which is most meaningful and essential—the truth. This notion transcends left or right, white or black, woman or man, and is about the compromised soul of our species. But this now presents a timely juncture, an opportunity to wake up to our most inherent inner nature, by loving more deeply our brothers and sisters.

We have all these incredible tools! Altered states of mind give us the perspective to make changes necessary to cultivate altered traits, like compassion, kindness, empathy, and altruism—this notion gives our world much hope for a better tomorrow.

Do the work and traits will follow—trust in science. Again, we have learned more about the brain in the last 10 years than the prior 2,000 combined. And the technologies that support our science are exponential, meaning they are doubling every year: Moore's Law—Wow!

There are transformational shifts happening every day: we are wired to transform and undertake personal revolutions; altered states equate to altered traits, psychologists have known this for the past hundred years. These elevated states of mind are a disruptive technology that forces change, often challenging the status quo by mirroring what needs to be seen on an individual and collective level just the same.

Sacred Hearts Club

In the preceding pages we looked at the underlying issues: Bullshit, Inc. Against the advice of others, I have broached taboo topics like the Church's sex abuse, the Industrial Military Complex, and Big Pharma's role in our mental health crisis; the systems that don't properly serve the evolution of our people.

Are we a sick people because of our own collective ignorance? Our sicknesses: addiction, obesity, heart disease, cancer, depression, PTSD—the list goes on and on. Could our troubles with mental health be a result of our having a faulty societal code? I think so.

We are a bunch of sinners! We have been sinning as individuals and as a collective. To sin was originally defined as "missing the mark." So, we have been trying our best but missing the mark. What are we to do? Give up—stop trying? Absolutely not. Let's error-correct and get this work done. In finding more sustainable and loving practices that are agreeable with our nature and aren't compromised and corrupted by Bullshit, Inc., we can rebuild this all from the ground up.

An integral part of any solution is uniting our people by highlighting our shared humanity, our innermost desire to live happy, healthy, and strong lives, free from oppression and fear. We all have this in common; let us build around this shared humanity. I suspect that fiercely defending our spiritual and cognitive liberties by fostering a wave of flow, bringing forth creative solutions to expand our networked circles of influence to better serve our planet and those in need, might be a good place for us to start.

Alongside my healing journey and extensive work with our U.S. veterans overcoming trauma, the research signals that people that heal in this sort of "Ritualized Surrender" report increased feelings of well-being in their baseline reality, as well as increased feelings of compassion, creativity, and joy. This (www.youtube.com/watch?v=23iF9z9yVFA) video is Jason Silva's most exceptional and captures in 6 minutes the full essence of a mystical/peak experience. Silva's visual wonder is laced with his lyrical genius, reminding us of the practical benefits of these once misunderstood and demonized transformational experiences.

Acclaimed spiritual teacher Michael Singer, the author of *The Untethered Soul*, asserts: "God is ecstasy." That is a bold declaration! And perhaps that is why these ecstatic healing technologies and psychedelic medicines are so effective in healing trauma?

These healing medicines set in motion a healing process. Effectively, they wake up something within. The result: potentially a society of fearless do-gooders who live more aligned with brotherly love. In time, this movement may make honest all of our deceptive ills. I personally believe that spirituality and these medicines are big data for the mind, ancient healing tools for transformation, lovingly graced to a struggling people. If we are talking about exponential technologies, what does this mean? Bullshit, Inc. is in trouble, a fierce army of conscious do-gooders are coming to make honest the errors in our ways by changing the system from within.

Strategic technologies and practices are made available for those who wish to transform—psychedelics most definitely are not required. Movement, breath and sex are some of the most powerful ways to generate flow and to heal. And are not subject to the possibility that with one stroke of the pen, psychedelic research could be shut down and all this progress halted. This happened before, it could very well happen again. Always diversify!

Thankfully, there is no right or wrong way—dogma is out—our missteps of yesteryear no longer serve our evolution. Spiritual grandmaster and author of *Outwitting The Devil*, Napoleon Hill, said it best when observing this essential governing principle: "No matter what you call the first cause, operator or creator, there is just one plan, there is just one set of natural laws, and it is up to every individual to discover what those natural laws are and adjust themselves favorably to them."

Whatever you call that power doesn't matter. Who really cares?! What does matter is the obedience to that truth—does one listen to that still voice that lies within our hearts, in those moments of silence?

A life-saving realization gleaned on my travel journey is that we all must walk our own path in our own way. I would never suppose that I know what is right for a given individual. Further, anyone who does presuppose anything about what is best for another ought be scrutinized as to their intentions. In time, dogmatic over-identification will be seen for what it really is—a mental illness—that's right, an affliction of the mind with the underlying foundation of "I am right! You are wrong!" This insane and obsolete narrative underpins separation and threatens our existence and global family, but should be treated with compassion and forgiveness.

In the years to come the fundamentalists will die off, paving the way for a sort of "Newmanity," one where we properly know our stance in relation to our fellow man. Where abundance reigns and peace is possible. I am a dreamer, that is true. I don't dream of a Utopian world, but a world where we collectively rally, coming together and committing to the right action needed to right this ship. Dreamer or not, I know the power of exponentials and what that may mean. Can this safely happen without a similar backlash to the one in the '60s and '70s? I think so. This is a latent power that has truth on its side. It is a slow burn.

Who knows what the future holds? For all of us, the magic is in the day-to-day, in the *present moment*, whichever way you access it. Tomorrow, many of these words and notions may be obsolete; I may think differently about everything then. This is part of our constantly evolving and contradictory nature: I am a contradiction; that is, I am a human.

As humans, we are meaning-making machines. We have been blessed with imaginations; some think them our greatest gifts. Former GE executive Beth Comstock shares in her book *Imagine It Forward: Courage, Creativity, and the Power of Change* a detailed map about how to infiltrate large organizations from within. She knows a thing or two about bureaucratic maneuvering from her time atop large American corporations. Beth graciously shares innovative and enthusiastic ideas that can be applied across industries. Her progressive notion of the imagination gap really resonates: "get comfortable with not knowing, with living in the in-between of what was and what will be." How can we apply this to the lessons in *Worth the Fight*? Psychedelics supercharge your imagination, but in order to effectively channel this thought energy, we must have a worthy objective to direct toward or we'll just be people making shit up as we go, creating more confusion, disrupting the efforts of the people who are doing great, healing work with these still-in-question technologies and tools of transformation. In many respects, after a healing experience, one has to man this very same gap in their own lives; they are not yet what they see, but are no longer what they were.

Collective change is impossible without ruthless accountability at the individual level; relearning to trust ourselves by cultivating that which was lost and compromised during the wrong turns of yesteryear. We all must embrace the slow climb with patience and humility, manning the imagination gap in our lives with the knowing that we are well-equipped with the exponential tools that indeed make us divine: meditation, psychedelics, flow. In bravely doing so, we can create ripples of "beyond," love so powerful and positive effects unquantifiable, something so incredibly just that wants only good for all living beings, man and all other sentient beings just the same. This power, this intelligence that is beyond words, governs our natural world and every cell in our human bodies. Do your work, whatever that means to you, and I'll see you on the way up. Awakening to this truth may be the fuel that has been overlooked. The fuel that could be the impetus that shines the light on all the solutions that we can't see right now; the *abundance* that lies dormant begging to come out and play. Tread lightly—Let's do this!

COME TOGETHER

"We are so much stronger together!"

— WIM HOF

In the mega bestseller *Originals*, Adam Grant, explores in depth many "originals" that have moved our world by creating positive social change. Grant enlightens us that iconic filmmaker Francis Ford Coppola once noted, "The way to come to power is not always to merely challenge the establishment, but first make a place in it and then challenge and double cross the establishment." By slowly stalking the prey, this double-crossing will be a blinding punch of love, justice, and truth: a bright light of a compassionate forgiveness, effectively a check and balance for our errant ways, making right the mistakes and errors of our past, an awakening to all that is possible as a species when a tipping point of passionate, inspired lovers of life standing in truth is reached. Heal, get right, get fit for service, then start a not-for-profit or conscious business or go back to school or do your yoga teacher training—whatever calls you! The model: find a way to help others who are stuck in overcoming the very same challenges you have moved beyond—BE the model of change. In *From Shock to Awe*, inspired U.S. veteran Matt Kahl is just that. He implores his fellow servicemen and servicewomen to heal and get right, then, run for office in an effort to create positive change from within. Our veterans know war, carnage, and despair and can speak to the horrors so that hopefully, in time, we can finally see a planet at peace. Kahl's message of hope is powerful and what I believe to be a solution to all that ails our world. That's right, healing the hearts and minds of our struggling but resilient war veterans, those who have honor, integrity, and courage, trusting in them to do what is right. I would bet it all on psychedelic G.I. Joe as a viable solution to our challenging times, their leadership is unmatched and their vulnerable spirit will inspire the world around them. We have the strongest, most enviable democratic container and freedoms that invite this long-game approach. "You don't owe our nation anything, you owe it something." These wise words are from Miguel Chapero Junger (Sebastian Junger's dad). When you find that "something" you love to do, work will be like a ceremony, truly a labor of love with infinite rewards. Find a role on Team Faith and play that role, however large or small, with all your heart and soul. We need you!

Train. You are Neo and have access to tools that supercharge your creativity, learning, and productivity. Breath, movement, sex, and, yes, psychedelics and plant medicines surely help kickstart the healing and transformative process. Most importantly, know that you have the support of a growing brotherhood and sisterhood of humanity. Again, there are over a million conscious businesses worldwide that are doing "the work" within the system, playing their part in creating the better world we want for our children and generations to come. Those brave conscious warriors who are working tirelessly to make our world better often run circles around the fundamentalists whose hands are frozen and paralyzed by hypocrisy, leaving them listless and stuck in front of the TV, resistant to change, infected by a plague of inaction, gripping too tightly to a dying paradigm. Really, this is how change works and how it has always worked, although we tend to think we are special because it is us, and this is now. This has all been done before. People once thought the world was flat and the sun revolved around the Earth. This is progress.

We might be able to pull this off together if we can come together over what is shared. What is it that you and I share together?

A desire for peace? Perhaps a duty to do what is right by our veterans struggling with mental health? In coming together, to heal a damaged part of our collective psyche? Transmuting by redirecting a wrongly perceived negative into a national treasure positive?

"Veterans are the light at the tip of the candle, illuminating the way for the whole nation. If Veterans can achieve awareness, transformation, understanding and peace, they can share with the rest of society the realities of war. And they can teach us how to make peace with ourselves and each other, so we never have to use violence to resolve conflicts again."

This illuminating quote is shared a second time for good reason. From my vantage point, there is no shared humanity greater than the suffering of our U.S. veterans, who are checking out at more than 22 per day. Our nation's warriors are struggling needlessly with post-traumatic stress, depression, and traumatic brain injury when there are medicines that work. Many are sick, scared, confused, and in pain, stuck in endless loops of hellishly traumatic memories. They know darkness; therefore, they can know light. Our veterans, our protectors, our greatest hidden power.

If you agree with these words, and really want peace, to be a part of a grassroots movement to help right this wrong, please share this book with a friend or family member, someone who might be struggling. Consider engaging one of the not-for-profit organizations that *Worth the Fight* is supporting by donating *ALL* book proceeds to psychedelic research and the relief of adult survivors of child sex abuse, which, as we've come to find out, are sadly many of our war veterans in dire need of our love and support. You can make a difference—come together—in our shared humanity we are infinitely strong! We can bring positive change by cleaning up *our* messy mental health and, in doing so, rightly challenging and in time bringing to its knees, Bullshit, Inc.

Join the slow march toward a peaceful planet—bring on the Star Wars! BELIEVE.

Thank you for reading these words. They are all that I have to give.

ACKNOWLEDGMENTS

Thank you to my mother, Nancy Simpson, for the steadfast love and encouragement and for always believing in me. Thank you to all of my friends and confidants that have been listening to me test these very ideas: Bethann Olsavsky, Nick Fulton, Lisa Henderson, Heidi Hrastnik Berke, Robert Voloshin, and Kam Knight, I am ever grateful for the help in editing and initial feedback.

So much gratitude for friends and family that actively supported me through my personal transformational healing journey and with the writing of this book: John Gottschall, Steve Blentlinger, Caleb Rozina, Natalie Wright, Chris Huxtable, Colleen & Mike DelFava, Mandy Bojar, Lorena Santacruz, Julia Penn & Eugene Dumas, Brian Michalek, Patti Bielecka, Atticus, Josh Kaplan, Lola Wright, Dawn Applegate, Sara Rivera, Serena Keith, Todd Collins, Justin Walker, Molly Rose, Tony Lehnen, Hanna Morfogen, Shawn Dorgan, Ben Simpson, Vera Haene, Brian Cole & Emmie Cerow, Bob Simpson, John Moony, Nick & Dana Gunn, Bill & Betty Simpson. And the many, many others who have touched my life and heart—I am truly blessed and grateful.

Thank you to my veteran friends Ryan LeCompte, Kaine Marzola, Jimi Reed, Cam Dupre, Chris Fesmire, Dan Kasza and Juliana Mercer. Your warrior spirits have inspired me to find my own.

My coach, Carla Samson, thank you for holding incredible space that allowed me to do things my way. You are a superstar!

Nicole and Vismay, thank you for the incredible healing work you are doing at Florestral. I am truly blessed to have had the opportunity to cross paths in this cosmic journey. Thank you for the unconditional love you give our world.

Thank you to Alex Seymour, the "Psychedelic Marine" and first mover who many years back started this movement to heal our world's war veterans with psychedelic plant medicines.

Thank you to Steven Kotler for your inspiring work around flow. And for generously sharing your gifts via the Flow Genome Project: Flow for Writers Workshop.

Thank you to Chris Ryan, PhD, my hero, for helping to move forward the important conversation about sex.

Thank you to Ann Maynard and Rochelle Deans for your help with the editing process. This couldn't have happened without your assistance and attention to details. And for honest feedback that has helped me to grow as a writer.

Thank you to my book coach: Azul Terronez, AKA "the book whisperer" for keeping the book publishing logistics on track. For believing in this work and my message.

AFTERWARD

LOVE IS ALL I GOT!

I knew something bigger was at play a few months after returning home from my initial healing retreat in Costa Rica. I wrote about synchronicity earlier, the series of events that had me feeling called to heal with ayahuasca in spite of all the fearful conditioning and would-be obstacles: that date with Jess, my time at the pizza parlor with CK, and that fortuitous article about U.S. veterans overcoming PTSD and mental health challenges with psychedelics as medicine. All of those pale in comparison to this happenstance encounter.

For 86 days (I checked the Apple records) *before* my transformational healing experience in Central America, I awoke each morning to a love song: "Love Is All I Got," a catchy tune I adopted as my waking alarm clock. It was most certainly a groovy way to start the day, a testament of my earnest intentions to have more love in my life. "Love Is All I Got" was a pop hit by Sebastian's band, yes, the skinny, 20-day-coconut-water-fast, Sebastian from the UK I talked about in chapter 5. He was the front-man/lead singer of a band called the Crystal Fighters—I connected the dots months after my return home to Chicago from Florestral.

What were the chances that Sebastian would be my alarm clock? That the two of us, and a group of 30 other brave souls, would be going through this ayahuasca healing ritual together? What is the likelihood that I would partake in this powerful rite of passage and fiery transformation in a foreign land, side by side with Sebastian, engaging this sacred plant medicine for the first time, united by an unexplainable higher power and intelligence?

All of this has been strange; at times, hair-raising bizarre. And a great challenge to quantify. Thankfully, the more I meditate, the more I find these favorable chance happenings and the more I feel at peace with my interconnectedness with all that surrounds me. These events, these signs, lovingly reinforce my path by counterbalancing much of the lingering doubt I've needed to overcome to do this work.

Legendary Swiss psychiatrist and psychoanalyst Carl Jung first coined the term "synchronicity" and defined it as such: meaningful connections across time or space between an inter-psychic event and something that happened in the material world. Einstein called this phenomenon "spooky action at a distance."

These synchronicities have always felt like a loving hug from the Universe. Like little breadcrumbs reminding me that I am on my way—little boosts to keep me moving forward in the direction of my dreams.

I don't give much thought to these encounters anymore, having surrendered to the idea that there is indeed an infinite intelligence at work. Humbly I play my role in all this.

In *Worth the Fight*, I made bold assertions, like our global family coming together to finally see a peaceful planet in the next generation or two. While that is my hope and prayer, the reality is that we still have much work to do. While I am bullish on world peace, the reality exists that we are currently a fractured global family that has problems playing nice with each other. I'd be delusional to ignore our current plight. Our U.S. military has a budget that is greater than the next 25 countries combined. Wow! Surely in time, we will pare that back and focus more on our home turf. Lord knows we have enough pressing problems that need addressed as we wake up to many of the harsh realities I've discussed in the preceding pages.

In summer of 2018, I parted ways with Veterans for Entheogenic Therapy (VET), but in no way have I parted with this mission to eradicate veteran suicide. My work was done with VET; there was no longer anything I could provide in our efforts to push that boulder uphill after our fundraising efforts were stymied by a fearful climate and organizational challenges. With Michael Pollan's book *HOW TO CHANGE YOUR MIND* making such a big splash, having every 50-something white person in America rethinking psychedelics as viable medicines, we may get a second chance at this work, to do what is right for our U.S. veterans in dire need of healing modalities that work.

Waking Up the Giants

Since engaging this work with our veterans, serving as their self-appointed civilian ambassador, I often wondered: *what kind of people are we to turn our backs on our veterans in need?* I think we've been a scared and misinformed people that haven't had full access to all the pertinent details needed to make more transparent decisions. It is my hope and prayer that these words will have our populace a little less fearful and a little more willing to explore healing the hearts and minds of our war veterans, not just as a moral obligation but a potentially viable solution to our times of discord. I believe in psychedelic GI Joe and what they can teach all of us.

If we solve the tragic veteran suicide epidemic, I believe that in the process we may solve a whole host of other challenges at the same time: our mental health challenges as a nation, war, child sex abuse, and possibly even the environmental challenges that may very well have our species in peril. This is how exponentials work. When you treat the deepest root of the problem with a loving antidote, in time, the branches will grow with a graceful vibrancy, making way for an abundant yield far beyond what our linear minds can comprehend.

Time is ticking. Twenty-two U.S. veterans take their lives *each* day, *every* day. Together we can put an end to this needless suffering.

Join the movement. Your voice matters. We need you!

Please know that half of all *Worth the Fight* proceeds will be donated to the Heroic Hearts Project, to further their efforts in organizing healing retreats for our veterans who struggle with treatment-resistant PTSD. You can follow the book's fundraising progress at worththefightbook.org. Twenty-five percent has also been pledged to MAPS to further their efforts of leading the movement of psychedelics as medicine and their pioneering work with MDMA-assisted therapy. The remaining amount of *Worth the Fight* funds will be disbursed to other organizations that push forward this important work and conversation.

RESOURCES

Erowid.org. A nonprofit educational organization whose mission is to share transparently anything and everything about psychoactive plants and compounds that can produce altered states of consciousness.

Reset.Me. An online resource created by former CNN news reporter Amber Lyon who suffered from work-related PTSD, subsequently healing herself with ayahuasca and psilocybin, courageously leading the charge in objective journalism for natural medicines and psychedelics.

Psychedelic Support. If you are reading these words and struggling with mental health: Please consider applying for one of the many clinical trials that are seeking volunteers. This research is "on like Donkey Kong" as prestigious universities and organizations are researching: MDMA, psilocybin, LSD, cannabis, ketamine, ibogaine, and salvinorin for a variety of conditions—including PTSD, depression, smoking, opioid addiction, cocaine addiction, alcohol use disorders, cancer, fear, anxiety, HIV/AIDS, and OCD. And YES, healthy normals, long-term meditators, and religious professionals qualify for some clinical trials.

https://psychedelic.support/resources/how-to-join-psychedelic-clinical-trial/

Hummingbird Healing Center in Iquitos, Peru, is an additional trusted resource for those looking to heal trauma or address emotional challenges. Without question, this is the strongest medicine I have ever drunk. Jim Davis is a humble servant of the divine doing incredibly important work. He and his ayahuasceros hold safe space at their sanctuary of peace. This is highly recommended if one wants to brave the Amazon Rainforest to either drink ayahuasca or San Pedro. Jim is a veteran of the U.S. Air Force and generously offers U.S. veterans half off retreat expenses.

Featured Not-For-Profits:

MAPS, the Multidisciplinary Association of Psychedelic Studies, is the pace-car in the "psychedelics-as-medicine movement" toward a saner mental health for our nation and world. MAPS is a nonprofit research and educational organization applying steadfast scientific rigor and objectivity to their paradigm shifting approach towards healing and mental health.

The Heroic Hearts Project (HHP). Heroic Hearts Project is a registered 501(c)3 non-profit that connects military veterans struggling with mental trauma to ayahuasca therapy retreats, healing the hearts and minds of our U.S. veterans in need who suffer from treatment-resistant PTSD. Led by former Army Ranger and Cornell grad Jesse Gould.

TO CONTACT ME:

Next Level Transformations (NLTRANS.ORG): Hire me for coaching or speaking engagements. Or just reach out to say hi.

ABOUT THE AUTHOR

Matthew Simpson humbly serves as the self-appointed civilian ambassador to our nation's veteran suicide tragedy and epidemic. He brings very diverse experiences to the table: leadership in corporate America, free spirit world travels, extensive healing with psychedelics and plant medicines. He generously shares his personal transformation and awakening to spiritual principles in hopes of inspiring others to look within to find their truest purpose and calling.

Thank you to all of the artists who favorably impacted this creative project. I am grateful for the inspirational music, your loving words, and high resonant beats.

WORTH THE FIGHT PLAYLIST

True to Myself:	*Ziggy Marley*
The Fruitful Darkness:	*Trevor Hall*
Sound of Settling:	*Death Cab for Cutie*
Stay Awake:	*Jose Gonzales*
Whatever It Takes:	*Imagine Dragons*
Once Was One:	*Portugal. The Man*
From the Ground Up:	*Ayla Nereo*
Anything Can Happen:	*Ellie Goulding*
Unharnessed:	*Leah Song*
Road Home:	*MC Yogi*
Hold The Line:	*Broods*
Love Is Mystical:	*Cold War Kids*
Worth The Fight:	*Broods*
Something to Believe In:	*Young the Giant*
Angel By the Wings:	*SIA*
Kill Em With Kindness:	*Selena Gomez*
Wider Circles:	*Rising Appalachia*
Writing to Reach You:	*Travis*
Love of the Game:	*Welshly Arms*
Coming of Age:	*Foster the People*
Play It Right:	*Sylvan Esso*
When I Grow Up(feat. Amae Love):	*The Human Experience*
We are the People:	*Empire of the Sun*
Come Together:	*Gary Clark, Jr.*
Love Is All I Got:	*Crystal Fighters*
Waking Up the Giants:	*Grizfolk*